# CRAFTS IN THE EARLY ISIN PERIOD

# ORIENTALIA LOVANIENSIA ANALECTA

Volume 1: EDWARD LIPINSKI, Studies in Aramaic Inscriptions and Onomastics I.

Volume 2: JAN QUAEGEBEUR, Le dieu égyptien Shaï dans la religion et l'onomastique.

Volume 3: P.H.L. EGGERMONT, Alexander's Campaigns in Sind and Baluchistan and the Siege of the Brahmin Town of Harmatelia.

Volume 4: WINAND M. CALLEWAERT, The Sarvāṅgī of the Dādūpanthī Rajāb.

Volume 5: EDWARD LIPIŃSKI (ed.), State and Temple Economy in the Ancient Near East I.

Volume 6: EDWARD LIPIŃSKI (ed.), State and Temple Economy in the Ancient Near East II.

Volume 7: MARIE-CHRISTINE DE GRAEVE, The Ships of the Ancient Near East (c. 2000-500 B.C.).

Volume 8: WINAND M. CALLEWAERT (ed.), Early Hindī Devotional Literature in Current Research.

Volume 9: FRANS L. DAMEN, Crisis and Religious Renewal in the Brahmo Samaj Movement (1860-1884).

Volume 10: R.Y. EBIED - A. VAN ROEY - L.R. WICKHAM, Peter of Callinicum, Anti-Tritheist Dossier.

Volume 11: AGNES RAMMANT-PEETERS, Les pyramidions égyptiens du Nouvel Empire.

Volume 12: SIMONE SCHEERS (ed.), Studia Paulo Naster Oblata I. Numismatica Antiqua.

Volume 13: JAN QUAEGEBEUR (ed.), Studia Paulo Naster Oblata II. Orientalia Antiqua.

Volume 14: E. PLATTI, Yaḥyā ibn ʿAdī, théologien chrétien et philosophe arabe.

Volume 15: E. GUBEL - E. LIPIŃSKI - B. SERVAIS-SOYEZ (ed.), Studia Phoenicia I-II.

Volume 16: W. SKALMOWSKI - A. VAN TONGERLOO (ed.), Middle Iranian Studies.

Volume 17: M. VAN MOL, Handboek Modern Arabisch.

Volume 18: C. LAGA - J.A. MUNITIZ - L. VAN ROMPAY (ed.), After Chalcedon. Studies in Theology and Church History.

Volume 19: EDWARD LIPIŃSKI (ed.), The Land of Israel: Cross-Roads of Civilizations.

Volume 20: SHELLEY WACHSMANN, Aegeans in the Theban Tombs.

Volume 21: K. VAN LERBERGHE, Old Babylonian Legal and Administrative Texts from Philadelphia.

Volume 22: E. LIPIŃSKI (ed.), Phoenicia and the East Mediterranean in the First Millennium B.C.

ORIENTALIA LOVANIENSIA
ANALECTA
——— 24 ———

# CRAFTS IN THE EARLY ISIN PERIOD:

## A STUDY OF THE ISIN CRAFT ARCHIVE FROM THE REIGNS OF IŠBI-ERRA AND ŠŪ-ILIŠU

BY

MARC VAN DE MIEROOP

*Uitgegeven met de steun van de Universitaire Stichting Van België*

DEPARTEMENT ORIËNTALISTIEK
LEUVEN

1987

D/1987/0602/36

ISBN 90-6831-092-5

Printed in Belgium by Orientaliste, Leuven.

# CONTENTS

## ACKNOWLEDGEMENTS

I would like to thank many persons for their various contributions to this study:

G. Beckman, M. Civil, B.R. Foster, W.W. Hallo and P. Steinkeller for commenting extensively on the whole or part of various stages of the manuscript;

J. Black, M. Cooper, S. Dalley, G.Th. Ferwerda, D. Frayne, J.P. Grégoire, B. Hrouda, Th. Jacobsen, D. Loding, M. Stol, M. Walker, R. Whiting, N. Yoffee, and R. Zettler, for suggestions and information; all errors are my sole responsibility.

For permission to include unpublished material I am grateful to the following scholars:

W.W. Hallo, curator of the Yale Babylonian Collection, gave me free access to the tablets in his care, and the permission to publish them;

P.R.S. Moorey allowed me to study and copy the tablets from the Ashmolean Museum. They were brought to my attention by N. Yoffee and J.P. Grégoire, and are quoted by courtesy of the Visitors of the Ashmolean Museum. I am grateful to J.P. Grégoire for the permission to quote Ash 1932-274 and 280;

G.Th. Ferwerda allowed me to use his transliterations of the tablets in the de Liagre Böhl Collection in Leiden. They were brought to my attention by M. Stol, and are quoted with the permission of E. Van Donzel;

I.J. Gelb allowed me to use his transliterations of tablets in the Chicago area. They were brought to my attention by P. Steinkeller;

P. Steinkeller informed me about a tablet from the Zion Research Library, now in the Harvard Semitic Museum. It is quoted with the permission of W.L. Moran;

J.A. Brinkman, curator of tablets, gave me permission to study tablets from Nippur in the Oriental Institute of the University of Chicago.

A. Sjöberg, curator of tablets, allowed me to study Nippur texts from the University Museum of the University of Pennsylvania.

I would like to take this occassion to thank my first teachers in Ancient Near Eastern studies: Professors E. Lipiński, P. Naster and H. Sauren.

Financial support for this research was partly provided by Yale

University, and by the Alexander Kohut Foundation, for which my sincere thanks. I am especially grateful to the "Universitaire Stichting van België" for making possible the publication of this book.

Publications which became available to me after the summer of 1985 could not be considered in this study. These include the important contributions by J.M. Durand in *ARM* XXI, Paris, 1983, and by G. Th. Ferwerda, *A Contribution to the Early Isin Craft Archive (TLB/SLB* V), Leiden, 1985.

New York, 1986 Marc VAN DE MIEROOP

# LIST OF TABLES

# LIST OF FIGURES

# LIST OF ABBREVIATIONS

Bibliographical abbreviations are according to *Chicago Assyrian Dictionary* N/1 (Chicago, 1980): pp. VII-XXI, with the following additions:

R. Borger, *Zeichenliste* = Borger, Rykle
  1978 *Assyrisch-babylonische Zeichenliste* (*AOAT* 33), Kevelaer.

V. Crawford, *Terminology* = Crawford, Vaugh Emerson
  1948 *Terminology of the Leather Industry in Late Sumerian Times,* unpubl. Ph.D. diss., Yale Univ.

R.J. Forbes, *SAT* I = Forbes, R.J.
  1964 *Studies in Ancient Technology* I, 2nd edition, Leiden.

R.J. Forbes, *SAT* IV = Forbes, R.J.
  1964 *Studies in Ancient Technology* IV, 2nd edition, Leiden.

R.J. Forbes, *SAT* V = Forbes, R.J.
  1966 *Studies in Ancient Technology* V, 2nd edition, Leiden.

J.P. Grégoire, *AAS* = Grégoire, Jean-Pierre
  1970 *Archives administratives sumériennes,* Paris.

D. Snell, *YNER* 8 = Snell, Daniel
  1982 *Ledgers and Prices* (*YNER* 8), New Haven.

Other abbreviations:

I.D. = Iddin-Dagan
I.E. = Išbi-Erra
I.S. = Ibbi-Sîn
Š.i. = Šū-ilišu

# INTRODUCTION

Crafts and craftsmen are important to any pre-industrial society, since they provide tools, furniture, cloth, and many other daily necessities. They are important as well to the historian for they demonstrate the technological abilities of the society under study. Unfortunately, information concerning crafts from ancient Mesopotamia is partial, for it pertains only to lists of objects and types of craftsmen derived from textual evidence, and artifacts — almost exclusively remnants of pottery, stonecutting, and metalwork — discovered through archaeological excavations. There exists, however, almost no information on the processes by which these objects were manufactured. Archaeological remains of workshops are rare for the historical period in early Mesopotamia, and only two known archives contain records describing activity in a workshop.

Two factors hinder the archaeological identification of workshops: the perishable nature of most tools used in manufacture and the difficulty of discerning the relationship between small objects with particular crafts. Thus there have been discovered, to my knowledge, only three buildings from early Mesopotamia which can be identified, with more or less certainty, as workshops. Moreover, one group of objects indicates the remains of the workshop of a copper smith. In the northern section of Uruk, an area of 9 meters by 5.5 meters which appears to be part of a metal workshop, dated in the Late-Uruk period (ca. 3400-3100 B.C.), has been uncovered. The only remnants are channels with holes on both sides in which molds for metal objects could have been placed[1]. The smelted metal was probably made to flow through the channels, and scooped up by several persons who poured it into the molds.

In the Early Dynastic-Old Akkadian period two establishments can be connected with workshops. The first is the so-called "Northern Palace" in Tell Asmar, located in the northernmost part of the tell inside the city walls[2]. The building is preserved in two archaeological levels; in the earlier level it was L-shaped, measuring 32 meters by 38 meters; later, it

[1] H.J. Nissen, *Bagh. Mitt.* 5 (1970): p. 114-116, and *Wirtschaft und Gesellschaft*: p. 8-10.

[2] S. Lloyd, *OIP* 88: p. 181.

was almost rectangular, measuring 72 meters by 30 meters[3]. The large number of drains and waterworks, and the presence of large vats, led Delougaz to believe that the building was used as a workshop, probably for leatherwork, which requires large quantities of water to soak the hides. The Old Akkadian tablets found there mention the woman's house and textile industry, which may indicate that the building was also used for that activity[4].

In Tello, north of the "Tell des Pilliers", an area called "Région des Bassins" was uncovered in 1904[5]. In that area a number of metal points protuding vertically from the ground were found. They seem to have been used to peg wet hides to the ground in order to facilitate the scraping of the skins[6]. The presence of basins and drains in the neighborhood also supports this conjecture[7].

In Tell edh-Dhiba'i, a site close to Tell Harmal, remains of a copper smith's shop, dating from the early second millennium, have been found. Unfortunately, all metal tools have disappeared, and only clay objects were preserved. These include a number of clay pipes and moulds, the use of which can be reconstructed from modern parallels[8]. The publication does not indicate in what building these tools were found.

Textual evidence for crafts in ancient Mesopotamia is also limited. There exists a large number of records of institutions which receive manufactured products from which can be compiled lists of these products and of the craftsmen, but only two archives of workshops themselves are known. The largest archive was excavated in Ur and dates from the latter part of the Third Dynasty. In the so-called "Registrar's office", room 8 of the É-dub-lá-maḫ complex, a large group of texts was found[9]. Although it was originally thought that these were found *in situ*, it became clear subsequently that they were used as fill for a Kassite building[10]. These texts constitute records of four activities: (1) accounts of monthly offerings to Nanna by the king, (2) accounts of transactions pertaining to wool and the textile industry, (3) accounts of working materials for craftsmen, and lists of their atten-

[3] *OIP* 88: pls. 36 and 37.

[4] *OIP* 88: p. 196-198. I can identitify none of these tablets in I.J. Gelb, *MAD* 1.

[5] G. Cros, *Nouvelles fouilles de Tello,* Paris, 1910: p. 100-108.

[6] H.E.W. Crawford, *World Archaeology* 5 (1973-4): p. 236.

[7] Cf. G. Cros, *Nouvelles fouilles*: p. 101 plan D.

[8] L. al-Gailani, *Sumer* 21 (1965): p. 37f. and pls. 6f.

[9] *AJA* 57 (1953): p. 128 n. 1, IIId Campaign.

[10] Th. Jacobsen, *AJA* 57 (1953): p. 125f.

dance, and (4) records of payments to individuals and groups[11]. Other texts, found in different locations, can be classified in these groups. Most of these texts were published in *UET* 3 and *UET* 9.

Of particular interest for the study of crafts are groups (2) and (3). Group 2, the records of wool transactions, does not actually constitute the archive of a single workship, but originates from several institutions involved in the textile industry. The texts allow us to follow the different steps in this industry: the receipt of wool in a "wool office"; its expenditure to overseers of weavers located in villages around Ur; the accounts of weighed cloths received by the fullers, who after handling, deliver them to the gá-nun-maḫ; and the disbursement of the finished cloth by this office[12].

The third group of texts forms the archive of a workshop. Although it has been studied from different perspectives, it is not yet clear exactly which texts in fact belong to it. The workshop whose activities are recorded in this archive has been reconstructed on the basis of the large inventory text *UET* 3: no 1498, which "incidentally was found outside the Registrar's office"[13]. This text shows that the workshop was divided into eight departments: the houses of the metalworkers (é-tibira), the goldsmiths (é-kù-dím), the stone cutters (é-zadim), the carpenters (é-nagar), the blacksmiths (é-simug), the leatherworkers (é-ašgab), the felters (é-túg-du$_8$), and the reedworkers (é-ad-KID)[14]. Several receipt texts can be connected with these departments[15]. A group of so-called worker lists records the attendance of six types of craftsmen: metalworkers, goldsmiths, stone cutters, carpenters, leatherworkers, and reedworkers[16], with some associated professions[17]. The whole workshop was supervised by an overseer, Ir-Nanna, and by a šabra, Aḫuwaqar[18].

There is dispute over the question whether the archive is part of the royal or the temple administration. Th. Jacobsen[19] argues for the first possibility based on indications from all the tablets found in the

[11] Th. Jacobsen, *AJA* 57 (1953): p. 126f.

[12] Th. Jacobsen, "On the textile industry at Ur under Ibbī-Sîn", in *Tammuz*: p. 216-229. Cf. W.W. Hallo, *Jones AV*: p. 4-13.

[13] Th. Jacobsen, *AJA* 57 (1953): p. 127.

[14] Cf. D. Loding, *A Craft Archive from Ur*, Univ. Microfilms, Ann Arbor, 1974: p. 57-136.

[15] *id.*: p. 181-195.

[16] *id.*: p. 243-259.

[17] *id.*: p. 226-233.

[18] *id.*: p. 196.

[19] *AJA* 57 (1953): p. 127f.

"Registrar's office": the accounts of offerings for Nanna deal with royal offerings, the wool used in the textile industry is property of the palace, and the worker lists mention erín, a term translated "royal serfs" by Jacobsen. This last point has been refuted, since what he read as IGI-ERÍN-AK, is now read as $kurum_7$-ak = *piqittum*, "inspection", without reference to the erín[20]. D. Loding argues for temple control over the workshop, because Aḫuwaqar, the official supervising the administration, is a šabra, a title often associated with the temple administration. The workshop may have been related to the gá-nun-maḫ, which in its turn is part of a temple, and workmen of the workshop are said to be active in the *Giparu*, which she calls also a temple[21]. Although she admits that the evidence is far from conclusive, she suggests that crafts in Ur were controlled by the temple[22]. From the evidence presented by both scholars, it seems that Jacobsen's thesis has more validity, if it is true that all the texts from the "Registrar's office" originally were kept by the same administration[23]. This cannot be proven without a detailed study of all the texts; thus, so far, the evidence is inconclusive. The Ur workshop has also been studied extensively by H. Limet in his study of Sumerian metallurgy, which includes some remarks about the organization of the workshop[24]. We are, however, still in need of a comprehensive treatment of this archive, which makes use of all the relevant texts. Too much emphasis has been put upon *UET* 3: no 1498, while the individual receipt texts have been largely neglected. Many problems such as the extent and the periodicity of the archive, and the types of texts, still have to be discussed. Based on such information a reconstruction of the workshop can be attempted.

The second archive from a workshop comes from the city Isin in the reigns of the first two kings of its First Dynasty, Išbi-Erra (I.E.) and Šū-ilišu (Š.i.). In this work, the documents of this archive will be studied through the so-called archival approach: not as individual texts but as belonging to a larger body, which includes all the known texts. The Isin

[20] D. Loding, *op. cit.*: p. 23 n. 38.

[21] The *Giparu* is, however, not exactly a temple, but the official residence of the *enu*-priest and the *entu*-priestess, cf. R. Harris, *RlA* 3 (1957-71): p. 377-9; P.N. Weadock, *Iraq* 37 (1975): p. 101-128.

[22] *id.*: p. 27-33. In conversation Dr. Loding reiterated that the evidence does not allow one to draw any definite conclusion on this point.

[23] Dr. Jacobsen told me, however, that we cannot determine whether all texts originate from one administration or not without a detailed examination of the officials, which lies beyond the scope of the present study.

[24] *Métal*: esp. p. 166-180.

archive is more suitable for this approach than the Ur texts, since it consists of only 920 texts, while the Ur texts may be more than 2000 in number[25]. Although many texts of the Isin archive have by now been published in handcopies, they have never been systematically studied for the information they yield on the economy. V. Crawford, who published most of the texts in *BIN* 9, studied in his dissertation the terminology of the leather industry contained in them[26], and L. Matouš gave a short review of the material[27]. As will become clear from this study leather-work in the workshop has received disproportionate emphasis, since this was Crawford's main interest. Other aspects of the workshop will appear when all texts are taken into account.

First, the limits and content of the archive and its place of origin will be determined. Then a typology of its texts will be established and their periodicity will be studied. The main object of this study will be to reconstruct, as far as possible, the activities of the workshop: the process of manufacture, the raw materials used, the artifacts produced, and the function of the craftsmen and the supervisory personnel. Finally, the position of the workshop in the economy of the city Isin will be discussed.

[25] In the British Museum there are still a number of unpublished texts of this archive, and in the University Museum of the University of Pennsylvania more uncatalogued texts of this archive exist (communication, Dr. Loding).

[26] *Terminology of the Leather Industry in Late Sumerian Times*, unpubl. Ph.D. dissertation, Yale University, 1948.

[27] *BiOr*. 13 (1956): p. 135-140.

CHAPTER I

# THE EARLY ISIN CRAFT ARCHIVE: DEFINITION, TYPOLOGY, AND CHRONOLOGY

## A. *Definition of the archive*

The texts under study here are generally referred to as the "Early Isin texts". This term stemmed from the texts' origin in the Early Isin period[1], but since L. Matouš argued their provenience from the city of Isin itself[2], the term now refers also to their place of origin[3]. These tablets were brought to light by illicit diggers, however, and thus their archaeological context is unknown. In this first section, the content of this archive and its place of origin are defined through evidence from the texts themselves.

### 1) Definition of the archive

The archive[4] under study consists of 920 texts dating from the reigns of Išbi-Erra (2017-1985 B.C.) and Šū-ilišu (1984-1975 B.C.) of Isin; these record the activities of a craft workshop. 780 dated texts from the first two reigns of the Early Isin period belong to the archive of this workshop. They all date from I.E. 4 through Š.i. 3, a period of thirty-three years (cf. Appendix A). To determine whether a text belongs to the archive or not, the following procedure was used: from the worker lists (discussed in detail in chapter III) a list of names of workmen, active in the workshop, was derived. Account texts with their names were considered to be part of the archive. The names of the officials in these account texts — e.g., Nanna-kiag and Šū-Ninkarak (see chapter III) — were traced through the other texts. Other names found with those

[1] V. Crawford, *Sumerian Economic Texts from the First Dynasty of Isin* (*BIN* 9), New Haven-London, 1954; T. Fish, "Kuš Texts of the Isin Period", *MCS* 5 (1955): p. 115-124.

[2] "Zu den ältesten ökonomischen Texten aus Isin", *BiOr*. 13 (1956): p. 136f.

[3] M. Gallery, *AfO* 27 (1980): p. 7.

[4] The term "archive" is used here to indicate "a collection of administrative documents stored for long-term retention in a place that need not be the office of their origin or receipt", following B.R. Foster, *Umma in the Sargonic Period,* Hamden, 1982: p. 41, based on J. Papritz, *Archivalische Zeitschrift* 55 (1959): p. 11-50.

officials were then traced through the corpus and for each text it was thereby decided whether or not it belongs to the archive.

On the basis of proposography and subject matter, 140 undated texts, or texts where the year date is broken, were assigned to the archive, which brings the total number of texts to 920. All of them are written entirely in Sumerian[5], closely related to that of the Ur III economic texts. All of the tablets were acquired on the antiquities market, and most of them are now in the Nies Babylonian Collection at Yale University.

2) Publication history of the archive

Part of this corpus was published previously in handcopies and most of the remainder will appear in the near future. At the moment the following published texts are known to me:
a) 534 texts from the Nies Babylonian Collection and one from the Yale Babylonian Collection were published by V. Crawford in 1954[6]. *BIN* 9: no 475, an undated letter to Puzur-Kiš[7], has mistakenly been included in this corpus. The subject of the letter, sprouted malt (?), and the language, Akkadian[8], are alien to the Isin workshop archive. The occurrence of the names Tūram-ilī and Šū-Eštar is not sufficient reason to assign the letter to the archive, since both are common names elsewhere. L. Matouš[9] and I.J. Gelb[10] argue against the inclusion of *BIN* 9: nos 127 and 145 to the Isin archive, citing as evidence the use of Drehem month names, as opposed to the use of Nippur months in the rest of the corpus. This conclusion seems mistaken since the personal names in these texts, Nūr-Ea (127 and 145), Lu-Nanna, Nūr-Eštar, Adad-bani, Šū-Ea, and Šū-Ninšubur (145) are well known from other, almost contemporary, texts of the archive. Although the texts of *BIN* 9 were copied with extraordinary accuracy, some collations were needed (see Appendix B).
b) eleven texts from a private collection in Baghdad copied by T. Fish[11]. Unfortunately the copies seem often to be inaccurate.

[5] I.J. Gelb, *JNES* 20 (1961): p. 131f.

[6] *Sumerian Economic texts from the First Dynasty of Isin* (*BIN* 9), New Haven-London, 1954.

[7] See W.W. Hallo, *BiOr*. 26 (1969): p. 175.

[8] I.J. Gelb, *JNES* 20 (1961): p. 131.

[9] *BiOr*. 13 (1956): p. 137.

[10] *JNES* 20 (1961): p. 131.

[11] "Kuš Texts of the Isin Period", *MCS* 5 (1955): p. 115-124.

c) one text from the Rosicrucian Egyptian Oriental Museum in San José, California, published in transliteration only (*SET* no 291)[12].
d) two Isin texts belonging to the collection of F.M.Th. de Liagre Böhl copied by W.W. Hallo[13].
e) two texts in a private collection published by B. Kienast[14]. In the same collection exists a large tablet (Pf 5) with an inscription of the time of Iddin-Dagan written over an older inscription, largely illegible, dated to Išbi-Erra 26.
f) one text in the collection of Ugo Sissa[15] is dated I.E.33; the mention of the name Buqqušum in line 25 makes its assignment to the Isin archive most likely[16].
g) one text in a private collection published by K. Oberhuber[17].
h) one text in the collection of the Biblical Institute in Rome[18].
i) sixteen texts in that part of the Piepkorn Collection now in the Oriental Institute of the University of Chicago published by R.D. Freedman[19]. Three others texts (A, B, and C) included in the publication are difficult to assign to the Isin archive, but Freedman is convinced they belong there[20]. The subject of text A, beer and its ingredients, is not otherwise attested in the Isin archive, and since the date of the text could also be Ibbi-Sîn 2, it seems safer to assign the text to that reign. Text B, not dated, contains personal names unknown in the Isin archive. The only exception is the name Nadi, which is common elsewhere, and thus this text is probably not part of the archive. Text C was dated as possibly Š.i. 8 by Freedman[21]. He admits that the date seems unlikely since no other texts from the early Isin period after Š.i. 3 are known, but mentions that R.W. Whiting identified the text as early Isin from Adab[22]. Dr. Whiting rejects, however, the identification as early Isin

[12] A handcopy of the text by J. Snyder was made available to me by M. Cooper, who will publish it in a forthcoming issue of *ASJ*.

[13] *TLB* 3: nos 68 and 175. Collated by H. Waetzoldt, *OrAn.* 15 (1976): p. 329-32.

No 68 (p. 330): rev 4: Hallo's copy KI is more likely than Waetzoldt's suggestion ÉŠ since the name is certainly ᵈNanna-ki-ág.

No 175 (p. 332): obv 2, 4, 5: gín at the end; obv 2f.: beginning now missing; rev 1: sukkal-maḫ maškim; rev 5: at the end -ta over erasure.

[14] *JCS* 19 (1965): p. 42, Pf 3 and 4.

[15] W.F. Leemans, *JCS* 20 (1966): p. 38-42, no 5.

[16] For Buqqušum see chapter III.

[17] "Eine Tontafel aus der Zeit Išbi'erras von Isin", *Or* NS 36 (1967): p. 426-8.

[18] *MVN* 4: no 143.

[19] *JAOS* 98 (1978): p. 251-265. For collations of Freedman's copies, see Appendix B.

[20] *JAOS* 98 (1978): p. 259.

[21] *Ibid.*: p. 260.

[22] *Ibid.*: p. 259 n. 2.

"from Adab" as a misunderstanding of his words by Freedman, although he does not hesitate to identify the text as early Isin and not Šulgi 4 (personal correspondance)[23]. This text shows some connections with those from the Isin craft archive, for instance the mention of Adda-kalla[24], but the subject matter of the text does not show any connection with the workshop. Hence, the text probably belongs to another archive of this period.

j) one text in a private collection in Japan published by T. Gomi[25].

k) two texts in Burlington, Vermont published by B. Lewis and F.R. Jewell[26].

l) nine texts in the Australian Institute of Archaeology in Melbourne published by B.R. Foster and M. Van De Mieroop[27].

The following groups of unpublished texts are known to me at the moment:

a) a search through the Nies Babylonian Collection, partly based on a catalogue of year dates prepared by A. Goetze, yielded 288 unpublished texts belonging to the Isin archive. They will be published by me in *BIN* 10.

b) twenty-seven texts in the Ashmolean Museum in Oxford. They were brought to my attention by Norman Yoffee. All of them, except Ash 1932 — 274 and 280 will be published by me in *BIN* 10. The two remaining ones will be published by J.P. Grégoire. The text are quoted by courtesy of the Visitors of the Ashmolean Museum.

c) twenty texts in the Liagre Böhl collection in Leiden. Their existence was already noted by F.M. de Liagre Böhl[28], and they were brought to my attention by M. Stol. During a short stay in Leiden in the summer of 1983, I was able to look at about ten of them. The texts will be published by G.Th. Ferwerda, who kindly allowed me to use his transliterations, and are quoted here with the permission of Dr. E. Van Donzel.

[23] Letter May 13, 1982.

[24] Also attested in *BIN* 10: no 49 (IV/-/Š.i. 1).

[25] "Ein frühaltbabylonischer Text in Japan", *The Ancient Orient Museum* 3 (1981): p. 41f. and Pl. XIX.

[26] "Sumerian economic texts from the Robert Hull Fleming Museum of the University of Vermont", *ASJ* 4 (1982): p. 53-68, nos 16 and 17.

[27] "Early Isin texts in the Australian Institute of Archaeology", *ASJ* 5 (1983): p. 43-57.

[28] *Mededeelingen uit de Leidsche Verzameling van spijkerschrift-inscripties* I, Amsterdam, 1933: p. 22f. See also, A.A. Kampman, *Symbolae Biblicae et Mesopotamicae F.M. Th. de Liagre Böhl dedicatae,* Leiden, 1973: p. 221. The texts are now edited by G.Th. Ferwerda, *A Contribution to the Early Isin Craft Archive* (*TLB/SLB* V), Leiden, 1985.

d) three tablets in the Chicago area[29] were communicated to me by I.J. Gelb and P. Steinkeller.
e) one text in the Harvard Semitic Museum, previously belonging to the Zion Research Library (no 134) was brought to my attention by P. Steinkeller, and will be published by me in *BIN* 10.

3) Origin of the archive: city

The origin of the Isin archive is unclear since none of the texts were discovered as the result of scientific excavations. The current excavations at Išan Baḫriyat, the site identified as Isin by the inscriptions found there, have uncovered few remains from the Isin I period[30], none of them from the early Isin period[31], although the excavations reached pre-Sargonic levels[32]. The excavators found some epigraphic material of the Isin I period[33], but nothing from the reigns of Išbi-Erra and Šū-ilišu[34]. The site was looted extensively by illicit diggers before the official excavators arrived[35], so it is possible that the early Isin texts were removed by them.

L. Matouš attempted to prove that the tablets originate from Isin itself[36] by comparing the pantheon attested in the *BIN* 9 texts with that from the later Old Babylonian texts from Isin[37]. The gods Ninkarak, Ninisina and Damu are indicative; they appear both in the early and the later Isin texts. He also proposes that the often mentioned temple of Dagan in *BIN* 9 is the same as the later Dagan temple é-ki-tuš-ki-gar-ra in Isin. D.O. Edzard[38] reaches the same conclusion based on other indications in the texts; he excludes several cities (e.g., Nippur) because of the mentions of "to the city x", and thinks that the frequent mention

[29] Mr. Sheldon tablet, Lindblom High School 1 and 2. Inquiries have failed to located these tablets.

[30] B. Hrouda, *Isin - Išan Baḫriyat* I, München, 1977: p. 149; "Ergebnisse der Ausgrabung in Isin (4. Kampagne, Winter 1975-76)", *Sumer* 34 (1978): p. 87.

[31] B. Hrouda, "Isin: Archäologisch", *RlA* 5 (1976-1980): p. 192: only building activity of Enlil-bani.

[32] *Isin - Išan Baḫriyat* I: p. 147; *Isin - Išan Baḫriyat* II, München, 1981: p. 199.

[33] The earliest published epigraphic material from the Isin I period dates from the reign of Išme-Dagan (1953-1935 B.C.), cf. C.B.F. Walker - C. Wilcke, *Isin - Išan Baḫriyat* II; p. 93. See also D.O. Edzard, *Isin - Išan Baḫriyat* I: p. 88; C.B.F. Walker, *Sumer* 34 (1978): p. 98, and "Bericht über die 5. Kampagne in Isin/Išan Baḫriyat", *Sumer* 36 (1980): p. 79.

[34] Note, however, that on the surface of the tell an inscription of Šū-ilišu has been found, published by C. Wilcke, *Or.* NS 54 (1985): p. 304-308.

[35] *Isin - Išan Baḫriyat* I: p. 12.

[36] *BiOr.* 13 (1956): p. 136f.

[37] Studied by F.R. Kraus, *JCS* 3 (1951): esp. p. 59-88.

[38] *Zwischenzeit*: p. 59 n. 273. Cf. W.W. Hallo, *JCS* 18 (1964): p. 66 n. 19.

of the king, the palace, and uru "the city" in the early Isin texts proves their provenience from the capital city.

An additional indication of the provenience is the frequent mention of work on the wall (ki-sá-a) in the texts dated from I/-/I.E.16 through IV/-/I.E.17[39]. This activity can be connected with the year date I.E. 17, mu bàd *Eštar-tarām-Išbi-Erra* ba-dù[40]. Although building activity on walls is attested in earlier year dates of Išbi-Erra[41], and there exists no text which locates a wall with this name in Isin, it is most likely that this building activity in I.E.16 took place also in the city Isin.

The city name Isin seldom appears in the archive. L. Matouš and D.O. Edzard knew only of the phrase túg $^{d}$Nè-eri$_{11}$-gal Ì-si-in-na-šè "for the garment of Nergal of Isin" (*BIN* 9: no 84: 3). In the rest of the material two new references have come to light, both problematic. In *ASJ* 5: p. 56 no 6: l. 3 (XI/18/I.E.15) baskets for drawing water (gi-gur-a-ba[l-a]) are delivered kiri$_6$ $^{d}$Iš-bi-mu-ba-ni Ì-si-in$^{ki}$-šè. The translation of this line is difficult. It is possible that the name of the garden is Išbimu-bani-Isin with an unknown theophoric element Išbimu. An emendation of the text to kiri$_6$ $^{d}$Iš-bi⟨-Èr-ra⟩-mu-ba-lí⟨-iṭ⟩ Ì-si-in$^{ki}$-šè "for the garden of Išbi'(erra)-muballi(ṭ) in/of Isin", seems more acceptable since it was common practice to abbreviate names of kings[42]. The second occurrence of Isin is in the unusual text *BIN* 10: no 48 (X/-/I.E.33) where deliveries of reed are recorded. Though this reference gives little additional information, line 5 reads: 2 Ul-luḫ Ì-si-in-na/$^{ki}$ "two (bales) from/for Ulluḫ (of) Isin"[43].

Museological arguments from the Nies Babylonian Collection strongly support an Isin origin for the early Isin texts. Most NBC tablets seem to have been acquired from the antiquities dealer E.S. David from 1933 through 1947, while NBC 7724 through NBC 7796 were acquired from Messayeh on February 12, 1936. The tablets were assigned num-

[39] *BIN* 9: Nos. 153, 155-7, 159-68, 170-1, 173, 175-6, 194, *BIN* 10: no 192, *JAOS* 98: p. 253 no 4, *ASJ* 4: p. 68 no 17, *ASJ* 5: p. 56 no 7, LB 1105.

[40] D. Frayne, *The Historical Correlations of the Sumerian Royal Hymns*, Univ. Microfilms, Ann Arbor, 1981: p. 337f.

[41] I.E.12: mu bàd-gal *Itil-pāšunu* ba-dù = mu bàd-gal Isin$^{ki}$ mu-dù; I.E.14: mu bàd *Libūr-Išbi-Erra* ba-dù.

[42] Cf. H. Hirsch, *AfO* 20 (1963): p. 19 n. 201, W.W. Hallo, *JCS* 18 (1964): p. 64 and n. 11.

[43] Perhaps the line reads DU$_7$ sukkal Ì-si-in-na$^{ki}$. Certainly a personal name has to be read for all the other entries of the text contain one. Another possible occurrence of the name Isin may be in the text Ash 1932-274. Line 23', in very fragmentary condition, may read á šu-du$_7$-a nin-AN[ ] N[IN ] Nanše?? / lu[gal Ì-]si-in$^{ki}$. The context is, however, too unclear to give additional information.

bers from 5602 through 10076. The Isin tablets published in *BIN* 7[44] have NBC numbers from 5316-5580, thus they immediately precede the early Isin texts. Since David and Messayeh were the main sources of tablets for the Yale Babylonian Collection in the first half of this century, it is likely that the *BIN* 7 tablets were acquired from them also. In the Louvre Museum a group of thirty-two Old Babylonian Isin texts was acquired from David on December 22, 1927[45] along with two Sargonic texts probably from the same site (AO 11130 and 11131). The Sargonic texts in NBC thought to be from Isin[46] have museum numbers close to the early Isin tablets[47]. It is thus clear that David in particular had access to tablets from Isin itself, and that he sold them to the Louvre Museum and the Yale Babylonian Collection.

The texts in the Liagre Böhl collection are said to come from Tell-Laḥm, a site S.W. from Ur[48]. This seems impossible since many of the texts date from the period that Ibbi-Sîn was still in power in Ur, and it seems unlikely that Išbi-Erra's could have had such close contacts with a city S.W. of Ibbi-Sîn's capital. Moreover, the geographical horizon suggests a provenance of the tablets closer to Nippur. The Ashmolean tablets were acquired by the Kish expedition, but it seems impossible that the texts come from an area that far north in Mesopotamia. Most indications seem thus to point towards a provenience in Isin itself.

4) Origin of the archive: institution

The content of the texts shows that they form part of the archive of a workshop. Since the texts register transactions with other institutions, we know their names — e.g., é-kišib-ba, é-gal, é-ì-rá-rá (see chapter IV) — but the name given to the workshop itself is less clear.

In the worker lists workmen are often recorded as šà giš-kin-ti gub-ba-àm, šà-giš-kin-ti, or giš-kin-ti gub-ba (see chapter III) in order to distinguish them from workmen active in another location or absent. The term giš-kin-ti is usually taken to refer to a type of "household personnel specialized in some professional activity"[49], but in the Isin

[44] Cf. F.R. Kraus, *JCS* 3 (1951): p. 48f. and 53-59.

[45] D. Charpin, *RA* 74 (1980): p. 189; I.J. Gelb, *MAD* 4 (1970): p. 128.

[46] Cf. I.J. Gelb, *MAD* 4 (1970): p. xi-xiv, under IN$^{ki}$.

[47] NBC 5803, 5897, 6879, 6922, 6934, 7021. Compare with *BIN* 9: p. 71-5.

[48] F.M. de Liagre Böhl, *Mededeelingen*: p. 22f. For the probable identification of Tell-Laḥm with ancient Kisiga, see P.P. Vértesalji, *RlA* 6 (1980-83): p. 431f.

[49] I.J. Gelb, *JNES* 24 (1965): p. 242. Cf. B. Hruška, *Gesellschaft und Kultur im alten Vorderasien* (ed. H. Klengel), Berlin, 1982: p. 106-108.

archive the Sumerian term used to indicate the craftsmen is gašam[50]. Since it is unlikely that two terms, giš-kin-ti and gašam, were used to indicate the workers[51], a derived meaning of giš-kin-ti as "workshop" is preferable. This derived meaning has been proposed by A.I. Tyumenev[52] based on the occurrence of giš-kin-ti-gu-la-šè in *UET* 3: no 841. B.R. Foster concurs with this opinion citing the Old Akkadian text *Nik.* 2: no 22, where the locative construction giš-kin-ti-a "in the workshop" occurs. Some additional references suggest the derived meaning[53].

In the Isin archive, the term occurs outside the worker lists, most often in the phrases níg-gál-la šà giš-kin-ti "supplies among the craftsmen" or more likely "supplies in the workshop", and níg-gù-dé giš-kin-ti "work assignment for the craftsmen" or "work assignment for the workshop". One reference strongly suggests that the term giš-kin-ti has to be translated "workshop", *BIN* 9: no 303:

| | | |
|---|---|---|
| Obv | 1 kuš-udu *a-lum* | 1 *alum*-sheep skin, |
| | 1 kuš-máš-níta kuš/ dùg-gan ti-bala | 1 male goat leather courier's pouch, |
| | 1 5/6 ma-na 5 gín / níg-U.NU-a síg-ud$_5$ | 1 5/6 mina 5 shekels goat's hair spun thread, |
| Rev 5) | šà giš-kin-ti-ta | from the workshop; |
| | 10 kuš-udu | 10 sheep skins, |
| | é-su-si-ig-ta | from the house of the hide flayers. |

The parallel use of the house of the hide flayers (é-su-si-ig) with the term giš-kin-ti, indicates that the latter probably also refers to a building.

One may thus conclude that the 920 texts belonging to the archive under study come from a workshop called giš-kin-ti, and that this workshop was located in the city of Isin itself during the reigns of Išbi-Erra and Šū-ilišu.

[50] Worker list 18: [kur]um$_7$-ak / gašam. In the Ur worker lists the term gašam is also used in the subscript: šà giš-kin-ti-me-éš / kurum$_7$-ak gašam-e-ne, see D. Loding, *A Craft Archive from Ur,* Univ. Microfilms, Ann Arbor, 1974: p. 20-26 and 197-260.

[51] Both terms would have to be translated "craftsman", for giš-kin-ti, cf. I.J. Gelb, *JNES* 24 (1965): p. 242. For gašam = *apkallum,* cf. J.P. Grégoire, *AAS*: p. 134f.

[52] *Gosudarstvennoe Hozjajstvo Drevnego Šumera,* Moscow-Leningrad, 1956: p. 314f.; cf. B.R. Foster, *Umma in the Sargonic Period,* Hamden, 1982: p. 10f.

[53] D. Loding, *A Craft Archive*: p. 137-146, gives a detailed list of occurrences of the term through the late Old Babylonian Period with economic, literary and lexical references. The derived meaning seems preferable in the following contexts: Pre-Sarg., *DP* no 503: giš-ùr giš-kin-ti-kam "it is the roofbeam of the workshop"; Ur III, *Nik* 2: no 117: reed bundles giš-kin-ti-nagar-šè "for the workshop of the carpenters".

B. *Typology of the texts*

The texts in this archive are the usual Sumerian administrative types — receipts, disbursements, etc. — thus often very concise; they regularly contain only the most essential elements such as the object of the transaction and a personal name without any grammatical element or verb. This makes their interpretation difficult, and only from a study of the product and person involved, combined with information from other texts, we can determine whether the text in question records a receipt or a disbursement.

The activities of the workshop which are recorded can be divided into five steps; such a division was probably not made in antiquity, but, since most texts seem to record only one of these five steps, it will be used here for convenience. The first step consists of the issue of raw materials to the workshop and their receipt by a number of officials, step 2 the issue of these materials to the craftsmen, step 3 the manufacture of finished products, step 4 their receipt by officials of the workshop, and step 5 their disbursement to outsiders.

1) Step 1: The delivery of the raw materials

The first step accounted for in the workshop is the delivery of the unprocessed materials by a large number of institutions and individuals. For instance, many products are brought in from the central storage house (é-kišib-ba, e.g., *BIN* 9: nos 54, 69-85). Two basic types of texts recording this step can be distinguished; the most common type is written from the perspective of the workshop, and records receipt of the materials by its officials. The second type records the transaction from the viewpoint of the deliverer.

In their most explicit form the texts of the first type contain references to the following elements: the material delivered, the institution or individual who delivers it (ki...ta), the person in the workshop who receives it (PN1 šu ba-an-ti), the sealing official (kišib PN2), the conveyor (gìr PN3), and the date. E.g., *BIN* 9: no 57:

| | | |
|---|---|---|
| Obv | 3 kuš-gu$_4$-síg-mú | 3 hairy ox hides, |
| | 2 kuš-gu$_4$ | 2 ox hides, |
| | 1 kuš-gu$_4$-mu-3 | 1 hide of a three-year old ox, |
| | 5 kuš-máš-gal | 5 skins of full-grown goats, |
| | 7 kuš-máš-níta | 7 skins of male goats, |
| | 10 kuš-sila$_4$ | 10 lamb skins: |

Table I.1: Typology of the Isin texts

Step 1: *BIN* 9: nos 1-12, 14-15, 17-27, 29-33, 35, 40-87, 89-105, 107, 110, 112-113, 115-117, 120, 126-128, 151, 329, 476, 478-479, 493, 497-500, 505, 511, 517, *BIN* 10: nos 1-58, *JAOS* 98: p. 252 no 2, p. 254 no 6, p. 255 no 11, p. 256 no 13, *ASJ* 4: p. 67 no 16, *ASJ* 5: p. 43-57 nos 1-4, *MCS* 5: p. 117 no 3, p. 119 no 5, p. 122 no 8, p. 124 no 11, *TLB* 3: no 68, *JCS* 19: p. 42 Pf 4, Mr Sheldon tablet, LB 1105, 1123, 1128, 1948.

Step 2: *BIN* 9: nos 13, 16, 121-122, 124, 137-144, 147-149, 180, 188-189, 200, 203, 205, 207-210, 212, 460, 484, 501, 519, 524, 526, *BIN* 10: nos 59-71, *JAOS* 98: p. 253 no 5, *MCS* 5: p. 124 no 10.

Step 3: a) administrative texts: *BIN* 9: nos 468, 489, *MCS* 5: p. 115 no 1.
b) worker lists: *BIN* 9: nos 492, 504, 508, 513, 514, 515, 522, 527, 533, *BIN* 10: nos 208-312, Lindblom High School 2, LB 1118, 1119.

Step 4: *BIN* 9: nos 106, 129-136, 145-146, 181, 204, 246, 257, *BIN* 10: nos 72-86.

Step 5: *BIN* 9: nos 28, 34, 36-39, 88, 108-109, 111, 114, 118-119, 201-202, 206, 211, 214-245, 247-256, 258-328, 330-459, 461-467, 469-473, 477, 480-483, 485, 488, 490-491, 494, 496, 502, 506-507, 509-510. 512, 516, 518, 523, 525, 529-532, 534, *BIN* 10: nos 87-193, *JAOS* 98: p. 252 no 1, p. 253 nos 3-4, p. 254 no 7, p. 255 nos 9-10, p. 256 nos 12, 14, p. 257 nos 15-16, *ASJ* 4: p. 68 no 17, *ASJ* 5: p. 43-57 nos 5-9, *MCS* 5: p. 116 no 2, p. 118 no 4, p. 120 no 6, p. 121 no 7, p. 123 no 9, *JCS* 19: p. 42 Pf 3, *JCS* 20: p. 38-42 no 5, *The Ancient Orient Museum* 3: p. 41f., *TLB* 3: no 175, *Or* 36: p. 426, *MVN* 4: no 143, *SET* no 291, Lindblom High School 1, Ash 1932-274, Ash 1932-280, LB 1020, 1102, 1104, 1106, 1108, 1109, 1110, 1112, 1113, 1115, 1125, 1126, 1942, 1988.

Miscellaneous texts: *BIN* 9: nos 213, 474, 486, 487, 495, 503, 520, 521. 528. 535, *BIN* 10: nos 194-207, 313-314. *JAOS* 98: p. 254 no 8.

---

| | | |
|---|---|---|
| Rev | ki *Šu-Eš*$_4$*-tár*-ta | from Šū-Eštar |
| | *Šu-*$^{d}$*Nin-kar-ak* | Šū-Ninkarak |
| | šu ba-an-ti | received. |
| | gaba-ri kišib $^{d}$Nanna-/ki-ág | Copy. Sealed by Nanna-kiag. |
| | gìr $^{d}$Nanna-ma-ba | Nanna-maba (was) conveyor. |
| | iti gu$_4$-si-su | Month II, |
| | mu $^{\text{giš}}$gu-za bára/ $^{d}$Nin-urta mu-/na-dím | I.E. 25. |

The majority of the texts records the same information but omits the name of the conveyor (gìr), e.g., *BIN* 10: no 19:

| | | |
|---|---|---|
| Obv | 180 (sìla) ésir-é-a | 180 sila of bitumen |
| | é-kišib-ba-ta | from the storage house, |
| | *Šu-*$^{d}$*Nin-kar-ak* | Šū-Ninkarak |
| | šu ba-an-ti | received. |
| | gaba-ri | Copy. |

| | | |
|---|---|---|
| Rev | kišib $^{d}$Nanna-ki-ág | Sealed by Nanna-kiag. |
| | iti bára-zag-gar | Month I, |
| | mu-ús-sa bàd *Eš$_4$-tár-/tá-ra-am* $^{d}$*Iš-bi-/Èr-ra* ba-dù | I.E. 18, |
| LE. | u$_4$-3-kam | day 3. |

Other texts show a wide range of variations with the same elements, always omitting one or more of them. In their most concise form it is unclear whether they record step 1 or another step since they only mention the person receiving (*BIN* 9: no 126) or delivering (*BIN* 9: no 329, *BIN* 10 nos 10, 54).

It is remarkable that the large majority of these texts is called a copy (gaba-ri). They seem to have been drawn up by the administration of the workshop for its own reference while the original tablet was kept by the deliverer. The phrase kišib PN "sealed by PN" occurs almost always, but no tablet contains a seal impression. The seal must have been applied to the original tablet (see Chapter III, under "Sealing officials").

The second type of record of step 1 is written from the perspective of the deliverer. The frozen verbal form mu-túm "delivery" is used, and sometimes the name of the deliverer is included, e.g., *BIN* 9: no 505:

| | | |
|---|---|---|
| Obv | 4 1/2 sìla 5 gín / ì-giš | 4 1/2 sila, 5 shekels sesame oil |
| | mu-$^{giš}$ig-šè | for a door, |
| | [k]i *Li-bur-be-lí-*/ta | from Libūr-bēlī. |
| | [m]u-túm | Delivery. |
| Rev 5) | iti zíz-a u$_4$-26-kam | Month XI, day 25, |
| | mu $^{d}$*Iš-bi-Èr-ra* / lugal-e ugnim / lú SU.A ù / Elam bí-in-ra | I.E. 16. |

Libūr-bēlī, who delivers the oil is always associated to this commodity in the Isin archive, delivering it (e.g., *BIN* 10: nos 38, 44, *ASJ* 5: p. 54 no 3), or receiving containers for it (e.g., *BIN* 9: nos 393, 399, 429) and so he probably represents an institution dealing in oil. Such information, gathered from other texts, allows us to determine that the texts of this type record deliveries to the workshop, and not from it to another institution.

2) Step 2: Distribution of the materials to the craftsmen

The records of step 2 are hard to distinguish from those of step 1 or of step 5, since they contain the same elements. Only from the study of the personal names, can it be determined whether the texts record a delivery to the craftsmen or to another institution. If the recipients are known to be craftsmen (see the lists of craftsmen in chapter III), the text is a record of step 2. If the recipient does not belong to the craftsmen, the text is a record of step 5. Thus, forty-eight texts can be assigned to this step. Here too, the texts can be written from two different perspectives; they are either receipts by the craftsmen or deliveries by the officials to them.

The texts of the first type resemble the records of step 1, but from a study of the personal names it becomes clear that they record a transaction inside the workshop, e.g., *BIN* 9: no 501:

| | | |
|---|---|---|
| Obv | 1 gú síg-ud$_5$ | 1 talent goat's hair, |
| | ki $^{d}$Nanna-ki-ág-/ta | from Nanna-kiag |
| | Ur-$^{d}$Lugal-bàn-/da | Ur-Lugalbanda |
| Rev | šu ba-ti | received. |
| | iti gu$_4$-si-su | Month II, |
| | mu $^{giš}$gu-za / $^{d}$Nin-urta mu-/ dím | I.E.25. |
| seal impression: | Ur-Lugal-$^{d}$bàn[-da] | Ur-Lugalbanda |
| | dumu *A-ḫu-ba-a* | son of Aḫubā'a |

The text contains the same elements as do some records of step 1 (e.g., *BIN* 9: nos 110, 112), but since Nanna-kiag is an official of the workshop (see chapter III under "Supervisory Personnel") and Ur-Lugalbanda is the overseer of the felters, this text clearly records an internal transaction in the workshop. Moreover, the presence of a seal impression on the tablet distinguishes it from records of step 1. All the tablets of this type seem to be originals for the term "copy" (gaba-ri) does not occur on them.

The second type of records, written from the perspective of the officials, most often contains the frozen verbal form mu-túm "delivery", e.g., *BIN* 9: no 147:

| | | |
|---|---|---|
| Obv | 2 kuš-gu$_4$ ú-ḫáb | 2 red oxhides, |
| | 2 ma-na še-gín | 2 mina glue, |
| | mu-$^{giš}$ig-šè | for a door: |
| | ki *Šu-$^{d}$Nin-kar-/ra-ak*-ta | from Šū-Ninkarak. |
| Rev | mu-túm | Delivery. |
| | iti še-kin-kud | Month XII, |
| | u$_4$-25-kam | day 25. |

Šū-Ninkarak is a well known official of the workshop (see chapter III under "Supervisory Personnel"), and the products delivered are used inside the workshop for production of a door; therefore it is clear that this text records of a delivery to the craftsmen.

Many records of step 2 omit several elements such as the verb (e.g., *BIN* 9: nos 13, 207), the year date (e.g., *BIN* 9: nos 147-148), and the persons who deliver and receive (e.g., *BIN* 9: nos 180, 188-189), probably excluded because the texts were only records kept for internal use in the workshop.

In these disbursement texts the purpose for which the materials are issued is often given, e.g., in *BIN* 9: no 13, 1 kuš máš-gal / kuš du$_8$-ši-a-aš "a full grown goat skin, to be colored green", or in *BIN* 10: no 70, 1/3 ma-na še-gín / 1/3 sìla zì-šig$_{15}$ / $^{giš}$ig-dib-$^{d}$Inanna "1/3 mina glue, 1/3 sila coarse flour, for a panelled door of Inanna".

3) Step 3: Manufacture

The third step, the actual manufacture in the workshop, is illustrated only in a few account texts of the Isin archive. An example is *BIN* 9: no 489:

| | | |
|---|---|---|
| Obv | 140 gu$_4$-ú-ḫáb | 140 red ox(hides), |
| | 180 gu$_4$-mu-2-ú-ḫáb | 180 red (hides) of two year old oxen, |
| | 180 udu *a*⟨*-lum*⟩-ú-ḫáb | 180 red *alum*-sheep (skins), |
| | 10 udu-ú-ḫáb | 10 red sheep(skins), |
| | 90 máš-gal-ú-ḫáb | 90 red (skins) of full-grown goats: |
| | ì-bi 2 sìla 10 gín | its oil is 2 sila and 10 shekels, |
| | ú-ḫáb-bi 3 ma-na | its madder is 3 minas, |
| | *al-la-ḫa*⟨*-ru*⟩ 6 sìla | (its) alum is 6 sila, |
| | naga-bi 1/2 sìla | its alkali is 1/2 sila; |
| | 14 udu-gi$_6$ | 14 black sheep(skins), |
| | 11 máš-gal-gi$_6$ | 11 black (skins) of full-grown goats: |
| | ì-bi 100[+] sìla 4 gín | its oil is 100+ sila and 4 shekels, |
| | im-KÙ.GI 3 sìla | (its) ... is 3 sila, |
| | ì-ba-a-dé 1/2 sìla | (its) strained(?) oil is 1/2 sila, |
| | nu-úr!-ma 2 sìla | (its) pomegranate is 2 sila, |
| | 1/3 sìla 5 gín $^{giš}$gigir! kin-til-la | 1/3 sila 5 shekels (for a) chariot finished work; |
| | 50 gu$_4$ sí[g-mú?] | 50 hairy? ox(hides), |
| | 240 udu *a-[lum]* | 240 *alum*-sheep (skins), |
| | 27 [ ] / 240 u[du ] | 27 [ ] / 240 [ ] sheep(skins), |
| Rev | 9 u[du ] | 9 [ ] sheep(skins): |
| | ì-bi 2 1/3 sìla 4 gín | its oil is 2 1/3 sila 4 shekels; |
| | 70 ⟨gín⟩ sa | 70 (shekels) catgut, |
| | 4 ⟨ma-na?⟩ 29 ⟨gín?⟩ še-gí[n] | 4 (minas) and 29 (shekels) glue: |
| | kin-ašgab | work of the leatherworkers. |

| | |
|---|---|
| 4 ⟨ma-na?⟩ še-gín | 4 (minas) glue: |
| kin-nagar | work of the carpenters. |
| 34 ⟨ma-na?⟩ 40 ⟨gín?⟩ ⟨še-gín??⟩ | 34 (minas) and 40 (shekels) (glue??), |
| 6 ma-na 10 gín níg-/ | 6 minas and 10 shekels goat's |
| ⟨U.⟩NU-a síg-ud$_5$ | hair thread. |
| (erasure of several lines) | |
| iti šu-numun-a mu-ús-sa nin-me-/an-ki[54] | Month IV, I.E. 21. |

This text is unique in the Isin archive since it only describes amounts of leather processed with the amounts of materials used. Presumably, however, the erasure of several lines before the date of the text contained the information usually found in disbursement texts.

Information concerning manufacture is indeed sometimes included in disbursement texts which list the type of craftsman who worked on a specific part of the finished product and the components of that product, e.g., *BIN* 9: no 349:

| | | |
|---|---|---|
| Obv | 1 $^{\text{giš}}$ig-mi-rí-za | 1 door made of small boards: |
| | še-gín-bi 2/3 ma-na | its glue is 2/3 mina, |
| | kin-nagar-kam | it is the work of the carpenters; |
| | kuš-gu$_4$-babbar-bi 1 1/3 | its white oxhides are 1 and 1/3, |
| | kuš-gu$_4$-síg-mú-bi 1/3 | its hairy oxhide is 1/3, |
| | kin-ašgab-kam | it is the work of the leatherworkers; |
| | ésir-é-a 15 sìla | (its) bitumen is 15 sila, |
| | im-bábbar-bi 4 ma-na | its gypsum is 4 minas, |
| | kin-ad-KID-kam | it is the work of the reedworkers; |
| Rev | ká é-an-za-gàr / bàd šà uru$^{\text{ki}}$ | for the gate of the tower of the wall of the city. |
| | gìr $^{\text{d}}$*Sîn-re'i* / rá-gaba | Sîn-rē'ī, the mounted messenger (was) conveyor. |
| | iti sig$_4$-a u$_4$-11-kam | Month III, day 11, |
| | mu-ús-sa nin-dingir / $^{\text{d}}$Lugal-ír-ra ba-/íl | I.E. 33. |

[54] This text is very concise and many key words seem to have been omitted. There are also large numbers of erasures on the tablet, indicating that the tablet is a draft. In lines 1-5, 10-11, and 17-20 all entries must refer to skins and hides although the word kuš is never used, since the term ú-ḫáb "red" never occurs as a specification of oxen, sheep or goats.

The sense of line 16 is obscure: the product measuring 1/3 sila and 5 shekels is not specified. The chariot ($^{\text{giš}}$gigir) seems to be the "finished work" (kin-til-la = *kintillû*, *CAD* K: p. 388f., *AHw*: p. 481, *šiprum gamrum*, *AHw*: p. 1245).

In lines 23, 25, and 27 it is unclear in what unit the še-gín "glue" is measured. Usually it is measured by weight, in mina and shekel, and presumably these measures can be reconstructed here. In 27 it is unclear whether še-gín is intended, but it seems most likely given the parallelism with 23 and 25. Possibly a textile-related product is intended, since the following line has goat's hair thread.

Although information about manufacture is included in several of these disbursement texts, it is clear that this was not a primary concern to the administration.

Yet, the attendance of the craftsmen of the four sections of the workshop was carefully recorded. 117 texts list the names of the craftsmen active on a particular day, their profession, and sometimes a short notation about their activity. Two additional texts give similar information; but in a more concise form. *BIN* 10: no 313 only gives the names of reedworkers, and *BIN* 10: no 314 lists the days of absence of certain craftsmen. These texts, which will be referred to as the worker lists, are our main source of information about the craftsmen and will be discussed in detail in chapter III.

4) Step 4: Receipt of the finished products

The delivery of finished products by the craftsmen to the officials of the workshop is also poorly documented. Only thirty texts can be considered records of this step with more or less certainty. Some of these record amounts of finished products delivered by one or more craftsmen, and two give also the amounts they are in arrears, e.g., *BIN* 10: no 80:

| | | |
|---|---|---|
| Obv | 13 $^{gi}$banšur mu-túm / la(l)u$_6$ 2 | 13 reed trays delivered, in arrears 2: |
| | *Ili-ra-bí* | Ilī-rabi; |
| | 14 mu-túm la(l)u$_6$ 1 | 14 delivered, in arrears 1: |
| | *Ku-bu-lum* | Kubbulum; |
| | 7 mu-túm la(l)u$_6$ 4 | 7 delivered, in arrears 4: |
| | Lugal-ab-ba | Lugal-abba; |
| | 11 mu-túm *Šu-$^{d}$/Adad* | 11 delivered: Šū-Adad; |
| Rev | 18 mu-túm la(l)u$_6$ 2 | 18 delivered, in arrears 2: |
| | *Šu-$^{d}$Adad* min | Šū-Adad bis; |
| | 10 mu-túm la(l)u$_6$ 1 | 10 delivered, in arrears 1: |
| | Kù-$^{d}$Nanna | Ku-Nanna; |
| | 15 mu-túm *Šu-Eš$_4$-tár* | 15 delivered: Šū-Eštar; |
| | [10] mu-túm la(l)u$_6$ 1 | [10] delivered, in arrears 1: |
| | [*Puz*]*ur$_4$-$^{d}$En-líl* | Puzur-Enlil; |
| | *Puzur$_4$-Eš$_4$-tár* | (for) Puzur-Eštar. |
| | 98 mu-túm / la(l)u$_6$ 11 | (Total:) 98 delivered, in arrears 11: |
| LE. | (erasure) LUM | |
| | $^{[gi]}$banšur / mu-túm | reed trays delivered. |

All the workmen mentioned are reedworkers and the text lists their work quota, i.e. the amount of finished products they delivered, and the amount they had yet to complete. Several other texts list the amounts finished without the amounts in arrears (*BIN* 9: nos 131, 133, 135, 145, and *BIN* 10: no 72). Only in the last text is mention made of who received the product — HA̯.LA-ša, the overseer of those felters who produced the delivered goat's wool.

The products of the felters were sometimes weighed and a special document was drawn up, e.g., *BIN* 10: no 76:

| | | |
|---|---|---|
| Obv | 1 ébiḫ síg-ud$_5$ | 1 goat's hair heavy rope, |
| | ki-lá-bi 11 1/3 ma-na | its weight is 11 1/3 minas, |
| | u$_4$-7-kam | on day 7; |
| | 1 ébiḫ síg-ud$_5$ | 1 goat's hair heavy rope, |
| | ki-lá-bi 8 1/3 ma-na | its weight is 8 1/3 minas, |
| | u$_4$-8-kam | on day 8; |
| Rev | mu-$^{\text{giš}}$ig-šè | for a door. |
| | ì-lá Ur-$^{\text{d}}$Lugal-bàn-/da | Ur-Lugalbanda weighed. |
| | iti sig$_4$-a | Month III, |
| | mu bàd $^{\text{d}}$*Iš-bi-/Èr-ra ri-im* / $^{\text{d}}$*En-líl* ba-dù | I.E. 19. |

The person weighing is the overseer of the felters and, although the purpose for the manufacture of the rope is given, the text does not record its disbursement. Several texts, however, record together the weighing and delivering of products (steps 4 and 5), e.g., *BIN* 8: no 129, *BIN* 10: nos 85-86.

5) Step 5: Disbursement of finished products

The last step, the disbursement of the finished products, is the best documented, and more than 497 texts record it. Most of them are written from the perspective of the officials of the workshop, and record distribution by them. In the most complete records of this type, the following elements are included: the finished products, the person or institution to whom they are distributed (x-šè), the conveyor (gìr) of the recipient, the official of the issuing workshop (ki-PN-ta ba-zi), the general conveyor (gìr) of the workshop, the comptroller (maškim), and the date. Some of the tablets contain one or more seal impressions, most often from the conveyor representing the workshop. Some of the records of this type are extensive since they deal with several issues at once, e.g., *BIN* 9: no 415:

| | | |
|---|---|---|
| Obv | 1 [+ $^{\text{kuš}}$]dùg-gan $^{\text{giš}}$ban | 1+ leather bags for bows: |
| | kuš-udu-*a-lum*-bi 7 | their *alum*-sheep skins are 7, |
| | $^{\text{giš}}$ban ba-an-gar | bows are put in it; |

| | | |
|---|---|---|
| | 6 $^{gi}$pisan-gíd-da | 6 long boxes: |
| | ésir-é-a-bi 8 sìla | their bitumen is 8 sila, |
| | $^{giš}$gag-ban ba-an-gar | arrow-heads are put in it; |
| | gìr $^{d}$*Iš-bi-Èr-ra-*/zi-kalam-ma | Išbi'erra-zikalama (was) conveyor |
| | 1 $^{kuš}$e-sír é-ba-an | 1 pair of sandals: |
| | kuš-gu$_4$-ú-ḫáb-bi 5 gín | its red oxhide is 5 shekels, |
| | šu-e-sír-bi šà-ba | its shoe-mold is included, |
| | še-gín-bi 1/2 gín | its glue is 1/2 shekel, |
| | sa-bi 1 gín | its catgut is 1 shekel; |
| | 1 $^{kuš}$[u]mmu(d) | 1 waterskin: |
| | k[uš b]i 5 gín | its [ leat]her is 5 shekels; |
| Rev | $^{d}$*Iš-bi-Èr-ra-ša-/am-ba-la-ṭi-im* nar | (for) Išbi'erra-šam-balāṭim the singer. |
| | 4 $^{kuš}$ummu(d) | 4 waterskins: |
| | éš síg-ud$_5$-bi 1/3 ma-na | their goat's hair rope is 1/3 mina; |
| | kaskal Bar-sí-pa$^{ki}$-šè | (for) those who go on a |
| | gin-na-me | trip to Borsippa; |
| | gìr *Ma-nu-um-ki-ì-lí-a* / lú-kin-gi$_4$-a | Mannum-kī-ilija, the messenger (was) conveyor. |
| | sukkal-maḫ maškim | The sukkal-maḫ was comptroller. |
| | ki *Šu-$^{d}$Nin-kar-ak*-ta | Issued by |
| | ba-zi | Šū-Ninkarak. |
| | gìr *Bu-qú-šum* / ù Lú-ša$_6$-ga | Buqqušum and Lušaga (were) conveyors. |
| | iti sig$_4$-a | Month III, |
| | mu en $^{d}$En-líl-lá / ba-íl | I.E. 24, |
| LE. | u$_4$-16-kam | day 16. |

Most texts do not include all these elements. Very frequent is the absence of the name of the general conveyor after the phrase "issued by PN". On some of these texts (e.g., *BIN* 9: no 382, 401 and 451) the seal of Buqqušum — who acts as general conveyor of the workshop (see chapter III under "Supervisory Personnel") — is impressed, indicating his supervision over the transaction.

Most common are texts which only list the products and the outside conveyors who picked them up (e.g., *BIN* 9: nos 270, 272-274, 277-279). Only from other texts we know that these conveyors were not active inside the workshop and that the texts record expenditures, e.g., *BIN* 9: no 315:

| | | |
|---|---|---|
| Obv | 4 $^{dug}$šáman / ì-du$_{10}$-ga | Of 4 bowls for fine oil, |
| | kuš-udu-ú-ḫáb-bi 2/3 | the red sheepskin is 2/3, |
| | ka-tab-šè | for the lids. |
| | gìr $^{d}$Nanna-/ì-ša$_6$ | Nanna-iša (was) conveyor. |
| Rev | u$_4$-18-kam | Day 18, |
| | iti še-kin-kud | month XII, |
| | mu en $^{d}$Inanna / máš-e ì-pàd | I.E. 13. |

The conveyor mentioned here, Nanna-iša, is not associated with the workshop, but has the function of cupbearer (sagi, cf. *BIN* 9: no 389), and is always mentioned in relation to bowls and leather bags for oil in the rest of the Isin archive (e.g., *BIN* 9: nos 276, 317, 319).

More than 300 texts of this first type of disbursement are found in the Isin archive. Of them only forty-three are called a copy (gaba-ri). These are mostly "Sammeltafeln" listing several deliveries, sometimes over several days (*BIN* 9: nos 240, 307, 326, 327, 360) or months (*BIN* 9: nos 389, 512), but sometimes on the same day (*BIN* 9: nos 39, 325, 380, 408). These texts were probably compiled from several individual tablets and thus they were called copies.

Closely related to this type of texts are eight texts which contain the participial construction zi-ga "expended", with mention of the conveyor (*BIN* 9: nos 369, 463, 466, 492, *BIN* 10: no 191, *JCS* 20: p. 38-42 no 5), or of the name of the recipient (*BIN* 9: no 386, *BIN* 10: no 90).

A second type of disbursement text is written from the perspective of the recipient. They most often list the object, the name of the official of the workshop who delivers it (ki-PN1-ta), and the recipient's name (PN2 šu ba-an-ti). The texts are often sealed by the recipient, e.g., *BIN* 9: no 111:

| | | |
|---|---|---|
| Obv | 21 $^{kuš}$*ga-ba-/bu-um* | Of 21 shields |
| | kuš-gu$_4$-bi 6 | the oxhides are 6; |
| | ki $^{d}$Nanna-ki-ág-/ta | from Nanna-kiag, |
| Rev | $^{d}$*Iš-bi-Èr-ra-/ma-lik* | Išbi'erra-mālik |
| | šu ba-an-ti | received. |
| | iti bára-zag-gar | Month I, |
| | mu $^{giš}$gu-za $^{d}$/Nin-líl-lá ba-dím | I.E. 28. |
| Seal impression: | $^{d}$*Iš-bi-/Èr-ra* | lugal-ma-/da-na |
| | dingir-kalam-ma-/na | $^{d}$*Iš-bi-* |
| | lugal-kal-ga | *Èr-ra-ma-lik* |
| | Išbi-Erra | king of his land |
| | god of his land | Išbi'erra-mālik |
| | mighty king | |

Nanna-kiag is the official of the workshop who is responsible for the expenditures in I.E. 28 (see chapter III under "Supervisory Personnel"). Since none of these texts is said to be a copy (gaba-ri), most of the records of step 5 were originals kept in the archive of the workshop.

6) Miscellaneous texts

A special group of texts records days on which there were no transactions in the workshop. They are *BIN* 9: no 528, *BIN* 10: nos 197-

204, and *JAOS* 98: p. 254 no 8. Twice we have two copies of this record: *BIN* 10: no 197 = no 198 and no 199 = 200:

| | |
|---|---|
| Obv u$_4$-10-kam nu-ub-tuk | On day 10 no transactions (lit. of day 10 there is none), |
| iti ne-ne-gar | Month V, |
| mu-ús-sa nin-dingir / $^{d}$Lugal-ír-ra / ba-íl | I.E. 33. |
| Rev uninscribed | |
| Seal impression: *Bu-qú-šum* | Buqqušum |
| (only on no 200) dub-sar | the scribe |
| dumu *A-bu-bu* | son of Abūbu |

Five of these have a seal impression, probably to make them official. Note that all of these texts date from the fifth and sixth month of I.E. 33; of month V days 4, 10, 12, 18, 22, and 24 are recorded thus, of month VI day 10. These texts seem to indicate that on these days the workshop did not obtain any material, nor expended any products, and that no records were kept.

Another group of texts, closely related to these, seems to record the days that tablets were written in one month (*BIN* 9: no 521, *BIN* 10: nos 205-206), e.g., *BIN* 9: no 521:

| | | |
|---|---|---|
| Obv | u$_4$-1-kam | day 1 |
| | u$_4$-2-kam | day 2 |
| | u$_4$-6-kam | day 6 |
| | u$_4$-7-kam | day 7 |
| | u$_4$-8-kam | day 8 |
| | u$_4$-9-kam | day 9 |
| | u$_4$-10-kam | day 10 |
| | u$_4$-11-kam | day 11 |
| | u$_4$-12-kam | day 12 |
| Rev | u$_4$-14-kam | day 14 |
| | u$_4$-18-kam | day 18 |
| | u$_4$-19-kam | day 19 |
| | u$_4$-24-kam | day 24 |
| | u$_4$-25-kam | day 25 |
| | u$_4$-28-kam | day 28 |
| | u$_4$-30-kam | day 30 |
| | im-bi 16-àm | its tablets are 16: |
| | iti gan-gan-è | Month IX, |
| | mu $^{d}$*Šu-ì-lí-šu*/ lugal-e giš-nir $^{d}$Nanna | Š.i. 2 |

Among the other special texts are a letter (*BIN* 9: no 486) and tablet basket tags (pisan-dub-ba: *BIN* 9: no 503, and probably *BIN* 9: no 487 and *BIN* 10: no 196). Certain other texts are unique (e.g., *BIN* 9: no

520) and their function is not evident. For some of them it is unclear whether they belong to the archive or not.

7) Conclusions

Hence, almost all texts of the Isin archive are records of one of the five steps in the transactions of the workshop. Step 1, the issue of raw materials to the workshop, is documented by a large number of texts recording receipts of these materials. Most texts of this type are said to be copies (gaba-ri). The second step, the distribution of the raw materials to the craftsmen, is less well documented. The texts are either receipts by the craftsmen or records of deliveries by the officials who received the materials from outside the workshop. Since these texts are very similar to records of step 1 and 5, they are often difficult to recognize. The third step, the manufacture, is scarcely documented in the account texts, but we are well informed about what craftsmen were active through the worker lists. The next step, the receipt of the finished products from the craftsmen (step 4), is also poorly documented. There are a number of texts giving the work quota of some types of craftsmen, and some records of the weighing of products of the felters. Step 5, disbursement of the finished products, is the best documented. A large number of texts records issues of the finished products by officials of the workshop to their outside destinations. These texts seem to be mostly originals kept in the archives of the workshop. In addition to these records, there exists a small number of miscellaneous texts, mostly recording on what days transactions took place and when there was no activity.

This survey shows that the administration of the Isin workshop was most accurate in recording the transactions of the workshop with the outside: records of receipts of raw materials and deliveries of finished products were meticulously kept, while activities inside the workshop were not always written down. These records were kept together in baskets with labels such as *BIN* 9: no 503. Probably each month a list was made of the days on which transactions were concluded, and special tablets recorded the days on which no transactions occurred.

Moreover, it becomes clear that two types of records were kept, originals and copies. The tablets recording expenditures were originals and often have a seal impression, while the receipt texts are copies without sealing. The originals of those were probably kept by the issuing institution.

Because of this emphasis of the records we have actually little information about what took place inside the workshop. Only from fragmentary information, mostly from the lists of materials used in the finished products, can we discern what type of craftsmen were active in the manufacture of certain products. Detailed information about the manufacture, such as the consecutive steps in the production, the time involved, the exact amounts of materials used etc., is not available.

### C. *Chronology of the archive*

The recovered part of the Isin archive stems from a rather short period of time; all texts date from the years I.E. 4 to Š.i. 3, a period of thrity-three years. The distribution of the texts over that period of time is very uneven (see table I.2 and figure 1). In table I.2 the numbers of texts found in each year are listed; first the total number of texts from each year is given and then the percentage that number represents in the entire archive. Then the archive is divided following the five steps described in section B. The number of records of each type is given for each year, and the percentage that number represents in the total number of records of that step. Thus the ten records of step 1 in I.E.19 represent 5% of all the records of step 1. For step 3, the three account texts are separated from the worker lists which are an entirely different type of document. In the last two columns of the table the number of miscellaneous texts and their percentages are given. For all these groups it is also recorded how many texts have a date which is uncertain because it is partly broken, how many were not dated by the scribes, and how many have lost their date. In figure 1 some of this information is put out as a line graph. Figure 1a records the percentages of the total number of texts per year. In figure 1b the same is given for the records of step 1 (continuous line), step 5 (dotted line), and the worker lists (broken line). The other groups of texts are not recorded because they are too few in number.

It is clear that the total number of texts varies greatly from year to year. The largest number of dated texts is from I.E.13 (seventy-four texts), but there are more undated texts (112 texts). The smallest number of texts is found in I.E. 4, 5, and 31 (one text each). The graph in figure 1a shows a very irregular curve with alternate ups and downs, which V. Crawford interpreted as an indication that the texts do not represent a

| year | total | | step 1 | | step 2 | | step 3 | | | | step 4 | | step 5 | | misc. | |
|---|---|---|---|---|---|---|---|---|---|---|---|---|---|---|---|---|
| | | | | | | | account | | worker | | | | | | | |
| I.E. | # | % | # | % | # | % | # | % | # | % | # | % | # | % | # | % |
| 4 | 1 | .1 | 1 | .5 | | | | | | | | | | | | |
| 5 | 1 | .1 | | | | | | | | | 1 | 3.3 | | | | |
| 6 | 9 | .9 | | | | | | | | | | | 9 | 1.8 | | |
| 7 | 24 | 2.6 | 1 | .5 | | | | | 17 | 14.5 | 1 | 3.3 | 5 | 1 | | |
| 8 | 16 | 1.7 | 1 | .5 | | | | | 9 | 7.7 | 1 | 3.3 | 5 | 1 | | |
| 9 | 18 | 1.9 | | | 2 | 4.1 | | | 7 | 6 | 3 | 10 | 5 | 1 | 1 | 3.7 |
| 10 | 11 | 1.2 | 2 | 1 | | | | | 6 | 5.1 | | | 3 | .6 | | |
| 11 | 17 | 1.8 | 7 | 3.5 | 2 | 4.1 | | | 5 | 4.3 | | | 3 | .6 | | |
| 12 | 26 | 2.8 | 12 | 6 | 1 | 2 | | | 2 | 1.7 | | | 11 | 2.2 | | |
| 13 | 74 | 8 | 12 | 6 | 3 | 6.2 | 1 | 33 | 8 | 6.8 | 2 | 6.6 | 48 | 9.6 | | |
| 14 | 44 | 4.8 | 5 | 2.5 | 1 | 2 | | | 9 | 7.7 | 2 | 6.6 | 27 | 5.4 | | |
| 15 | 38 | 4.1 | 3 | 1.6 | 3 | 6.2 | | | 9 | 7.7 | | | 23 | 4.6 | | |
| 16 | 61 | 6.6 | 15 | 7.6 | 10 | 20.8 | | | 1 | .9 | 2 | 6.6 | 33 | 6.6 | | |
| 17 | 20 | 2.2 | 6 | 3 | | | | | 1 | .9 | | | 12 | 2.4 | 1 | 3.7 |
| 18 | 15 | 1.6 | 6 | 3 | 1 | 2 | | | 1 | .9 | | | 6 | 1.2 | 1 | 3.7 |
| 19 | 53 | 5.7 | 10 | 5 | 1 | 2 | | | | | 1 | 3.3 | 40 | 8 | 1 | 3.7 |
| 20 | 17 | 1.8 | 5 | 2.5 | | | | | 1 | .9 | | | 11 | 2.2 | | |
| 21 | 30 | 3.2 | 12 | 6 | | | 1 | 33 | 2 | 1.7 | | | 13 | 2.6 | 2 | 7.4 |
| 22 | 54 | 5.8 | 21 | 10.6 | 2 | 4.1 | | | | | | | 30 | 6 | 1 | 3.7 |
| 23 | 29 | 3.1 | 13 | 6.6 | 1 | 2 | 1 | 33 | | | | | 14 | 2.8 | | |
| 24 | 15 | 1.6 | 9 | 4.5 | | | | | | | 1 | 3.3 | 5 | 1 | | |
| 25 | 40 | 4.3 | 15 | 7.5 | 3 | 6.2 | | | | | 1 | 3.3 | 21 | 4.2 | | |
| 26 | 22 | 2.4 | 6 | 3 | | | | | | | | | 16 | 3.2 | | |
| 27 | 11 | 1.2 | 1 | .5 | | | | | | | 2 | 6.6 | 8 | 1.6 | | |
| 28 | 14 | 1.5 | 3 | 1.5 | | | | | | | 1 | 3.3 | 10 | 2 | | |
| 29 | 2 | .2 | | | | | | | | | | | 2 | .4 | | |
| 30 | 4 | .4 | 4 | 2 | | | | | | | | | | | | |
| 31 | 1 | .1 | | | | | | | | | | | 1 | .2 | | |
| 32 | 4 | .4 | 1 | .5 | | | | | | | 1 | 3.3 | 2 | .4 | | |
| 33 | 46 | 5 | 6 | 3 | | | | | | | 1 | 3.3 | 29 | 5.8 | 10 | 37 |
| Š.i. | | | | | | | | | | | | | | | | |
| 1 | 23 | 2.5 | 4 | 2 | 1 | 2 | | | | | | | 18 | 3.6 | | |
| 2 | 12 | 1.3 | 1 | .5 | | | | | | | 1 | 3.3 | 9 | 1.8 | 1 | 3.7 |
| 3 | 24 | 2.6 | 2 | 1 | 4 | 8.3 | | | | | | | 16 | 3.2 | 2 | 7.4 |
| uncertain | 4 | .4 | | | | | | | | | | | 4 | .8 | | |
| no date | 112 | 12.2 | 9 | 4.5 | 13 | 27 | | | 36 | 30.8 | 7 | 23.3 | 41 | 8.2 | 6 | 22.2 |
| broken | 28 | 3 | 5 | 2.5 | | | | | 3 | 2.6 | 2 | 6.6 | 17 | 3.4 | 1 | 3.7 |
| total # | 920 | | 198 | | 48 | | 3 | | 117 | | 30 | | 497 | | 27 | |

Table I.2: Chronological distribution of the texts of the archive

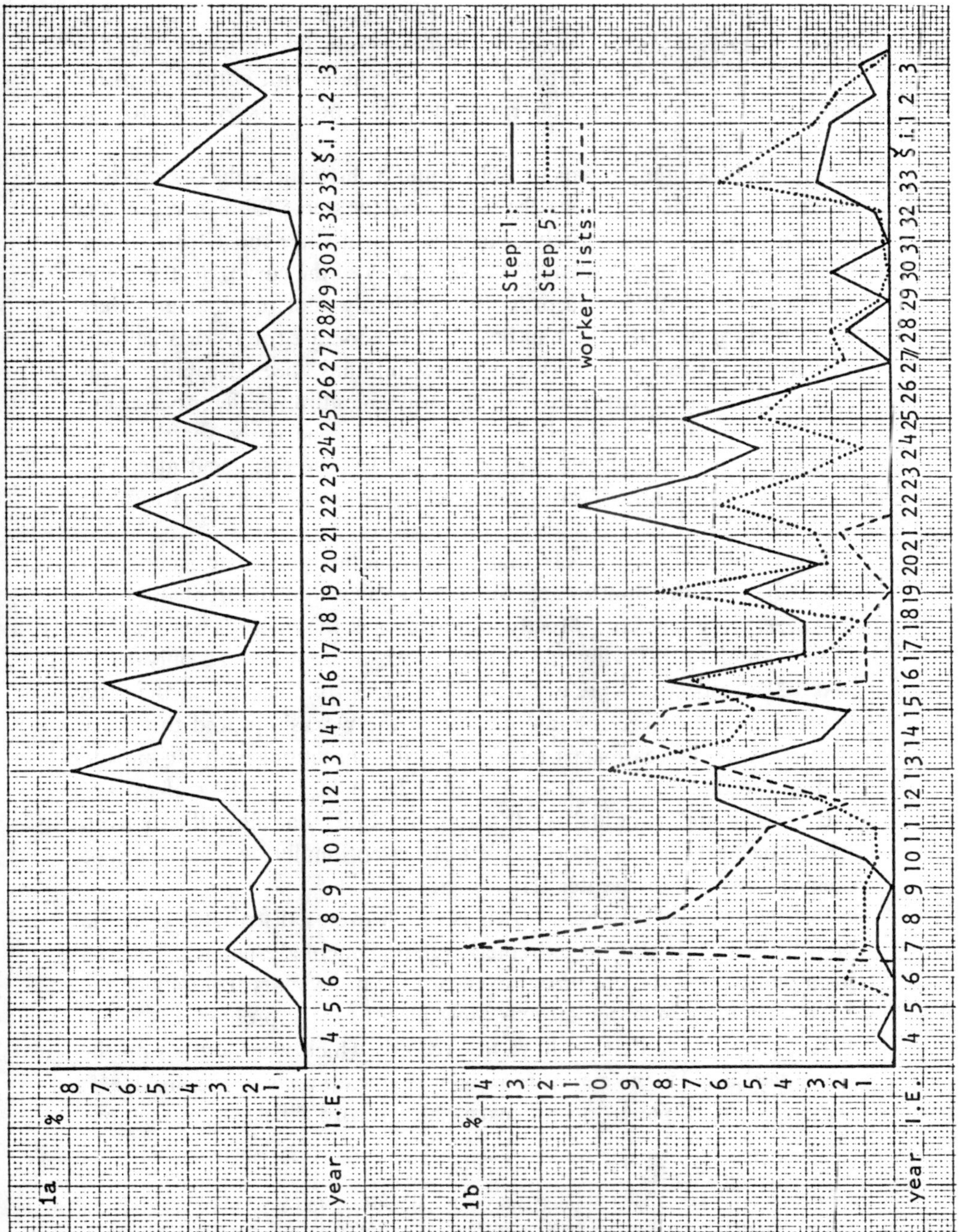


Figure 1a: Line graph of percentages of texts of the Isin archive per year
Figure 1b: Line graph of percentages of records of step 1 and 5, and of the worker lists per year

single large archive, but rather a series of small archives[55]. Since the tablets were recovered unsystematically by people who probably did not clear out the entire archive room or rooms and did not bother to collect fragments, however, this distribution seems more likely due to the accident of recovery.

The curves of the records of steps 1 and 5 show the same distribution of ups and downs (see figure 1b). The curve for step 5 follows that of the total number of texts closely, which is logical since most texts of the archive are records of this step. The similarity of the curves of step 1 and step 5 shows that these records were probably kept together and were recovered together. If they had been kept in separate rooms or areas, the distribution of recovered texts per type would have been dissimilar. This is the case for the worker lists which show an entirely different distribution over time. They are best represented in the early years of the archive, with a second peak in I.E. 14 and 15, and disappear after I.E. 21. This distribution shows that they were kept separate from the account texts.

From table I.2 it is clear that a large number of texts is undated (12.2%). The distribution of these texts over the different steps is, however, very uneven. Mostly undated are the records of steps 2 (30.8%) and 4 (23.3%), while of the records of steps 1 and 5 only 4.5% and 8.2% respectively are undated. This seems to indicate that the texts of steps 2 and 4 were for internal use in the workshop, and thus very concise, while those of steps 1 and 5 record transactions with the outside and had to be more complete (cf. section B). A large number of worker lists are also undated (30.8%). It seems, however, that they all date from I.E. 6 and that the year date was left out intentionally (see discussion of their chronology in chapter III).

In each year the number of texts is rather evenly distributed over the months. Some months are extremely well documented, such as I/-/I.E.16 from which we have seventeen texts, but for most years from which we have a sufficient number of texts most months are represented.

It is remarkable that we have few records which were written on the same day. Besides the eleven groups of duplicate texts in the archive[56], there are only three groups of texts which record different transactions

[55] *BIN* 9: p. 16.

[56] *BIN* 9: no 344 = no 345, no 356 = no 357, no 363 = *ASJ* 5: p. 57 no 9, *BIN* 9: no 376 = 377, *BIN* 9: no 380 = *JAOS* 98: p. 256 no 12, *BIN* 9: no 403 = no 404, no 448 = no 449, no 515 = *BIN* 10: no 208, *BIN* 10: no 107 = Lindblom High School 1, *BIN* 10: no 197 = no 198, no 199 = no 200.

on the same day: *BIN* 9: nos 778 and 208, I/7/I.E.16, *BIN* 9: nos 137 and 141, XII/3/I.E.16, and *BIN* 9: nos 159 and 204 both XIII/-/I.E.16. In addition, there are two lists of transactions over several days, which include a day from which we have another document; *BIN* 9: no 360 has an entry for IV/6/I.E.14, the date of *BIN* 9: no 257, and *BIN* 9: no 296 for V/5/I.E.16, also recorded in *BIN* 9: no 157. All these elements seem to indicate that the workshop did not require a large administration and that only a few records were written each day. From some texts we actually know that on some days no transactions at all were recorded (see section B under "Miscellaneous texts"). All the preserved records of days without transactions date from a short period of time; we have records for days 4, 10, 12, 18, 22, and 24 of month V and for day 10 of month VI of I.E.33. From other years we do not have any of these texts, but we may assume that they existed. Three texts in the archive record on what days in a certain month tablets were written (*BIN* 9: no 521, *BIN* 10: nos 205-206). The number of days with tablets is rather low, sixteen, fifteen, and twenty days respectively. This low number of records does, however, not indicate that there was little activity in the workshop, but, with most texts recording several transactions, only that few documents were drawn up.

It is thus difficult to estimate what part of the archive is recovered. While it is probable that for each year of the lifetime of the workshop only a small percentage of the texts is preserved, on the other hand the total number of texts may not have been extremely large.

CHAPTER II

# MATERIALS AND PRODUCTS

The types of texts discussed in the previous chapter give limited information about aspects of the production process in the workshop, since their main purpose is to record transactions with other institutions; our information is mostly limited to a list of materials acquired by the workshop, and of products issued by it. Some indications about the materials used by each type of craftsmen — carpenters, leatherworkers, reedworkers, and felters — and how they were employed can, however, be derived from the texts.

## A. *Materials*

### 1) Carpenters (nagar)

The prime material used by carpenters, wood, is attested infrequently in the Isin archive. It seems to have been mainly used for doors (e.g., *BIN* 10: no 186: 2 $^{giš}$ig / $^{giš}$ù-suḫ$_5$-bi 6, "two doors, their logs of fir(?) tree are six") and furniture (e.g., *BIN* 9: no 374: $^{giš}$gu-za sìr-da-ḫa-lu-úb, "a sedan-chair of oak(?)"), possibly only for certain parts such as the legs (cf. *BIN* 9: no 374: giš-nú umbin-bi $^{giš}$taškarin, "a bed with legs of boxwood"). Most often attested is $^{giš}$ù-suḫ$_5$, commonly translated as "fir tree"[1], but which was probably another type of tree[2]. One text records the delivery of 4080 willow-trees(?) ($^{giš}$ma-nu[3], *BIN* 9: no 531), a product commonly used in Mesopotamia[4].

As adhesives, the carpenters used barley flour (dabin) and glue (še-gín), often combined[5]. Related to še-gín are a-še-gín, probably a

[1] E.g., D. Snell, *YNER* 8: p. 222.

[2] The translation "fir tree" is impossible, since $^{giš}$ù-suḫ$_6$ was cultivated in Southern Mesopotamia, where the fir tree cannot grow, cf. M. Stol, *On Trees, mountains and millstones in the ancient Near East*, Leiden, 1979: p. 18.

[3] For the translation "willow", see P. Steinkeller, "Foresters of Umma" (forthcoming). M. Civil prefers the translation "ash tree" (letter Feb. 24, 1984).

[4] A.L. Oppenheim, *Eames Coll.*: p. 54 n. 71.

[5] E.g., *BIN* 9: no 341: 1 $^{giš}$gu-za-má-laḫ$_6$ / še-gín-bi 10 gín / dabin-bi 5 gín / kin-nagar, "1 boatman's chair, its glue is 10 shekels, its barley flour is 5 shekels, the work of the carpenters".

solution of še-gín in water[6], and white še-gín (še-gín-babbar, perhaps to be read še-gín-ḫád, "dried še-gín"), both used for doors in combination with še-gín (a-še-gín, e.g., *BIN* 9: nos 153-157, še-gín-babbar, e.g., *BIN* 9: no 157).

Only one text mentions tools used by the carpenters: in *BIN* 9: no 374 toothed knives (ba-zú) are issued[6a]. No other tools for the carpenters, or any other craftsmen, are ever mentioned. This may be because tools were property on hand which is not accountable, or because the tools were owned by the craftsmen who brought them with them to the workshop (cf. chapter III).

The carpenters seem thus to have been specialized in the production of doors, furniture, etc., using wood and glue.

2) Leatherworkers (ašgab)

The early Isin texts are rich in information on leatherwork, although their study shows that only specific steps of the tanning process are documented. Leatherwork includes three main stages: the preparation of the skins for tanning, the actual tanning procedure, and the finishing. Although the processes in each stage are varied and often complicated, they can basically be described as follows. During the preparation for tanning the skins are cleaned after the flaying of the animals[7] by soaking them in "liquors containing vegetable infusions, e.g., the macerated stalks of plants, twigs, leaves, flour, beer, wine, grape juice and possibly stale water or urine containing bacteria"[8]. Then the skins are unhaired which can be done in different ways: by sweating them in warm and damp chambers, by immersing them in a lime solution, or by scraping them[9]. Impurities, flesh and remains of hair are then removed by scudding the skins with a knife. Further treatment depends on the kind of leather one wants to obtain. When a soft and flexible leather is needed, the skins are treated with infusions of dung, a process called "bating"[10]. Another process used is called "drenching" in which the

[6] It is remarkable that a-še-gín in the Isin texts is always attested as used for work on the wall (ki-sá-a), especially for its doors. The relationship between the two is unclear.

[6a] Perhaps $^{giš}$ba-z[u] in *BIN* 10: 120 refers to the same object.

[7] When the skins have to be temporarily preserved before being processed, they are cured in order to stop their decay, cf. R. Reed, *Ancient Skins, Parchments and Leathers*, London-New York, 1972: p. 49f.

[8] R. Reed, *Ancient Skins*: p. 49f.

[9] R.J. Forbes, *SAT* V: p. 4.

[10] R. Reed, *Ancient Skins*: p. 55-60.

hides are treated with an acid liquor with barley, flour, soured dough, or the husk of cereals[11].

The actual tanning is the treatment of the skins with certain chemical reagents to produce leathers, which are imputrescible, water resistant, and flexible. Three main types of tanning are known:

vegetable tanning through the use of tannic acid infusions
from certain barkes, leaves, woods or nuts,
mineral tanning with mineral salts, mainly alum,
oil tanning with oils and fats[12].

After tanning, the leather is dyed to give it color and fat-liquored to make it water resistant, durable and flexible.

Not all the techniques of leather production described above are attested in Mesopotamian sources. Since no description of tanning procedures is preserved in the cuneiform source material[13], it is often hard to equate the ancient terminology of products and procedures with our understanding of the tanning process. Many attempts to translate such terms are found in the Assyriological literature[14], but they are often contradicting and confusing. In the following section I will present the information from the Isin material with only minor references to other sources. My conclusions thus cannot be considered valid for the entire history of leatherwork as attested in the cuneiform sources.

Many types of skins are used in the Isin workshop: most attested are hides of oxen (gu$_4$), goats (máš), sheep (udu), and lambs (sila$_4$), but also used are those of equids (anše and dúsu), wild oxen (am), stags (lulim), gazelles (mašda), wild sheep (šeg$_9$-bar), pigs (šaḫ) and lions (ug). Each of the common types of hides is attested in many variations; the different types of animals (e.g., máš, máš-gal, máš-níta) known from the Sumerian cattle texts can be distinguished.

A skin is usually accounted for as a unit. Sometimes only one-half or one-third of a skin is used, mostly of oxen (e.g., *BIN* 9: no 346) and goats (e.g., *BIN* 9: no 395), but also of sheep (*BIN* 9: no 275). Oxleather is accounted for also by weight (e.g., *BIN* 9: nos 103, 190). Sometimes

[11] R. Reed, *Ancient Skins*: p. 60.

[12] R.J. Forbes *SAT* V: p. 5, M. Sigrist, *JCS* 33 (1981): p. 144f.

[13] Two texts from the first millennium B.C., however, prescribe tanning of goat and ox leather for ritual purposes (cf. M. Stol, *RlA* 6 [1980-83]: p. 530). The described acts are probably partly unusual, but must basically reflect daily practices.

[14] Very useful for the study of leatherwork are two recent articles: M. Sigrist, *JCS* 33 (1981): p. 141-190, and M. Stol, *RlA* 6 (1980-83): p. 527-543. Sigrist bases himself almost entirely on the evidence of the Ur III texts from Umma, while Stol makes use of the entire cuneiform corpus and many additional sources.

small amounts of leather, primarily used for objects such as the lids of vessels (e.g., *BIN* 9: no 403) or cushions (e.g., *BIN* 9: no 440), were accounted for as leather scraps (kuš-zag-bar)[15].

Certain sequences of texts accounting for deliveries to the workshop give information concerning the quantity of hides used in the workshop. For the first month of I.E. 16, the following texts record deliveries of hides:

| | | | |
|---|---|---|---|
| *BIN* 9: | no 78 | = day 7 : | 15 oxhides |
| | no 69 | = day 9 : | 10 oxhides |
| | no 58 | = day 13: | 50 dehaired skins of full-grown goats |
| | | | 15 dehaired sheepskins |
| | | | 21 hairy sheepskins |
| | no 75 | = day 15: | 2 oxhides |
| | no 73 | = day 19: | 9 oxhides |
| | | | 8 hides of three-year old oxen |
| | | | 5 hides of two-year old oxen |
| *BIN* 10: | no 12 | = day 25: | 13+? oxhides |
| | | | 1? young [ ] hide |
| | | = | 62+? oxhides, 50 goatskins, 36 sheepskins, and 1 young [ ] hide |

Even from the surviving evidence which is far from complete, it becomes clear that large amounts of leather were handled in the workshop.

At the delivery of skins a distinction is made between haired and dehaired ones, e.g., *BIN* 9: nos 63 and 101. Only a minority of them are said to be haired (kuš-síg-mú): this is most often the case with oxhides (e.g., *BIN* 9: nos 3, 4, 6), but also with goatskins (*BIN* 9: no 207), sheepskins (*BIN* 9: nos 58, 93, *MCS* 5: p. 115 no 1) and those of stags (lulim, *BIN* 9: no 63) occur. The only information about the treatment of these skins appears in one text where oil is used to cover forty of them (*MCS* 5: p. 115 no 1). They seem to be used mainly for the production of doors (e.g., *BIN* 9: nos 15, 349, 350).

Other skins brought into the workshop are called kuš-a-GAR-nag-a. This term seems to indicate that the skins are "drunk" or "eaten"[16] by the a-GAR. This seems to be a mixture of water and flour[17], which is used for "drenching" in the pretannage stage of leatherwork (cf. above).

[15] Cf. B.R. Foster, *Umma in the Sargonic Period,* Hamden, 1982: p. 18 l. 15, for accounting of bread by morsels.

[16] Only in the Isin texts the term a-GAR-nag-a is attested. In the Ur III texts the term is always a-GAR-kú-a.

[17] Cf. M. Stol, *RlA* 6 (1980-83): p. 531. In Ur III texts the phrase še zì-a-GAR-kú-šè "barley for flour for the a-GAR-kú-a" sometimes occurs, e.g., *MVN* 3: no 259.

Although "drenching" is not the process that removes the hair from skins in our understanding of leatherwork, it seems that it was regarded as such in the Isin period since the drenched skins are distinguished from the haired ones[18]. Possibly this confusion resulted from the fact that several stages of the preparation for tanning were undertaken simultaneously.

These skins were thus prepared for tanning when they entered the workshop. This seems to be the case for most skins, although they appear in the texts without the specification síg-mú or a-GAR-nag-a. In none of the texts of the Isin archive there is any mention of products or processes used in the preparation for tanning. Moreover, the fact that the specification kuš-a-GAR-nag-a is almost always used only when a distinction has to be made with hairy skins[19], suggests that the skins were usually dehaired, and that the scribes did not regard it necessary to mention this condition.

In the workshop itself the skins were tanned and dyed. Both processes seem to be interwoven and thus they will be discussed together. Four different colors of leather are produced in the workshop: white, black, red and green.

White leather (kuš-babbar) is not obtained with a dye, but through tanning with alum[20]. The early Isin material does not explicitly confirm this, but we know that alum (*allaḫarum*) was used in the workshop for mineral tanning, and thus its use for the production of white leather seems likely.

Two texts give clear information about the materials used for the production of black and red leather: *BIN* 9: no 489 and *BIN* 10: no 130[21]. For black leather (kuš-$gi_6$) the products listed are oil (ì), im-KÙ.GI, strained (?) oil (ì ba-a-dè), and pomegranate (nu-úr-ma)[22]. The oil and strained oil were probably used for the oiling of the leather after the tanning. Pomegranate is a product which can be used for

[18] It is, however, also possible that the unhairing of the skins was done by simply soaking them, cf. M. Levey, *Chemistry and Chemical Technology in Ancient Mesopotamia,* Amsterdam, 1959: p. 66.

[19] Only in three Isin texts skins are specified as a-GAR-nag-a when no hairy skins are mentioned in the same text, *BIN* 9: nos 87, 112, and 116.

[20] R. Reed, *Ancient Skins*: p. 62-64, R.J. Forbes, *SAT* V: p. 7.

[21] For a transliteration and translation of *BIN* 9: no 489, see p. 13f.

[22] The same combination of products appears for the production of a throne in *BIN* 9: no 182.

[23] For pomegranate as tanning material, see H. Hoffner, *Alimenta Hethaeorum*, New Haven, 1974: p. 119f., R. Reed, *Ancient Skins*: pp. 86, 88, and 91, and J.A. Wilson, *Modern Practice in Leather Manufacture,* New York, 1941: p. 388.

vegetable tanning[23], and im-KÙ.GI, literally meaning "gold colored earth" was used to produce the black color[24].

These two texts indicate that red leather (kuš-ú-ḫáb) is produced with a different series of materials: oil (ì), madder (ú-ḫáb), and alum (*allaḫarum*), with an alkaline plant (naga) added in *BIN* 9: no 489. The oil was again probably applied after the tanning. The purpose of the alkaline plant is unclear, but since it is only attested in one text, it does not seem to have been essential for the production of this type of leather. *allaḫarum* is almost certainly alum[25] which was used for mineral tanning in antiquity[26]. ú-ḫáb has commonly been equated with gallnut which was an important tanning product in the Ancient Near East[27]. Since the color of the leather is said to be ú-ḫáb, it seems, however, more likely that the product is used as a dye. From comparison of the early Isin texts with later Mesopotamian sources (cf. Glossary s.v. ú-ḫáb), it is clear that ú-ḫáb corresponds to the Akkadian *ḫūratu*, which is to be translated as madder, Latin *Rubia tinctorum*, a product used as red dye[28].

The only information available concerning the production of green leather (kuš-du$_8$-ši-a), is that copper (urudu) was used (*BIN* 9: nos 107, 187, 455, 460). From copper an acetate was produced which was used to dye textiles and leather green in antiquity[29]. *BIN* 9: no 455 lists some amounts of copper needed to color one skin: 4 1/3 gín (= c. 36 grams, l. 1) and 4 gín (= c. 33 grams, l. 4). It is remarkable that in the few instances where the type of skin is specified, it is always goatskin (*BIN* 9: nos 13, 187, 193, 234, 435, 470, *BIN* 10: no 83). In the other instances where green leather is mentioned, the type of skin is not specified[30].

We can thus distinguish between the following groups of materials used by the leatherworkers to process leather: tanning materials, dyes, and oils. To the first group belong alum and pomegranate. Alum (*allaḫarum*) was used for mineral tanning. In the Isin texts two other

[24] Cf. *BIN* 9: no 198, *BIN* 10: nos 83 and 150 where the phrase im-KÙ.GI ba-gi$_6$, "blackened with im-KÙ.GI".

[25] M. Stol, *RlA* 6 (1980-83): p. 533.

[26] R. Reed, *Ancient Skins*: p. 61-64.

[27] E.g., F. Thureau-Dangin, *RA* 17 (1920): p. 27-30.

[28] M. Stol, *RlA* 6 (1980-83): p. 534f.

[29] M. Stol, *RlA* 6 (1980-83): p. 534.

[30] The absence of specification of the type of skin is especially strange when it appears in texts where the skins with other colors are specified, e.g., *BIN* 9: no 426, ll. 2-3: kuš-gu$_4$-ú-ḫáb-bi 5 gín / kuš-du$_8$-ši-a-bi 1/3.

variants of the product are known: A-*allaḫarum* and A-*allaḫarum liqtum*. Although the first is usually considered a variant writing of *allaḫarum*, with a phonetic complement, significantly it is only attested in texts recording deliveries to the workshop (*BIN* 9: nos 80, 81, 82, 104, 105, *BIN* 10: no 33)[31], while *allaḫarum* is only attested as the material used in production. A-*allaḫarum liqtum* is also a product delivered to the workshop (*BIN* 9: no 83, *BIN* 10: no 33); the specific meaning of *liqtum* "collected" remains unclear. Pomegranate (nu-úr-ma) was used for vegetable tanning. *BIN* 10: no 24 mentions a delivery to the craftsmen of the pomegranate kernel (peš!-$^{giš}$nu-úr-ma) and of moist(?) pomegranate ($^{giš}$nu-úr-ma-duru$_5$, measured as a liquid); they can both be used as tanning materials[32].

Three materials were used for coloring; im-KÙ.GI for black, copper for green, and madder for red. Of the last product two variants are mentioned in *BIN* 9: no 84, moist(?) madder (ú-ḫáb-duru$_5$) and dried madder (ú-ḫáb-ḫád)[33], both weighed. Since the text records only their receipt by the workshop, their special function is unclear. The term e-rí-na, attested in the Isin texts with sheep and goat leather (e.g., *BIN* 9: nos 37, 343, 445) seems to be a general indication for skins treated with an extract of roots ($^{giš}$erina (MUŠxMUŠ) = *šuršum*), but also a variant of ú-ḫáb, since it is equated with *ḫūratu* in Ḫḫ III 495[34]. The skins specified as such are often used in products that have to be water resistant, such as covers (e.g., *BIN* 9: nos 37, 445), jars (e.g., *BIN* 9: no 343) and containers (e.g., *BIN* 9: nos 364, 425), which may indicate a secondary meaning "water resistant" for the term e-rí-na.

The last group of products was used to oil the leather, in order to prevent it from becoming hard and stiff[35]. Most commonly used is oil (ì), but sometimes sesame oil (ì-giš, *BIN* 9: no 37, *BIN* 10: no 83, *MCS* 5: p. 115 no 1), or mutton-fat (ì-udu, *BIN* 10: no 51) are attested. Another variant found four times in the Isin archive is ì ba-a-dé, which seems to indicate strained oil. This term occurs three times between im-KÙ.GI and pomegranate (*BIN* 9: nos 182, 489, *BIN* 10: no 130) and once the term seems to specify the type of oil which is used (*BIN* 10: no 150: ì ba-a-dé ì-bi 10 gín). Since it is only found in connection with black leather, it may have had a special function in its preparation.

[31] The last text has in line 2: 5 ma-na ŠU.URU.GÁ / A-*al-la-⟨ḫa-⟩ru*, the meaning of which is unclear to me.

[32] Cf. J.A. Wilson, *Modern Practice in Leather Manufacture*, New York, 1941: p. 277.

[33] B. Landsberger, *JCS* 21 (1967): p. 169.

[34] M. Stol, *RlA* 6 (1980-83): p. 535, M. Sigrist, *JCS* 33 (1981): p. 162f.

[35] Cf. J.A. Wilson, *op. cit.*: p. 468, M. Stol, *RlA* 6 (1980-83): p. 535.

Two additional materials are used by the leatherworkers: alkaline plants and glue. The first, naga or naga-si-è, is rarely attested in the archive[36], and its function is not clear. In *BIN* 9: no 489, it is used for the production of red leather. The second product, glue, is attested more often, used by both leatherworkers and carpenters[37]. It is possible that the glue was produced from scraps of leather, and thus a product of the leatherworkers[38]. Moreover, glue is used in a large variety of objects produced by the leatherworkers, such as boats (e.g., *BIN* 9: nos 426, 428), water bags (e.g., *BIN* 9: nos 421, 423), and doors (e.g., *BIN* 9: no 164)[39]. It is used when small scraps of leather have to be applied (*BIN* 9: no 106, *BIN* 10: no 63).

Another animal product used by the leatherworkers is catgut (sa). It is measured by weight, and used mainly for sandals (e.g., *BIN* 9: nos 397, 415), but also for bags (e.g., *BIN* 9: no 421), covers (e.g., *BIN* 10: no 116), chariots (e.g., *BIN* 9: no 193), and the harness of a donkey (e.g., *BIN* 9: nos 429, 430). Although there is no record of the delivery of this material, it is unlikely that it was prepared in the workshop itself, for there are no deliveries of complete slaughered animals or texts recording the production of catgut.

From this survey it becomes clear that the leatherworkers in the Isin worshop were not responsible for the entire process of leather manufacture. There is no evidence for the preparation of the hides before tanning. Since this stage probably took place elsewhere, it is not documented in the texts of this archive. The omission of these stages, which made tanning such an ill-smelling industry and required that the tanners work in a special section of the city in the first millennium[40], made it possible for the leatherworkers in the Isin workshop to work in the same building as the carpenters, reedworkers, and felters. Similarly, the excavated remains of leather workshops in Tell Asmar and Tello (cf. Introduction) are located among other buildings.

### 3) Reedworkers (ad-KID)

Reed is a widely used material in Mesopotamia, since it is available in abundance while wood is very rare[41]. In the Isin archive only four texts,

[36] naga: *BIN* 9: nos 37 and 489; naga-si-è: *BIN* 9: nos 81 and 82.
[37] Cf. the distinction between kin-ašgab and kin-nagar with glue in *BIN* 9: no 193.
[38] Cf. M. Levey, *Chemistry*: p. 77f.
[39] Cf. M. Sigrist, *JCS* 33 (1981): p. 158f.
[40] R.J. Forbes, *SAT* V: p. 38, M. Levey, *Chemistry*: p. 65.
[41] N. Postgate, in *L'archéologie de l'Iraq* (ed. M.T. Barrelet), Paris, 1980: p. 101-109.

however, mention deliveries of reed to the workshop. One of these (*BIN* 10: no 45) dates from the ninth month of I.E. 33, and two others (*BIN* 10: nos 47-48) from the tenth month of that year. In two of these texts *BIN* 10: nos 45 and 47) the amounts delivered add to 76 1/2 talents (gú), i.e. 2,295 kilograms. This suggests that large quantities of reed were used in the workshop. The reed is delivered in bundles (sa-gi) and bales (gu-kilib). In *BIN* 10: no 48 a bale is said to contain 130 bundles, a much larger amount in comparison to those attested in the Ur III texts from Umma[42]. In *BIN* 10: no 47 one delivery is specified as processed reed (gi-ra).

Other materials used by reedworkers are derived from the date-palm[43]: in *BIN* 9: nos 490, 519, *BIN* 10: no 78, and *JAOS* 98: p. 255 no 9, date palm spines (peš-murgu) and palm fronds (zé-na) are delivered for baskets and for a table[44].

Two other materials used by the reedworkers in the Isin archive are bitumen (ésir) and gypsum (im-bábbar). The former is attested numerous times, especially in the form of ésir-é-a. Often large quantities are delivered to the workshop: e.g., 2 gur and 80 sìla (*BIN* 10: no 15), 1 gur and 60 sìla (*BIN* 10: no 31), and 1 gur (*BIN* 9: no 511, LB 1128). It is used to coat ($sub_6$ = TAG) doors (e.g., *BIN* 9: nos 343, 378) and tables (e.g., *BIN* 10: no 170). As an adhesive[45], it may be used in the production of reed mats (gi-kid, e.g., *BIN* 9: nos 332, 451, KA-gìr[46], *BIN* 10: no 107). It is also used to waterproof[47] ships (e.g., *BIN* 10: nos 30, 129) and baskets (e.g., *BIN* 9: no 395, *ASJ* 5: p. 56 no 6). Bitumen is used in smaller quantities in the production of flutes ($^{gi}$gíd, e.g., *BIN* 9: nos 359, 365, 368) and to coat vessels (e.g., *BIN* 9: nos 417, 457). The dried variant (ésir-é-a-ḫád) is only attested once (*BIN* 9: no 139) with no indication of its use.

Gypsum (im-bábbar) is not a tanning material[48], but is used by the reedworkers: in *BIN* 9: no 349 both bitumen and gymsum are called "work of the reedworkers" (kin-ad-KID) and in *BIN* 9: nos 250 and 251

[42] A.L. Oppenheim, *Eames Coll.*: p. 46, seven to twenty-five bundles per bale.

[43] N. Postgate, in *L'archéologie*: p. 99-101.

[44] Cf. N. Postgate, in *L'archéologie*: p. 101.

[45] Cf. R.J. Forbes, *SAT* I: p. 95-98.

[46] KA-gìr is usually equated with *padānum*, "road". Here, however, it may be a variant of KA-gir, KA-$gir_4$, a type of reed mat or something for which reed mats are made (M. Civil, letter Feb. 24, 1984).

[47] Cf. R.J. Forbes, *SAT* I: p. 90-95.

[48] Contra, L. Matouš, *BiOr.* 13 (1956): p. 137, and M. Stol, *RlA* 6 (1980-83): p. 531, who thinks it is a product used to dehair skins.

both products are received by Ku-Nanna and Ilī-TAB.BA-ì known to be reedworkers (cf. chapter III). Gypsum is used for doors (e.g., *BIN* 9: nos 178, 346) and furniture (e.g., *BIN* 9: nos 201, 202), baskets (e.g., *BIN* 10: no 100, *JAOS* 98: p. 256 no 14) and chariots (kak-sal$_4$, e.g., *BIN* 9: nos 249, 250, 251). Its exact function is unclear, but gypsum may have been used for coloring.

The reedworkers thus work with reed and palm products, to which gympsum and bitumen are applied, as adhesive, for waterproofing, and perhaps for coloring.

4) Felters (túg-du$_8$)

The felters were responsible for making felt and ropes from wool, and for using them in the production of finished goods[49]. There are thus two levels to be distinguished in their labor: first they turn the wool, received from the outside, into felt, thread and ropes, and second, these products are used in the manufacture of objects. Several texts account for the receipt of wool (síg) by the workshop. Most common is ordinary wool (síg-gin, e.g., *BIN* 10: nos 9, 43), which probably is goat's wool (síg-ud$_5$, e.g., *BIN* 9: nos 500, 501). Often the wool is combed (síg-ga-ríg-ak, e.g., *BIN* 9: no 524, *BIN* 10: no 42).

There is little indication in the texts about how felt (túg-du$_8$-a) was made. Different types of wool were used: combed ordinary wool (síg-gin ga-ríg-ak, e.g., *BIN* 9: nos 328, 341), and a type of wool called KA.AḪ (*BIN* 9: no 355). Felt is made by beating, rolling and pressing wool together until it forms a mat-like compact mass[50]. Different types of felt are attested in the Isin texts: felt without any specifications (túg-du$_8$-a, e.g., *BIN* 9: nos 361, 385), white(?) felt (túg-du$_8$-a-babbar, e.g., *BIN* 9: nos 129, 395), and a felt called SU.A (túg-du$_8$-a SU.A, e.g., *BIN* 9: no 129, *BIN* 10: no 85). The felt was used for several purposes: in mattresses (šà-tuku$_5$, e.g., *BIN* 9: nos 348, 351, *BIN* 10: no 66)[51], and as lining (šà-ra) of boots (e.g., *BIN* 9: nos 128, 428), sandals (e.g., *BIN* 9: nos 129, 397), belts (e.g., *BIN* 9: no 473), and containers (e.g., *BIN* 9: nos 361, 395)[52].

A second type of product made by the felters is spun thread (níg-U.NU-a / šà-U.NU-a), made from different types of wool. níg-U.NU-a is mostly produced from goat's wool (níg-U.NU-a-síg-ud$_5$, e.g., *BIN* 9:

[49] P. Steinkeller, *OrAn.* 19 (1980): p. 93.
[50] *Ibid.*: p. 89.
[51] *Ibid.*: p. 82.
[52] *Ibid.*: p. 93.

nos 30, 31), but also attested is wool of the uligi-sheep (níg-U.NU-a-síg-gi, *BIN* 10: no 74). A special type of thread is called níg-U.NU-a-*zibbatum*, (e.g., *BIN* 9: nos 142-144). šà-U.NU-a is less often attested (e.g., *ASJ* 5: p. 57 no 8); once it is specified as šà-NU.U-a-*zibbatum* (*BIN* 9: no 481)[53].

These products are used in mattresses (e.g., *BIN* 10: no 66, *ASJ* 5: p. 57 no 8) and covers (*ASJ* 5: p. 57 no 8). A common use seems to be for bags to carry metals ($^{kuš}$lu-úb-BÚR, e.g., *BIN* 9: nos 139, 141-144), and for waterbags ($^{kuš}$ummu(d), e.g., *BIN* 9: nos 382, 388). Thread is also used to wrap (kešda) precious metals (e.g., *BIN* 9: nos 30, 462). Several texts record the expenditure of thread, for instance, to the house of the goldsmiths (é-kù-dím, e.g., *BIN* 9: nos 206, 264). It seems thus that níg-U.NU-a and šà-U.NU-a, which were used as warp thread and woof thread in the textile industry, have to be considered more generally to be ropes or threads, especially since goat's hair rope (éš-síg-ud$_5$) and goat's hair thread (níg-U.NU-a-síg-ud$_5$) seem to alternate in the production of waterbags[54]. The exact difference between níg-U.NU-a and šà-U.NU-a is not clear, but it may refer to two different ways of spinning.

The third product manufactured and used by the felters is rope (éš), mostly made from goat's hair (éš-síg-ud$_5$). Sometimes the rope is specified as "heavy" (ébiḫ, e.g., *BIN* 9: no 526, *BIN* 10: no 84). These ropes can be long and heavy, as for instance, in *BIN* 10: no 161, where four ropes of twenty-four meters (4 gar) each weigh fifteen kilograms (29 1/2 minas). The product is always weighed, often by the overseer of the felters (e.g., *BIN* 9: no 453, *BIN* 10: no 76). Rope is used for the manufacture of furniture (e.g., *BIN* 9: no 246: throne, *BIN* 9: no 255: bed), bags (e.g., *BIN* 9: nos 391, 415), and sandals (e.g., *BIN* 9: nos 39, 327). It is also used to wrap (kešda) gold (e.g., *BIN* 9: no 29, *BIN* 10: 75) and musical instruments (*BIN* 9: no 458).

The felters were thus responsible for processing wool into felt, thread and rope, which were than used for the manufacture of other products. No information is available concerning other materials they may have used.

5) Additional materials

In addition to the materials listed above there are attested a few

[53] For šà-NU.U-a as variant of šà-U.NU-a, cf. H. Waetzoldt, *Textilindustrie*: p. 122.
[54] Note also the term éš níg-U.NU-a síg-ud$_5$ in *BIN* 10: no 114.

others which cannot be assigned with certainty to a particular craft. Tortoise shell (ba-sig$_4$) is delivered for a throne in one text (*BIN* 9: no 182), probably for inlay, and as such was possibly used by the carpenters. Glues made of flour are attested in several texts: flour (zì) used for a chair (*BIN* 9: no 340), coarse(?) flour (zì-sig$_{15}$) for doors (*BIN* 9: no 169, *BIN* 10: no 70), pea(?) flour (zì-gu) for a chair (*BIN* 9: no 203), and barley flour (dabin) for a door (*BIN* 9: no 172). They were probably used by carpenters or reedworkers.

It is thus clear that most materials were used by a specific type of craftsmen and that, although the products of the workshop were manufactured by several types of craftsmen, each worked only on specific parts. This shows a high level of specialization of the craftsmen in this workshop.

## B. *Products*

A wide range of products is manufactured in the workshop in its entirety or partially with the materials described above. They can be grouped into ten types: (1) containers, (2) footwear, (3) furniture, (4) weapons, (5) musical instruments, (6) vehicles, (7) doors, (8) mats and covers, (9) cloth, and (10) varia.

### 1) Containers

Three types of containers are attested in the Isin archive: bags, baskets, and vessels. Bags are made mainly from leather. The amount needed per bag varies, but for each type of bag it seems more or less standard; thus a bag called $^{kuš}$dùg-gan-túg is almost always made of two sheepskins (e.g., *BIN* 9: nos 411, 414). In addition to leather, other products are used for certain types of bags. For instance, goat's hair made into rope (éš-síg-ud$_5$) or thread (níg-U.NU-a-síg-ud$_5$) is used for waterbags ($^{kuš}$ummu(d), e.g., *BIN* 9: nos 382, 395), or for a bucket ($^{kuš}$*mašlium, BIN* 9: no 327). Sometimes catgut (sa) is used (*BIN* 10: no 130). A bag to carry metals ($^{kuš}$lu-úb-BÚR) is made of leather, thread, and bitumen (*BIN* 9: nos 139, 141). Certain bags are oiled (e.g., tùn, *BIN* 9: no 37).

Baskets are mainly made of reed (cf. the gi determinative), and covered with other materials. Bitumen is used for many types of baskets, probably as adhesive and for waterproofing: for instance, in *ASJ* 5: p. 56 no 6 baskets for pouring water ($^{gi}$gur-a-bal-a) are coated with bitumen. Gypsum (im-bábbar) is also applied (e.g., *BIN* 10: no 100, *JAOS* 98: p. 254 no 14). Some baskets are covered (si) with leather (e.g., *BIN* 9: nos 356, 452)[55] and rope can also be used in them (e.g., *BIN* 9: nos 326, 450).

Though attested in the archive, vessels are not manufactured in this workshop, since only a few texts record the expenditure of them (*JCS* 20: p. 40 no 5, *BIN* 9: no 411). Most texts record the manufacture of certain accessories for vessels: some of them are covered with leather ($^{dug}$šáman-kuš-si-ga, *BIN* 9: no 452, cf. *BIN* 9: no 360), others are pitched with bitumen, probably as a protective coating (e.g., *BIN* 9: no 532, *BIN* 10: no 173). Many texts record the manufacture of lids (ka-tab) and caps (SAGŠU) for a large variety of vessels (e.g., *BIN* 9: nos 190, 220-222). They are made of small amounts of leather, generally of white and red sheepskins. Since many more texts record the expenditure of lids than that of vessels, the lids must have been manufactured and disbursed separately.

2) Footwear

The information found in the published Isin texts concerning footwear has been gathered and discussed extensively in A. Salonen's *Fussbekleidung* and, since no markedly new information is found in the unpublished material, only a few remarks will be presented here[56].

The two attested types of footwear, sandals ($^{kuš}$e-sír) and boots ($^{kuš}$súḫub), are both produced in pairs (é-ba-an)[57]. In addition to leather, catgut (sa, e.g., *BIN* 9: nos 423, 425) and glue (še-gín, e.g., *BIN* 9: no 424, *BIN* 10: no 128) are used. The soles (KI.KAL) of boots are sometimes lined with felt (e.g., *BIN* 9: nos 428, 469)[58]. In two texts it is indicated that goatleather was used to produce straps (*zāḫirum*) of sandals (*BIN* 10: no 149 and Ash 1932-280)[59]. One phrase, not discussed by A. Salonen, occurs several times in connection with sandals in the Isin texts: šu-e-sír šà-ba, or shortened šu-bi šà-ba (*BIN* 9: nos 324, 325, 326, 327, 395, 415, 422, and Ash 1932-280), the translation of which

[55] Cf. M. Sigrist, *JCS* 33 (1981): p. 190.

[56] A detailed list of Sumerian terms for footwear is given by M. Stol, *RlA* 6 (1980-83): p. 538-540. See also M. Sigrist, *JCS* 33 (1981): p. 187f.

[57] Against A. Salonen's Ḫa$_x$-ba-an referring to the city Ḫamban.

[58] Against A. Salonen, *Fussbekleidung*: p. 89, where túg-du$_8$-a = "straps".

[59] *zāḫirum* is probably the same as *šāḫirum* known from the Old Assyrian texts, cf. *AHw*: p. 1132.

is unclear. For šu-e-sír the same products as for sandals and boots are used: leather — mostly from oxen, glue, and catgut. V. Crawford argued that the phrase means "its shoe-mold is included"[60] but this is not certain.

### 3) Furniture

The furniture produced by the workshop can be divided into three groups: chairs, tables, and beds. The chairs ($^{giš}$gu-za) also include thrones (dúr-gar), benches (giš-ḫum), and stools ($^{giš}$ŠU$_4$.A), all of which are found in several varieties[61]. Many different materials can be used for the manufacture of a chair. It can be made of wood (e.g. $^{giš}$gu-za-nita-šinig "a man's chair of tamarisk", *BIN* 9: no 499), or reed (e.g., $^{gi}$dúr-lugal "a reed chair for the king", *BIN* 10: no 87). Leather is used for cushions (ku-ša-nu-um, e.g., *BIN* 9: no 342) which are stuffed with wool (e.g., *BIN* 9: no 32). They are thus the combined work of several craftsmen in the workshop. Some chairs are said to be covered with silver (e.g., $^{giš}$dúr-kù-babbar-gar-ra, *BIN* 9: no 438), but this seems to have been done outside the workshop, for precious metals are not among the materials handled by it.

Tables can also be made of wood or reed. *BIN* 10: no 80 is an account of a quota of reed trays to be delivered by several reedworkers[62]. Although there is no indication of the time period involved, some idea can be gained about the productivity; in total ninety-eight trays are delivered and eleven are in arrears. The trays can be covered with bitumen (e.g., *BIN* 9: no 426, *BIN* 10: no 170). A related product is a table with drawers ($^{giš}$ka-kara$_4$) which is sometimes inlaid with gold (*BIN* 9: no 29).

Several types of beds (giš-nú, *majjaltum*) are produced by the workshop, from wood, leather, thread, or rope (e.g., *BIN* 9: nos 254, 255). The workshop also makes mattresses (šà-tuku$_5$, e.g., *BIN* 9: no 348, *BIN* 10: no 66), and their covers ($^{giš}$ZA.AN.KA, e.g., *BIN* 9: no 417, *ASJ* 5: p. 57 no 8). Here too, the efforts of several types of craftsmen in the workshop are required.

### 4) Weapons

A number of weapons and accessories are manufactured in their

[60] *Terminology*: p. 131-133.
[61] Cf. A. Salonen, *Möbel: passim.*
[62] For a transliteration and translation of this text, see p. 15.

entirety or partially in the workshop. Bows ([giš]ban) are treated with glue (e.g., *BIN* 9: nos 121, 124), spears ([giš]gíd-da) are made from poplar trees ([giš]íldag, *BIN* 10: no 125) and thread (níg-U.NU-a *zibbatum, BIN* 9: nos 194, 197), with bitumen applied to them (*BIN* 10: no 92). Battering rams ($gu_4$-si-AŠ) are covered with leather (*BIN* 9: nos 103, 125), with bitumen and thread (*BIN* 9: nos 197, 463). The workshop produces baskets and boxes for bows and arrows (*BIN* 9: no 415), and arrowholders (*parūtum, BIN* 9: nos 14, 274). Shields are made of leather ([kuš]*gababum*, e.g., *BIN* 9: nos 14, 106, [kuš]*tuksium, BIN* 9: no 312). A leather weapon holder or a weapon of unknown type, [kuš]Á, is delivered by the workshop to the armory (é-[giš]tukul, *BIN* 9: no 507, cf. *BIN* 9: nos 108, 109).

5) Musical instruments

In the workshop leather and glue are applied to several musical instruments: lyres or harps ([giš]zà-mi [*BIN* 9: no 352, *BIN* 10: no 82] and [giš]balag [*BIN* 9: nos 441, 445]), and unknown instruments — [giš]ŠÀ.TAR (*BIN* 9: no 496, *BIN* 10: nos 82 and 104) and *mārītum* (*BIN* 9: no 253). More information about musical instruments is not available, probably because only those specific parts were produced in the workshop.

6) Vehicles

Two major products of the workshop are vehicles: chariots and boats. Only one text, *BIN* 10: no 91, records the delivery of a fir(?) log three meters long (1 [giš]ù-suḫ$_5$ / gíd-bi 6 kùš) for a chariot ([giš]gigir). Most records mention leather[63], glue, bitumen, and oil to be used for chariots (e.g., *BIN* 9: nos 187, 198, 491). Certain texts record the production of certain parts such as the seat ([giš]gu-za-[giš]gigir, e.g., *BIN* 9: no 187), the side board (da-[giš]gigir, *BIN* 9: no 192), and the wheels (umbin-[giš]gigir, *BIN* 9: no 191).

For boats ([giš]má)[64] too, wood deliveries are rarely recorded (*BIN* 10: no 88), and reed not at all. The boats were waterproofed with bitumen (e.g., *BIN* 10: nos 30, 129)[65]. Leather is also used, probably for

[63] Cf. M. Sigrist, *JCS* 33 (1981): p. 182-4, for the use of leather in chariots.

[64] For the construction of boats, see M.C. De Graeve, *The Ships of the Ancient Near East* (*OLA* 7), Leuven, 1981: p. 91-93 for reed boats, and p. 99-106 for wooden boats.

[65] This caulking had to be done at least once a year, cf. R.J. Forbes *SAT* I: p. 90-95.

tarpaulins (*BIN* 9: nos 25, 26), and as decoration[66]. Black leather is used for the bench of a boat (giš-ḫum-má, *BIN* 9: no 184)[67].

7) Doors

Doors ($^{giš}$ig) are produced in large quantities by the workshop. Few texts, however, account for wood or reed used for them. According to *BIN* 10: no 186, six logs of fir(?) tree were used for two doors. Most texts record the use of leather (e.g., *BIN* 9: nos 77, 106), and glue (še-gín and a-še-gín, e.g., *BIN* 9: nos 55, 153). Certain doors made of reed ($^{giš}$ig-gi) are coated (sub$_6$ = TAG) with bitumen (e.g., *BIN* 9: nos 343, 532). Probably the doors are sometimes decorated (ḪI-lá) with oxhides of different colors (*BIN* 9: no 174, red and white, *BIN* 9: no 477, red)[68].

In addition to the door itself, the doorlocks ($^{giš}$sag-gul, e.g., *BIN* 9: nos 350, 382) and doorpivot ($^{giš}$nu-kúš, e.g., *BIN* 9: nos 442, 534) are mentioned. Both products are covered with bitumen, and for the locks, leather (*BIN* 9: no 382) and glue (*BIN* 9: no 442) are used for covering. Other parts are also produced: DU$_8$.IG, commonly translated as "key", but made of leather (*BIN* 9: nos 75, 463), and the doorhinge ($^{kuš}$A.SI, *BIN* 9: no 106).

8) Mats and covers

Mats ($^{gi}$kid, KA-gìr [*BIN* 10: no 107], *ḫurdum* [*BIN* 9: no 426])[69] are made of reed and coated with bitumen (e.g., *BIN* 9: no 359, *BIN* 10: no 158). The archive contains also records of skins used to cover (si) reed mats (e.g., *BIN* 9: nos 259, 354), the exact purpose of which is unclear. One text records the use of thread in mats, probably to tie them together (*BIN* 9: no 332).

Several types of covers are produced by the workshop. The large cover or tarpaulin ($^{kuš}$AB) is made of leather, catgut, thread, covered with bitumen, and used to cover boats (e.g., *BIN* 9: nos 37, 445). Smaller seem to be the covers (ka-dù) used for tables and shields, also made of leather (e.g., *BIN* 9: nos 434, 435).

*naḫbatum*, made of leather, catgut, and glue (e.g., *BIN* 9: nos 333,

[66] Cf. M. Sigrist, *JCS* 33 (1981): p. 181f.

[67] Possibly giš-ḫum = giš-ḫu-um, a structure on the boat to provide shade, cf. M Sigrist, *JCS* 33 (1981): p. 182 n. 159.

[68] Cf. M. Sigrist, *JCS* 33 (1981): p. 184f.

[69] For reed mats in general in the Ur III period, cf. A. Goetze, *JCS* 2 (1948): p. 165-202.

398), may also refer to a cover and used as such for musical instruments[70]. One text records the use of leather for a *puzirum* of musical instruments, probably also a cover (*BIN* 9: no 334).

9) Cloth

Some textiles seem to be treated in the workshop: alum and madder are used to shine (su) guzza-cloth (*BIN* 9: no 467), and a type of linen called gu-dim$_4$-ba, used for sandals (*BIN* 9: no 129), is treated with copper, probably to color it green (*BIN* 9: no 455).

10) Varia

In addition to these groups of products, a number of other products are manufactured or treated by the craftsmen in the Isin workshop: some, such as sieves ($^{gi}$ma-an-sim, e.g., *BIN* 9: nos 355, 433) are produced in their entirety, others, such as yokes ($^{giš}$šudun, *BIN* 9: nos 256, 437) are only covered with leather[71]. Bitumen is applied to several products, such as flutes ($^{gi}$gíd, e.g., *BIN* 9: nos 359, 365), and traverse beams ($^{giš}$dal, *BIN* 10: nos 109, 156). Perhaps leashes for dogs (éš-ur-gi$_7$-ra, *BIN* 10: no 101), and even for lions (éš-ur-maḫ, *BIN* 10: no 84) are made with goat's wool.

11) Conclusions

From this survey it is clear that the workshop was involved in the production of a large array of objects, but mostly manufactured only part of them. Of vessels, for instance, only the lids were made. While furniture was mostly made in the workshop, certain details such as gold inlay had to be done elsewhere. Thus there seems to have been a chain of workshops, with only one of them documented by the preserved sources. Each workshop seems to have been specialized, so that, for instance, all work involving leather was done in the workshop studied here, and all that with precious metals elsewhere.

From the list of finished products it is also clear that the workshop produced for important institutions, especially the palace. Many products are said to be for the king (e.g., $^{kuš}$e-sír-babbar-lugal "white royal sandals" [*BIN* 9: no 129], $^{giš}$gigir-lugal "royal chariot" [*BIN* 9: nos

[70] L. Matouš, *BiOr*. 13 (1956): p. 138.
[71] Cf. M. Sigrist, *JCS* 33 (1981): p. 188.

186, 454, 459]), or for certain gods (e.g., [giš]gigir-[d]En-líl-lá "chariot of Enlil" [*BIN* 9: no 423], má-[d]En-ki "boat of Enki" [*BIN* 10: no 30]). Connections with these and other institutions will be discussed in detail in chapter IV.

The importance of the products also becomes clear from comparison of the data of these archival texts with year formulae and royal hymns. Such connections have been researched previously, most thoroughly by D. Frayne[72]. Frayne's results will be presented here in summary, with some additions from the published and unpublished material[73].

I.E. 6: mu giš-nú [d]Inanna ba-dím, "year that the bed of Inanna was fashioned".

Archival:
*BIN* 10: no 90: glue for the bed of the nin-priestess of Ninurta, cf. I.E. 7.

I.E. 7: mu nin-dingir [d]Nin-urta ba-ḫun/íl, "year that the nin-dingir-priestess of Ninurta was installed".

I.E. 15: mu-ús-sa bàd *Libūr-[d]Išbi-Erra* ba-dù, "year following the one that the wall Libūr-Išbi'erra was built".

Archival:
*BIN* 9: no 152: present of the Amorites, the day that Elam was smitten with the weapon, cf. I.E. 16.
*BIN* 10: no 124: *zamirītum* leaving Uruk, the day that Elam was defeated, cf. I.E. 16.

I.E. 16: mu [d]*Išbi-Erra* lugale lú SU.A ù Elam bi-in-ra, "year that Išbi-Erra the king defeated the SU.A people and Elam".

Hymns:
I.E. A: *STVC* 63 rev 13': Elam[[k]i] (Frayne)
I.E. B: col II 26: *Kindattu* lú Elam[ki] [...], "Kindattu the man of Elam" (Frayne).

Archival:
*BIN* 9: no 125: leather for a battering ram, cf. I.E. 16
no 194: thread for spears, cf. I.E. 16
no 197: thread and bitumen for a battering ram, thread for spears, cf. I.E. 16

[72] *The Historical Correlations of the Sumerian Royal Hymns* (2400-1900 B.C.), Univ. Microfilms, Ann Arbor, 1981: pp. 300-378, Išbi-Erra and Šū-ilišu; *AfO* Beiheft 19 (1982): p. 25-32.

[73] For the details on how these relations are established, see D. Frayne's dissertation. He follows the chronological scheme established by B. Kienast in *JCS* 19 (1965): p. 45-55, with minor changes. The scheme followed here is slightly different, as established in Appendix A. Frayne's results are indicated with his name. For references to the hymns I.E. A and B, see D. Frayne: p. 305.

no 463: thread and bitumen for a battering ram, cf. I.E. 16 (Frayne)
LB 1115: thread for spears, thread and bitumen for a battering ram, cf. I.E. 16
*BIN* 9: nos 153-157, 159-169, LB 1105: glue for doors in the wall, cf. I.E. 17
nos 170, 173: oxleather for doors in the wall, cf. I.E. 17 (Frayne)
*BIN* 10: no 127: poplar trees for spears for the wall, cf. I.E. 17
*BIN* 10: no 81: rope for door in the wall (date broken), cf. I.E. 17

Add perhaps:
*BIN* 9: nos 87, 138, 149: oxleather for doors, cf. I.E. 17?
no 158: leather and glue for a door, cf. I.E. 17?

I.E. 17: mu bàd *Eštar-tarām-dIšbi-Erra* ba-dù, "year that the wall named 'Eštar loves Išbi'erra' was built".

Archival:
*BIN* 9: nos 171, 175, 176, *JAOS* 98: p. 253 no 4: oxleather for doors in the wall, cf. I.E. 17 (Frayne)
no 167, *ASJ* 4: p. 68 no 17: glue for a door in the wall, cf. I.E. 17

Add perhaps:
*BIN* 9: no 158: oxleather and glue for a door, cf. I.E. 17?
*BIN* 10: no 126: glue for the ledge of a door, cf. I.E. 17?

I.E. 20: mu nin-me-an-ki $^{giš}$šu-nir-gal $^{d}$Inanna ba-dím, "year that Ninmeanki, the emblem of Inanna was built".

Archival:
*BIN* 10: no 68: glue for the emblem of Inanna (not dated), cf. I.E. 20

I.E. 21: mu-ús-sa nin-me-an-ki $^{giš}$šu-nir-gal $^{d}$Inanna ba-dím, "year after the one that the emblem of Inanna was built".

Archival:
*BIN* 9: no 435: woman's chair and bed ... ritual offerings (níg[collated] pi-lu$_5$-da) on the day that Ninzianna was made to lie down, cf. I.E. 22 (Frayne)

I.E. 22: mu Ninzianna dumu-SAL lugal máš-e in-pà, "year that Ninzianna the daughter of the king was called by an oracle".

Archival:
*BIN* 9: no 198: leather for the chariot of Enlil, cf. hymn of I.E. 23 (Frayne)
*ASJ* 5: p. 57 no 8: bed as present for the nin-dingir-priestess of $^{d}$N[in-gi$_5$-lí]-il*, cf. I.E. 23, *BIN* 9: nos 378 and 532.

* Nin-gi$_5$-lí-il seems to be a variant of the divine name Ningilina. Ningilina is attested in *BIN* 9: no 378, and Nin-gi$_5$-lí-il in *BIN* 9: no 532, both texts dated I.E. 23. For other variants of this divine name, cf. D.O. Edzard, *Zwischenzeit*: p. 66 n. 309.

I.E. 23: mu nin-dingir $^{d}$Lugalmarda ba-íl, "year that the nin-dingir-priestess of Lugalmarda was installed".

Hymn
I.E. B col III 1'-2': $^{giš}$gigir-maḫ ... lugale Isin[$^{ki}$-na] "the great chariot ... the king in Isin".

Archival:

*BIN* 9: no 532: baskets and a door for the house of nin-priestess of Ningilil; vessels for the temple of Lugalmarda, cf. I.E. 23 (Frayne)

no 534: doors for the house of the nin-dingir-priestess of Lugalmarda, cf. I.E. 23 (Frayne)

no 105: goat's wool for the throne of the *enu*-priest of Enlil, cf. I.E. 24 (Frayne, cf. D.O. Edzard, *Zwischenzeit*: p. 20 n. 85)

no 184: leather for sedan-chair of *enu*-priest of Enlil, cf. I.E. 24 (Frayne)

no 378: leather, glue and rope for the throne of Ningilina.

I.E. 24: mu en $^{d}$Enlila ba-íl, "year that the *enu*-priest of Enlil was installed".

I.E. 28: mu $^{giš}$gu-za $^{d}$Ninlila ba-dím, "year that the throne of Ninlil was built".

Hymn:

I.E. B col III 37'-38': [$^{giš}$gu-za] $^{d}$Ninlila a-xxx, "the throne of Ninlil ..." (Frayne)

Archival:

*BIN* 10: no 162: glue, thread, and bitumen to apply copper to the throne of Enlil; may be related to building of the throne of Ninlil in I.E. 28.

*BIN* 9: no 28: glue and leather for an arm-chair of Nanna and Ningal, cf. I.E. 29 (Frayne)

I.E. 29: mu $^{giš}$gu-za $^{d}$Nanna $^{d}$Ningal ba-dím, "year that the thrones of Nanna and Ningal were built".

I.E. 33: mu-ús-sa nin-dingir $^{d}$Lugal-irra ba-íl. "year after the one that the nin-dingir-priestess of Lugal-irra was installed".

Archival:

*BIN* 9: no 470: oxleather to wrap the emblem of Nanna, cf. Š.i. 2

Šū-ilišu's accession seems to have taken place shortly before the fashioning of the emblem of Nanna, and had to be commemorated in a year name. This explains why there is a one-year interval between the fashioning of the emblem and its commemoration in a date formula (cf. Appendix A).

Š.i. 1: mu $^{d}$*Šū-ilišu* lugal-àm, "the year that Šū-ilišu became king".

Archival:

*BIN* 9: nos 182, 201, 206: materials for the throne and throne-dais of Ningal, cf. Š.i. 2 (Frayne)

Frayne: p. 368, suggests that the dedication of the throne of Ningal took place at the same time as the fashioning of the emblem of Nanna, her consort, which is commemorated in the name of Š.i. 2. Since the emblem of Nanna was made in I.E. 33, however (cf. *BIN* 9: no 470), this suggestion seems to be mistaken.

Š.i. 2: mu $^{d}$*Šū-ilišu* lugale $^{giš}$šu-nir $^{d}$Nanna mu-na-dím, "year that Šū-ilišu the king fashioned the emblem of Nanna".

Royal inscription:

*UET* 8: no 62: ᵈNanna ... ᵈ*Šū-ilišu* ... ᵈšu-nir-gal mu-na-dím, "(for) Nanna ... Šū-ilišu ... built the emblem" (Frayne).

These frequent correspondences between the archival texts and the year names, with objects mentioned in the year names produced in the workshop or delivered on the occasion of an event commemorated in a year name, indicate the importance of the products of the workshop, and thus of the workshop itself in the official life of Isin.

CHAPTER III

# PERSONNEL

The labor personnel who provide the physical labor in the workshop, can be studied in a large number of texts of the Isin archive. One particular group, the worker lists, is extremely informative for the study of the workmen employed. A detailed examination of them in conjunction with information from other texts will be presented in the first part of this chapter. In the second part the information in the account texts will be examined to derive the functions of the persons supervising transactions in the workshop.

## A. Labor personnel: the craftsmen

The main source for the study of the craftsmen is a group of 117 texts which will be referred to as "worker lists", since they provide daily record of the names of the workmen active in each of the four sections of the Isin workshop. The following section will deal with (1) the form of these texts; (2) systems of accounting for a workday; (3) notations referring to work done in and outside the workshop; (4) notations referring to work not done; (5) notations referring to different people with the same name; (6) supervision of each section of the workshop, (a) carpenters, (b) leatherworkers, (c) reedworkers, (d) felters; (7) the composition of teams of workmen in each of the four sections; (8) chronology of the texts; (9) further information on craftsmen in the rest of the Isin archive. In the conclusions (10) the social status of the craftsmen and the system of employment will be examined.

### 1) *The form of the texts*[1]

The standard form of the worker lists includes four sections always in the same order: carpenters (nagar-me), leatherworkers (ašgab-me), reedworkers (ad-KID-me), and felters (túg-du$_8$). Text 27 is exceptional

[1] The texts are referred to by the numbers given in the final column of table III.1; the preceding columns give the date of the texts — the year of Išbi-Erra, the month and day — and their museum number or publication reference.

Table III.1: Temporal distribution of the worker lists

| date | | | text | | number |
|---|---|---|---|---|---|
| I.E. year | month | day | | | |
| 7 | M(1) | 15 | *BIN* 10: no | 208 | 1 |
| 7 | M | 15 | *BIN* 9: no | 515 | 2 |
| 7 | VII | 1 | *BIN* 10: no | 209 | 3 |
| 7 | VII | 4 | | 210 | 4 |
| 7 | VII | 6 | | 211 | 5 |
| 7 | VII | 21 | | 212 | 6 |
| 7 | VII | 24 | | 213 | 7 |
| 7 | VII | 26 | | 214 | 8 |
| 7 | VII | [–] | | 215 | 9 |
| 7 | VIII | 14 | | 216 | 10 |
| 7 | VIII | 17 (20?) | | 217 | 11 |
| 7 | VIII | 25 | | 218 | 12 |
| 7 | IX | 22 | | 219 | 13 |
| 7 | X | 4 | | 220 | 14 |
| 7 | X | 8 | | 221 | 15 |
| 7 | X | 9 | *BIN* 9: no | 513 | 16 |
| 7 | X | 12 | *BIN* 9: no | 514 | 17 |
| 8 | IV | 3 | *BIN* 10: no | 222 | 18 |
| 8 | V | 9 | | 223 | 19 |
| 8 | V | 10 | | 224 | 20 |
| 8 | V | 15 | | 225 | 21 |
| 8 | VI | 12 | *BIN* 9: no | 522 | 22 |
| 8 | VII | 1 | *BIN* 10: no | 226 | 23 |
| 8 | VII | 8 | | 227 | 24 |
| 8 | XIII | 12 | | 228 | 25 |
| 8 | XIII | [–] | | 229 | 26 |
| 9 | IV | 16 | | 230 | 27 |
| 9 | VII | 10 | | 231 | 28 |
| 9 | VII | 18 | | 232 | 29 |
| 9 | VII | 25 | | 233 | 30 |
| 9 | VIII | 23 | *BIN* 9: no | 533 | 31 |
| 9 | IX | 26 | *BIN* 10: no | 234 | 32 |
| 9 | XI | 14 | | 235 | 33 |
| 10 | III | 4+ | | 236 | 34 |
| 10 | V | 6 | | 237 | 35 |
| 10 | V | 30 | | 238 | 36 |
| 10 | VI | 26 | | 239 | 37 |
| 10 | VIII | 21 | | 240 | 38 |
| 10 | [–] | 15 | *BIN* 9: no | 492 | 39 |

(1) iti kin-$^{d}$Nanna

| date | | | text | | number |
|---|---|---|---|---|---|
| I.E. year | month | day | | | |
| 11 | IV | 15 | *BIN* 9: no | 508 | 40 |
| 11 | V | 23 | *BIN* 10: no | 241 | 41 |
| 11 | VI | [–] | | 242 | 42 |
| 11 | VII | 14 | | 243 | 43 |
| 11 | VII | 17 | | 244 | 44 |
| 12 | X | 26 | | 245 | 45 |
| 12 | XI | 24 | | 246 | 46 |
| 13 | V | 24 | | 247 | 47 |
| 13 | V | 30 | | 248 | 48 |
| 13 | VI | 5 | | 249 | 49 |
| 13 | VI | 27 | | 250 | 50 |
| 13 | VII | 8 | | 251 | 51 |
| 13 | VIII | 27 | | 252 | 52 |
| 13 | IX | 14 | | 253 | 53 |
| 13 | XIII | 2 | | 254 | 54 |
| 14 | VI | 2 | | 255 | 55 |
| 14 | VI | 17 | | 256 | 56 |
| 14 | VI | 28 | | 257 | 57 |
| 14 | VII | 6 | | 258 | 58 |
| 14 | VII | 20 | LB 1118 | | 59 |
| 14 | VII | 22 | *BIN* 10: no | 259 | 60 |
| 14 | VII | [–] | | 260 | 61 |
| 14 | VIII | 22 | | 261 | 62 |
| 14 | XII | 18 | | 262 | 63 |
| 15 | I | 18 | | 263 | 64 |
| 15 | I | 19 | | 264 | 65 |
| 15 | II | 15 | *BIN* 9: no | 527 | 66 |
| 15 | II | 28 | *BIN* 10: no | 265 | 67 |
| 15 | III | 10+ | | 266 | 68 |
| 15 | IV | 25 | | 267 | 69 |
| 15 | IX | 29 | | 268 | 70 |
| 15 | X | 7 | | 269 | 71 |
| 15 | X | 11 | | 270 | 72 |
| 16 | X | 7 | | 271 | 73 |
| 17 | V | 17 | | 272 | 74 |
| 18 | VI | 28 | *BIN* 9: no | 504 | 75 |
| 20 | V | 18 | *BIN* 10: no | 273 | 76 |

| date | | | | text | | number |
|---|---|---|---|---|---|---|
| I.E. | year | month | day | | | |
| | 21 | IX | 26 | | 274 | 77 |
| | 21 | XII | 22 | | 275 | 78 |
| | — | 11 | 4 | LB 1119 | | 79 |
| | — | VII | 8 | *BIN* 10: no | 276 | 80 |
| | — | VII | 16 | | 277 | 81 |
| | — | VII | 25 | | 278 | 82 |
| | — | VII | 27 | | 279 | 83 |
| | — | VII | 28 | | 280 | 84 |
| | — | VII | 30 | | 281 | 85 |
| | — | VIII | 3 | | 282 | 86 |
| | — | VIII | 11 | | 283 | 87 |
| | — | VIII | 22 | | 284 | 88 |
| | — | IX | 9 | | 285 | 89 |
| | — | IX | 16 | | 286 | 90 |
| | — | IX | 23+ | | 287 | 91 |
| | — | IX | 28 | | 288 | 92 |
| | — | IX | 28 | | 289 | 93 |
| | — | X | 4 | | 290 | 94 |
| | — | X | 10 | | 291 | 95 |
| | — | X | 20 | | 292 | 96 |
| | — | X | 23 | | 293 | 97 |
| | — | X | 30 | | 294 | 98 |
| | — | XI | 1 | | 295 | 99 |
| | — | XI | 10 | | 296 | 100 |
| | — | XI | 19 | | 297 | 101 |
| | — | XI | 22 | | 298 | 102 |
| | — | XI | 23 | | 299 | 103 |
| | — | XI | 26 | | 300 | 104 |
| | — | XI | 30 | | 301 | 105 |
| | — | XII | 21 | | 302 | 106 |
| | — | XIII | 7 | | 303 | 107 |
| | — | [–] | 5 | | 304 | 108 |
| | — | [–] | 22 | | 305 | 109 |
| | — | [–] | [–] | | 306 | 110 |
| | — | [–] | [–] | | 307 | 111 |
| | [–] | [–] | 6 | | 308 | 112 |
| | [–] | [–] | 17 | | 309 | 113 |
| | [–] | [–] | [–] | | 310 | 114 |
| | — | VI | 15 | Lindblom High 2 | | 115 |
| | — | VI | 28 | *BIN* 10: no | 311 | 116 |
| | — | VI | 29 | | 312 | 117 |

in that after these four groups six names are added under the heading nagar-lugal-me, "they are royal carpenters". Some sections are omitted when that part of the workshop was not active: for example, text 55 lists only carpenters and felters and text 78 only leather and reedworkers. Sometimes the type of workman is mentioned but no personal names are listed, which indicates that on that day no workers of such profession were active: for example, in text 69 the sections of reedworkers and felters do not contain any names and the subscript indicates that none was active that day[2]. At times, after a list of names, the profession is omitted probably by scribal error, as, for instance, in text 49 where "reedworker" is not mentioned although other texts indicate that three of the listed persons — Ilšu-êr, Lugal-kuzu and Ku-Nanna — are reedworkers[3]. After these four sections there is a subscript giving the date and often the total number of workmen — called guruš — present.

Eighty-one tablets list year, month and day[4], and thirty-six lack the year date. In sixty-six texts the total number of workmen present is given. In texts 62 and 76 the formula to record their presence is given but the scribe omitted the number. This information is often given on the left edge of the tablet. Text 18 has a special formula [kur]um$_7$-ak / gašam / u$_4$-3-kam / iti ... / mu ..., "inspection of the craftsman on day 3", abbreviated in text 115 as kurum$_7$-ak / u$_4$-25-kam / gub-ba-àm, "inspection of day 25, on duty"[5].

A second variety of worker lists is only represented by three examples, all lacking the year date (texts 115-117). In these texts the total number of workmen per section is given, but not their names, and in the subscript the total number of workmen in the workshop is given.

The number of personal names can vary from none to eighteen per section. Several notations precede or follow the names and will be studied in the following sections.

### 2) *Systems of accounting for a workday*

All personal names are preceded by a vertical wedge or a blank space regardless of whether or not there follows another notation. From the

[2] In text 69 two carpenters and one leatherworker are named and the summary on the left edge mentions a total of three workmen.

[3] See analysis of the reedworker section below.

[4] On eight tablets one or more of these elements is broken.

[5] For a recent discussion of this phrase, see D. Loding, *A Craft Archive from Ur*, Univ. Microfilms, Ann Arbor, 1974: p. 197 n. 1 and 23 n. 38.

texts which give the total number of workmen in the subscript it is clear that only those names with a vertical wedge are counted[6]. Texts 33 and 38 are exceptions in that personal names not preceded by a vertical wedge seem to have been counted in the total; in both cases the scribe seems to have counted the names, not the wedges[7].

Nine times a name is preceded by two wedges. In three texts (28, 33 and 113) the total number of craftsmen is given in the subscript. In text 113, where the double wedge occurs twice, the total does not take this into account, and so the scribe seems to have counted the number of names, not of wedges. In text 33, however, the total counts the workmen with double wedge twice. Text 23 is peculiar in that the wedges are not vertical but horizontal. The notation before the personal name seems to be 2 gú gi, as if the scribe wanted to indicate two talents of reed, but in the subscript the workman seems to have been counted twice[8].

Text 39 has a similar notation: 3 1/2 búr Puz[$ur_4$-$Eš_4$]-tár which accounts for 3 1/2 workmen in the total[9].

The wedges preceding the personal names account for man-days, i.e., the number of days that the workman was active. Since the worker lists are made up on a daily basis (cf. below) usually only one man-day at a time is accounted for. The importance of accounting for the number of days that a craftsman worked is also clear from *BIN* 10: no 314 where days of absence of a number of them are recorded (cf. below). The same notion of man-days is used in Ur III texts dealing with labor by guruš, where the formula × guruš $u_4$-y-šè does not count workmen but workdays. This also explains the occurrence of one half guruš[10].

### 3) *Notations for work done in and outside the workshop*

#### a) In the workshop

Other notations occur before or after the personal names or after a

[6] A similar system of accounting for workmen is already attested in the economic texts from Fara where wedges are used in lists of workmen with a total at the end. There too, persons who are not preceded by a vertical wedge are not included in the total, cf. J. Krecher, *ZA* 63 (1973): p. 163.

[7] Scribal errors occur: in text 93 the total number of vertical wedges is seventeen while the scribe noted eighteen. Since this text is a copy of text 92, we know that he inadvertently omitted the wedge before the name Adad-bani.

[8] This is not completely certain since the beginning of some lines in this text are broken and may have included other notations.

[9] For búr in this context, see below under 3.c.

[10] Cf. V.V. Struve, "Some New Data on the Organization of Labour ...", in *Ancient Mesopotamia* (ed. I.M. Diakonoff), Moscow, 1969: p. 128 and 130-133, for discussion of the Ur III material.

group of them. Very common is the phrase šà giš-kin-ti (gub-ba-àm). This is most frequently followed by a number of names of workman who are not on duty or active in another location. The term giš-kin-ti probably refers in this context to the building in which the work is done (cf. chapter I). The phrase should then be translated as "they are on duty in the workshop".

Some notations indicate that the workman did specialized work. With leatherworkers two special notations occur. Text 76 lists two leatherworkers as e-rí-na-íl-me prossibly referring to the carrying of waterproof skins, and in text 39 Ur-Sîn is preceded by the notation kuš-íl which seems to indicate that he carries hides[11].

With reedworkers a number of notations seem to refer to specific types of reedbaskets: $^{gi}$gur (text 4, 79), $^{gi}$gur-mušen (text 4), $^{gi}$gur-IN (texts 5, 10, 11, 12, 19, 22, 23, 24 and 43), $^{gi}$gurdub (texts 42, 44 and 51), and $^{gi}$gurdub-túg (text 33)[12]. The notation GI.MA.ŠA in text 32 may refer to a reed cover for boats[13]. GI.NAM.MA.AN in text 5 may stand for $^{gi}$ma-an-sim "a sieve", an item often referred to in the Isin texts. It seems that these reedworkers were active in the production of specific types of reedwork on the days recorded. It is peculiar that only in text 33 these notations are preceded by a vertical wedge and the workmen included in the total. Moreover, in text 79 all names preceded by $^{gi}$gur are said to be absent.

b) Outside the workshop

There are many references to workmen active in a location outside the workshop. They could work in the house of the singers, é-nar (texts 22 and 56), or that of the oilpressers, é-ì-rá-rá (texts 37, 45, 50 and 64). Work in temples of Dagan (texts 48, 49, 50, and 51)[14] and of Ninisina (text 5) is also recorded. In texts 25 and 26 é probably refers to an

[11] Possibly they set the hides on the racks for tanning or waterproofing.

[12] For $^{gi}$gur, see A. Salonen, *Hausgeräte* I: pp. 209-212. He does not mention $^{gi}$gur-mušen or $^{gi}$gur-IN. $^{gi}$gur-mušen may be a basket for birds; $^{gi}$gur-IN may contain the element in-nu = *tibnum*, "straw" (*AHw*: p. 1354), and be a "straw-carrying basket", or IN could possibly refer to "of the Isin type" since it is the old spelling of the city name, cf. most recently, D. Charpin, *RA* 74 (1980): p. 189. For $^{gi}$gurdub, see A. Salonen, *Hausgeräte* I: p. 235, s.v. $^{gi}$PISANxGI. He does not list $^{gi}$PISANxGI-túg but such a compound is very likely.

[13] Some relation may exist with the words $^{gi}$KID.MÁ.ŠÚ.A, $^{gi}$KID.ŠÚ.MÁ and $^{gi}$MÁ.ŠÀ.GA, all indicating a mat to cover boats, discussed by A. Goetze, *JCS* 2 (1949): p. 177-9, A. Falkenstein, *ZA* 57 (1965): p. 91, and M. Civil, *RA* 61 (1967): p. 67f.

[14] The texts date from a short time span, V/30/I.E. 13 - VII/8/I.E. 13.

unidentified temple. Some reedworkers work on the wall (šà ki-sá-a) in text 74[15]. Other workmen seem to have been assigned guard duty there since text 51 has PN en-nu bàd (ll. 8, 21 and 39), and other texts have the notation bàd, "wall" (texts 52 and 114). Text 2 mentions two reedworkers ki šabra and text 74 one reedworker ki Libūr-bēlī. They were probably working in the house or office of these persons.

Some craftsmen can be found in other cities[16]. Text 87 refers to one felter in Nippur and in text 30 a carpenter is said to be in the city Mur[17]. The notation kaskal only occurs with Adad-ellatī, the leatherworker, in texts 88, 89, 91-96 and 109, and may indicate that he is on the road to perform his work. The nature of this work is unclear but since the texts are in chronological succession[18], Adad-ellatī may have been sent out on a mission for several months.

Other notations refer to construction work, always in connection with carpenters. They are housebuilders (šitim), or active with the housebuilders (ki šitim [gub-ba]), or on duty doing construction work (ŠU.DÍM gub-ba)[19].

In texts 22, 23 and 24, Šū-Eštar bis is "called up for service" (zi-ga)[20]. ZI in texts 42 and 52 is probably the shortened form of this notation. It seems that the workmen recorded with ZI are sometimes considered active when preceded by a vertical wedge (text 42, 7, text 52), and sometimes inactive (texts 22, 23, 24 and text 42, 5-6).

### c) Agricultural activity

Several activities of the craftsmen are related to agriculture. Three

[15] Note that many texts record work for doors šà ki-sá-a: *BIN* 9: nos 153, 155-157, 159-168, 170, 171, 173, 175, 176 and 194, *BIN* 10: no 192, *JAOS* 98: p. 253, no 4, *ASJ* 4: p. 68, no 17, LB 1105. As in the case of worker list 74, all these texts are dated from I/–/I.E. 16 - V/–/I.E. 17. These building activities can be related to the year date I.E. 17, mu bàd *Eštar-tarām-ᵈIšbi-Erra* ba-dù, cf. D. Frayne, *The Historical Correlations of the Sumerian Royal Hymns*, Univ. Microfilms, Ann Arbor, 1981: p. 337.

[16] See C. Zaccagnini, *JNES* 42 (1983): p. 247-249, on sending workmen to other cities as documented in the Mari texts.

[17] Cf. *Répertoire Géographique* 2: p. 134.

[18] The texts date from VIII/22/– to X/20/–. The year will be discussed later. Text 90 does not record Adad-ellatī at all, presumably by omission of the scribe. text 109, where the month is broken, probably belongs in the same time period.

[19] šitim: texts 1, 80, 81, 83, 84, 86-89, 91-94, 96.
ki-šitim: texts 6, 9, 10, 11, 79, 90.
ŠU.DÍM: texts 95, 96, 97, 98.

[20] Cf. *UET* 3: no 1475 where the guruš stationed at the wall (l. 7) is listed as zi-ga in the subscript. zi-ga has the basic meaning of "levy", cf. A. Poebel, *AS* 14: pp. 71f.

texts mention hoeing in the field EZEN.SAR (text 112: $^{\text{giš}}$al-ak a-šà EZEN.SAR; text 44: a-šà EZEN.SAR). The exceptional text 47 probably mentions the same activity: nagar / ašgab / ad-KID / túg-du$_8$ / [$^{\text{giš}}$a]l-ak a-šà E[ZEN]/SAR/ date[21]. Lastly, in text 3 a reedworker is said to be ki-$^{\text{giš}}$al!. All references are found on tablets dated in months V (text 47) and VII (texts 3, 44)[22], which are among the months where hoeing (al-ak) is mainly recorded in agricultural texts from Ur III Umma[23]. Work related to irrigation is also attested: workmen can be stationed at the weir (kun-zi-da; text 1, 79)[24], and the IŠ sign which precedes several names in texts 2, 81, 100, 102 and 104 may be read saḫar and stand for kin-saḫar "earthwork" of agricultural texts from Umma[25]. The notation sig$_4$ in texts 10 and 11 probably refers to brickmaking. Work in the granary (šà gur$_7$) is attested for carpenters, reedworkers and a felter in texts 21 and 40. Agricultural work related to reed is also attested. The notation gi occurs with workmen of all four professions[26], mostly without the vertical wedge. Why this wedge is sometimes recorded and sometimes omitted is unclear, especially in text 51 where gi is twice preceded by it and once not. Exceptional is the indication 2 gú gi in text 28 (cf. above). Reed for fire, gi-izi, is also collected by craftsmen (text 45)[27]. The notation búr in text 39 probably refers to the plucking of the reed[28]. Some craftsmen are stationed at

[21] The first sign in ll. 1-4 is probably not the NU sign to indicate that none of the workmen were active, but a checkmark to indicate these men were accounted for. Similar checkmarks can be found in *TLB* 3: nos 75, 82 and 170 where they appear on the left edge of the tablet. It is unlikely that we have here a type of non-recording text such as the Ur III text published by E. Sollberger, *RA* 45 (1951): p. 116.

[22] In text 112 the month name is broken.

[23] J.W. Turner, *Early Mesopotamian Agriculture*, unpubl. Ph.D. diss., Yale Univ., 1981: p. 90.

[24] In text 79, 7 only the kun-sign is used, probably as an abbreviation.

[25] J.W. Turner, *op. cit.*: p. 250.

[26] Carpenters: texts 31, 33 and 53; leatherworkers: texts 42, 51, 53 and 76; reedworkers texts 18, 27, 28, 29 and 31; felters: texts 42 and 51.

For reedwork in agricultural texts from Ur III Umma, cf. A.L. Oppenheim, *Eames Coll.*: p. 45-8, J.W. Turner, *op. cit.*: p. 209-222.

[27] For discussions of the terms gi-izi/gi-zi cf. S.T. Kang, *SACT* II: p. 371f., E. Sollberger, *TCS* 1: p. 138 s.v. izi, D. Owen - G. Young, *JCS* 23 (1970): p. 96, and J.W. Turner, *op. cit.*: p. 221f. gi-izi as a term referring to fodder for animals is unlikely in the context of the early Isin archive.

[28] bu(r) is probably the main dialect word for Emesal zé(r), cf. BU.BU = Emesal zé-zé = *nu-su-ḫu*(*MSL* 4: p. 38: III 114), and gi-zé is well-known as "plucking reed", cf. A.L. Oppenheim, *Eames Coll.*: p. 117 n. 114, and C. Wilcke, *Lugalbanda*: p. 204f.

boats[29], which corresponds to the often attested work on boats in the rest of the Isin archive[30].

d) Enigmatic notations

In text 96 the number 30 (or KUR) precedes the name of a carpenter, and in text 39 the numbers 40 and 50 occur twice each (40: l. 6 and prob. l. 15, 50: l. 7 and prob. l. 16). In text 96 the workman is included in the total in the subscript, in text 39 the workmen are not. Text 62 lists in every section a number of workmen níg-kin-ezen without recording their names, perhaps indicating that they were involved in the preparation of a festival. In texts 54 and 57 the names of the leatherworker Nūr-Ea and of the felter Ilī-bani are followed by the GU sign, which may be a reference to an unknown profession[31]. Text 21, 18 ([ ]ZA.LI) and text 114, 25 ([ ]ŠA.AB) are unintelligible because of the breaks in the tablets.

4) *Notations referring to work not done*

Some notations indicate that the workman is not on duty. Frequently, nu-gub and its shortened form nu occur. Related to it is probably the phrase nu-LU-me found after a list of names in the leather and reedworker sections of text 31, while the parallel carpenter section has a number of names preceded by nu. Often craftsmen are recorded as ill (tu-ra). In more than half of the cases the name is not preceded by a vertical wedge (texts 3, 4, 7, 8, 91, 92, 93 and 106), while in the rest there is a vertical wedge (texts 32, 36, 40, 50, 52 and 83). Thus some of the ill craftsmen may still have accounted for a full day of work.

*BIN* 10: no 314 (undated) is a unique text listing the names of craftsmen and the number of days they were $la(l)u_6$[32]. This difficult term must be interpreted as "absent" here, since in the Ur examples guruš $la(l)u_6$ "absent" are distinguished from those gub-ba

[29] Text 8: one carpenter má-gub-ba; text 107: ad-KID-ma má-lugal gub-ba; text 35: five carpenters má-Ma-rí$^{ki}$; text 46 six guruš ki-má-a-ka.

[30] E.g., *BIN* 10: no 129 lists issues of bitumen for the large Dilmun boat and the large royal boat; *BIN* 9: no 37, and *MCS* 5: p. 122 no 8, list deliveries for covers for the royal boat.

[31] Oppenheim, *Eames Coll.*: p. 77 s.v. G34. This interpretation is very unlikely for professions other than the four listed are never mentioned.

[32] LAL.NI, for the reading see R. Borger, *Zeichenliste*: p. 182. P. Steinkeller, *Aula Orientalis* 2 (1984): p. 137-9.

"present"[33]. In *BIN* 10: no 314 the craftsmen are divided into four groups each with their overseer (ugula). The first three names are known as carpenters from the worker lists and their overseer is Ur-Lisina, the second group felters with their overseer ḪI.LA-ša[34], the third leatherworkers with overseer Lu-Nanna, and the last reedworkers with Ilšu-êr as overseer. Šū-Eštar, the leatherworker, is followed by a special notation, a-rá-1-kam, "for the first time". At the end of the text it is mentioned that Munanum, probably the carpenter of that name, was absent for fifteen days. Since the text is undated we do not know what period of time it covers.

5) *Notations to differentiate people with the same name*

Of interest is also the way in which workmen with the same name are distinguished from one another. This problem only arises when they belong to the same profession. Names such as Lugalkuzu appear in different sections of the worker lists, but are not distinguished from one another with a special notation since they belong to different professions. Only a few workers of the same profession share identical names: Ilī-bani, Nūr-Ea and Šū-Eštar. Most elaborate are the notations to distinguish the different reedworkers by the name of Šū-Eštar. This name is followed by šu, min, and šu.min. The notation tur is also used, for instance, with the leatherworker Nūr-Ea.

min is commonly used in lists of personal names to indicate a second person with the same name. The notation šu, is not attested outside the Isin lists, probably stands for šu-gi$_4$ "old", opposite of tur "young"[35].

[33] Cf. e.g., *UET* 3: no 490 where twice a summary is made of guruš gub-ba and la(l)u$_6$. The term la(l)u$_6$ is discussed at length by F.R. Kraus, *Edikt*: p. 89-95. B.R. Foster, *Umma in the Sargonic Period,* Hamden, 1982: p. 65, discusses the term in the Sargonic material; he proposes the translation "in arrears", i.e., "the amount that should have been delivered but had not been until the date of the document" and shows that in the Sargonic material the amount is always a positive one.

Basically this translation does coincide with the translation "absent" since the guruš recorded in the Isin and Ur worker lists were supposed to work a certain number of days (cf. below), and when absent they were in arrears in regard to their obligation. Cf. also in the Sargonic material, e.g., in *ITT* II: no 3081 (no copy) where a la(l)u$_6$ workers nu-mu-gub, "not on duty".

The term does occur with the usual meaning "in arrears" in the Isin texts *BIN* 9: no 130 where deliveries of glue by leatherworkers are recorded with the amount la(l)u$_6$, and in *BIN* 10: no 80 where for nine reedworkers the number of reed trays delivered and in arrears are listed. In the balanced account *BIN* 9: no 150 the hides la(l)u$_6$ are those left over after the transaction. Cf. D. Snell, *YNER* 8: p. 228, M. Powell, *Iraq* 39 (1977): p. 26f.

[34] For this name see below note 43.

[35] Suggestion of P. Steinkeller.

### 6) *Supervision of each section of the workshop*

From the worker lists it is clear that the workshop was divided into four parts corresponding to the four sections in the lists. Each section of the workshop was headed by an overseer (ugula), whose name appears in almost every text at the beginning of his section; in *BIN* 10: no 314 (cf. above) he is called ugula.

#### a) Carpenters (nagar)

For the carpenters the function of overseer was performed by Ur-Lisina in the year I.E. 7-15[36], and Ennum-Ea from I.E. 16 on[37]. Ur-Lisina is last mentioned in text 73 (X/7/I.E. 16), not in the first place but at the end of the carpenter section as absent. In the rest of the archive Ur-Lisina is mentioned only once (*BIN* 10: no 123, X/–/I.E. 15)[38]. Ennum-Ea is mentioned several times from I.E. 25 until Š.i. 3 as delivering glue, gypsum and flour (*BIN* 9: nos 16, 169, 201, and 202) and as conveyor of chairs (*BIN* 9: no 499).

#### b) Leatherworkers (ašgab)

The foreman of the leatherworkers is Lu-Inanna, who is mentioned first in the leatherworker sections of all but ten texts[39]. In *BIN* 10: no

[36] He is mentioned first in all dated texts from that period and all undated texts, except eight. In six texts his name was probably recorded in the broken part of the tablet (texts 41, 43, 46, 63, 111 and 112), while in one text no carpenters are recorded at all (text 47). For unknown reasons he is also not mentioned in text 32 (XI/14/I.E. 9).

[37] He is recorded in the first place in text 73-75 and in text 113. In texts 76-78 no carpenters are recorded.

[38] It is interesting to note how the spelling of Ur-Lisina's name changes over time. Until text 28 (VII/10/I.E. 9) the spelling Ur-$^{d}$⟨Li-⟩si$_4$-na is common and from text 35 (V/6/I.E. 10) on the writing Ur-$^{d}$Li$_9$-si$_4$. si can replace si$_4$ in both spellings. In month VII of I.E. 11 the old spelling reappears (text 44). The plene writing Ur-$^{d}$Li-si$_4$-na occurs only a few times (texts 18, 30 and 34). Exceptional is the writing in text 16, dating from the day after text 15. While the texts are almost exact duplicates (text 15 has omitted Puzur-Sîn in the reedworker section), when text 15 has Ur-$^{d}$⟨Li-⟩si$_4$-na, text 16 has Ur-$^{d}$NIN-si$_4$-na! (as copied in *BIN* 9: no 513 [collated]). The text without year dates all have the plene spelling Ur-$^{d}$Li$_9$-si$_4$-na (si can replace si$_4$), except text 79 and 90 which have Ur-$^{d}$⟨Li$_9$⟩-si$_4$-na (si can replace si$_4$), and text 106 with Ur-$^{d}$Li$_9$-⟨si⟩-na.

[39] Two of those probably mention him in the broken part of the tablet (texts 29 and 46). In texts 64, 69 and 74 only one leatherworker is mentioned, and so no overseer seems to have been needed. Text 62 lists only one leatherworker in the workshop and six unspecified workers preparing the festival (níg-kin-ezen), Lu-Inanna most likely among them. In texts 35, 47 and 55 no leatherworkers are mentioned, and in text 75 Lu-Inanna is not mentioned.

314 the overseer of the leatherworkers is called Lu-Nanna, a name not attested in the worker lists. But Lu-Nanna occurs in *BIN* 9: no 145 (VIII/2?/I.E. 5), a record of deliveries of glue by six leatherworkers. Since Lu-Nanna is mentioned first and with the largest amount delivered, he must be the overseer of the group. This can be assumed through comparison with *BIN* 9: no 130 (–/–/I.E. 7) where deliveries of glue by ten leatherworkers are recorded; they are headed by Lu-Inanna who is their overseer in contemporaneous worker lists. Lu-Nanna may thus have been Lu-Inanna's predecessor.

Lu-Inanna is often attested as receiving hides in the rest of the Isin archive from I.E. 6 until I.E. 30, and perhaps also in Š.i. 1. In some texts he is explicitly called leatherworker (ašgab) (*BIN* 9: nos 24 and 469). His seal is known: Lú-Inanna / dumu Ur-tab-ba / [ ] (*BIN* 9: no 129). The Lu-Inanna "rider" (rá-gaba), attested during Š.i. 1 (*BIN* 9: nos 341 and 452) is probably someone else.

c) Reedworkers (ad-KID)

The overseer of the reedworkers is Ilšu-êr[40]. He is mentioned first in almost every reedworker section[41] and is called overseer in *BIN* 10: no 314. He appears only three times in the rest of the archive. In *BIN* 10: no 67 (XII/–/I.E. 15) Ilšu-êr the reedworker receives a *zamiritum*, and in *BIN* 10: no 130, l. 24 (VII/30/I.E. 19) we read: 8 [sìla ésir-é-a][42] / kin ad-[KID] / gìr Ìl-šu-[e-er], "8 quarts of bitumen, work of the reedworkers, Ilšu-êr was conveyer". Surprisingly he appears next in the same text in connection with feltwork 2/3 ma-na [níg-U.NU-a] síg-$ud_5$ / kin túg-d[$u_8$] / gìr Ìl-šu-e-[er], "2/3 minas of goat's hair thread, work of the felters, Ilšu-êr was conveyor". Perhaps he replaced the overseer of the felters on that day.

d) Felters (túg-$du_8$)

This position is not always in the same hands during the period covered by the worker lists. From I.E. 7 until I.E. 11 (texts 1-44), and in

[40] "His god is watchful", cf. *AHw*: p. 247 s.v. *êru*.

[41] His name is not mentioned in sixteen worker lists: in ten because no reedworkers are mentioned (texts 36, 37, 47, 55, 62, 63, 65, 69, 70 and 73), in four because the tablet is broken (texts 25, 32, 42 and 51), in text 72 probably because only one reedworker is listed, and for unknown reasons in text 75.

[42] Restored from summary section of the text.

the texts without year dates (79-111) ḪA.LA-ša[43] is mentioned first in the felter section[44]. In four texts (81-84) the name is written ḪI.LA-ša, which is also the name of the overseer of the felters in *BIN* 10: no 314[45]. From I.E. 12 on, the post is taken over by Ur-Lugalbanda who is mentioned previously in different positions in the list but never in the first place. From text 45 on, he appears as the head of most felter sections[46]. The change in foreman is also reflected in the rest of the archive. From I.E. 6 until I.E. 11 ḪA.LA-ša — sometimes specified as felter (*BIN* 10: nos 3, 60, and 72) — is found as conveyor or recipient of wool (*BIN* 10: nos 3, 60, 61, and 72), delivering felt (*BIN* 9: no 385) or cloth (*BIN* 10: no 73), or as weighing (*BIN* 10: no 74) or sealing (*BIN* 10: no 60) official. His seal is known, but unfortunately incomplete: ḪA.LA[-ša]/dumu Ga[ ] (*BIN* 10: nos 60, 61, and 72). He appears once afterwards in connection with rope (*BIN* 10: no 75, III/14/I.E. 15).

Ur-Lugalbanda is attested only from I.E. 12 to Š.i. 2, never specified as felter[47]. He is often recipient or conveyor of wool[48], and acts as weighing official and conveyor of rope[49]. and as conveyor of thread[50]. In other texts he delivers, receives, or weighs miscellaneous items such as rope, thread, glue, cloth, felt and a chair[51]. Two seals of Ur-Lugalbanda are known: Ur-$^{d}$Lugal-bàn-[da] / dumu *A-ḫu-ba-a* (*BIN* 10: nos 64, 69) and Ur-Lugal-$^{d}$bàn-[da] / dumu *A-ḫu-ba-a* (*BIN* 9: no 501)[52]. It is remarkable that both seals appear on tablets dated I.E. 25 (*BIN* 9: no 501, *BIN* 10: no 69).

[43] V. Crawford, *BIN* 9: p. 34 reads the name Zitta-ša, cf. also E. Kienast, *JCS* 19 (1965): p. 48. Because of the variant ḪI.LA-ŠA, however, I am not certain that the first two signs have to be read as a logogram.

[44] Except in text 79 where he is not mentioned at all.

[45] In text 81 Aḫubā'a is mentioned first, ḪI.LA-ša second.

[46] In texts 55 and 58 ḪA.LA-ša and in text 74 Šū-ilī are mentioned as the only felter; probably no overseer was needed. In text 76 Ur-Lugalbanda is mentioned second after Ilī-bani, probably by scribal error. Ur-Lugalbanda seems to have been added later. The text reads: *Ilī-ba-ni* túg-du$_{8}$ / Ur-$^{d}$Lugal-bàn-da / túg-du$_{8}$-me. In eleven other texts no felter at all is recorded (texts 47, 62-65, 68-71, 75 and 78).

[47] The specification of ḪA.LA-ša as felter was sometimes necessary since there is also a carpenter ḪA.LA-ša. For Ur-Lugalbanda this problem does not arise.

[48] Recipient: *BIN* 9: nos 128, 500, 501, 517, 524, 526, *BIN* 10: nos 9, 42, 43, 66, 69, conveyor: *BIN* 9: nos 105, 141, *BIN* 10: no 35, *JAOS* 98: p. 254 no 6.

[49] Weighing: *BIN* 9: nos 257, 453, *BIN* 10: nos 75, 76, 81, 84, conveyor: *BIN* 9: nos 255 and 265.

[50] *BIN* 9: nos 142, 143, 144, 205, 209, 483, and *BIN* 10: no 71.

[51] *BIN* 9: nos 249, 484, *BIN* 10: nos 64, 65, 71, 85, 86, *JAOS* 98: p. 252 no 2, and LB 1112.

[52] Cf. V. Crawford, *BIN* 9: pl. 93, seal O. The seal impression on *BIN* 9: no 484 is too faint to be legible at present. Crawford thought it was impressed with seal O. Also the impression on *BIN* 10: no 65 is too faint to determine what seal was used.

From this material we can safely conclude that each section of the workshop had a foreman who was present almost every day. The rest of the craftsmen, however, work in teams on alternating days.

### 7) *Composition of teams*

For every section a large number of personal names is attested: twenty-nine carpenters, thirty-two leatherworkers, forty-one reedworkers, and twenty-four felters. The names of workmen in each section differ from text to text. The changes are not solely chronological since, for instance, Šullulu the carpenter is attested in I.E. 7 month VII on days 1 and 4, but not on day 6, and again on days 21 and 24, but not on day 26. On some days workmen who were expected to work did not appear and were recorded as absent (nu-gub). The days that they are not accounted for cannot all be days of rest, for the days off duty would then be too numerous[53]. It seems that in each section of the workshop two teams of craftsmen alternated work. The system by which it was decided which team was to work remains unclear since a complete daily record is not extant; the composition of teams can nevertheless be recovered.

#### a) Carpenters (nagar)

In the carpenter section there were two teams of workmen. In each a certain hierarchy seems to have been indicated by the place the workman occupies in the section. When a worker is ill or absent, he is in most cases placed at the end of the list. Team I (see table III.2a)[54] seems to have been formed by Nadi[55], Erra-bani, Šū-Eštar (replaced by Lugal-kuzu), Munanum, Duššumum and Puzur-Ea; in team II (see table III.2b) the members were Ursig, Šullulu, Baga and Ḫalala. In addition there existed a group of workers who cannot be assigned to either team with certainty. The teams seem to have been regrouped when Ennum-Ea replaced Ur-Lisina as overseer in I.E. 15. From the tables it is clear that

[53] See W.W. Hallo, *HUCA* 48 (1977): p. 12f. for a discussion of days of rest, $u_4$-$du_8$-a. In Ur III Umma there were seven days of rest in one month. Here it seems that a workman was only active for fifteen days each month.

[54] The numbers under each name in tables III.2-4 give the position of the worker in the section of the worker list of that day. The name of the overseer is not given for he remains the same for both teams, cf. 6) "Supervision of each section of the workshop". The total number of craftsmen in the section, including the overseer, is given in the right hand column.

[55] The name may have to be read Na-sá, cf. L. Matouš, *BiOr*. 13 (1956): p. 140, although Nadi seems to be a normal Sumerian name (H. Limet, *Anthroponymie*: p. 495).

## Table III 2a: Team I of the carpenters

| text | Nadi | Erra-bani | Šū-Eštar | Lugalkuzu | Munanum | Duššumum | Puzur-Ea | other workers | To |
|---|---|---|---|---|---|---|---|---|---|
| 1 | 2 | 3 | 4 | | | | | | [illegible] |
| 5 | | 2 | 3 | | | | | | [illegible] |
| 8 | 2 | 3 | 4 | | | | | | 4 |
| 10 | 2 | 3 | 4 | | | | | | [illegible] |
| 12 | 3 | 2 | 4 | | | | | | [illegible] |
| 15 | 2 | 3 | 4 | | | | | | [illegible] |
| 16 | 2 | 3 | 4 | | | | | | [illegible] |
| 18 | 2 | 4 | 3 | | 6 | | | Zilakum(5), Allamu(7) | |
| 19 | 2 | 3 | 4 | | | | | | [illegible] |
| 20 | 2 | 3 | 4 | | | | | | [illegible] |
| 21 | 2 | 3 | 4 | | | | | | [illegible] |
| 22 | 2 | 3 | 4 | | | | | | [illegible] |
| 23 | 2 | 4 | 3 | | | | | | [illegible] |
| 24 | 2 | 4 | 3 | | | | | | [illegible] |
| 25 | 2 | 3 | 4 | | 6 | | | Ḫalala(5), Allamu(7), Zilakum(8) | [illegible] |
| 26 | 2 | 3 | 4 | | 5 | | | Šū-Erra(6), Ḫalala(7), Allamu(8) | [illegible] |
| 28 | 2 | 3 | 4 | | 6 | | | Šullulu(5), Ennum-Ea(7), Zilakum(8) | [illegible] |
| 29 | 2 | 4 | 6 | | 5 | | | Šullulu(3), 2 names broken(7-8), Allamu(9) | 9 |
| 31 | 2 | 3 | 6 | | 4 | | 5 | Allamu(7), Zilakum(8) | 8 |
| 32 | 2 | 3 | 5 | | 4 | | 7 | Zilakum(6), Allamu(8) | 8 |
| 33 | | 1 | | | 2 | | 3 | Zilakum(4), Ennum-Ea(5), Allamu(6) | 6 |
| 35 | 2 | 3 | 4 | | | 5 | 6 | Šū-Erra(7) | 7 |
| 36 | | | | | | | 3 | Zilakum(2) | [illegible] |
| 39 | 2 | 3 | 4 | | | 5 | 6 | Allamu(7) | 7 |
| 40 | 2 | 6 | 3 | | | 4 | 5 | | 6 |
| 41 | | | | | | 5 | 6 | 6 names broken(1-4, 7-8) | 8 |
| 45 | | 6 | | 2 | 5 | | 4 | Ennum-Ea(3), Šullulu(7) | 7 |
| 48 | | | | 2 | 4 | | | Ennum-Ea(3), Buzuzu(5), Rabī-ilī(6), Baga(7), Aḫuwaqar(8) | 8 |
| 50 | | | | 2 | 5 | | | Ibarriq(3), Allamu(4), Baga(6), ḪA.LA-ša(7) | 7 |
| 51 | 2 | | | 8 | 7 | | | Buzuzu(3), Šū-Erra(4), Baga(5), Ibarriq(6), Šullulu(9), Ennum-Ea(10) | 10 |
| 56 | | | | 3 | 4 | | | Ennum-Ea(2), ḪA.LA-ša(5) | 5 |
| 61 | | | | 3 | | | | Ennum-Ea(2) | 3 |
| 67 | 3 | | | | | | | ḪA.LA-ša(2) | 3 |
| 68 | 2 | | | | | | | | 2 |
| 72 | 2 | | | 4 | | | | Allamu(3) | 4 |
| 112 | | 1' | 5' | | | 2' | 3' | Šū-Erra(4'), several names broken | ? |
| 114 | 2 | 3 | 8 | | 7 | | 6 | Allamu(4), Zilakum(5) | 8 |

Table III 2b: Team II of the carpenters

| text | Ursig | Šullulu | Baga | Ḫalala | other workers | total # |
|---|---|---|---|---|---|---|
| 2 | 2 | 3 | | | | 3 |
| 3 | 2 | 3 | | | | 3 |
| 4 | 3 | 2 | | | | 3 |
| 6 | 2 | 3 | | | | 3 |
| 7 | 2 | 3 | | | | 3 |
| 9 | 2 | 3 | | | | 3 |
| 11 | 2 | 3 | | | | 3 |
| 13 | 2 | 3 | | | | 3 |
| 14 | 2 | 3 | | | | 3 |
| 17 | 2 | 3 | | | | 3 |
| 27 | 3 | 2 | | | Ennum-Ea(4), Zilakum(5), Allamu(6), Lu-Ningirsu(7) | 7 |
| 30 | 3 | 4 | 6 | 7 | Erra-bani(2), Lu-Ningirsu(5), Allamu(8), Ennum-Ea(9), Zilakum(10) | 10 |
| 34 | 2 | 3 | 4 | 5 | Zilakum(6), Lu-Ningirsu(7) | 7 |
| 37 | 2 | 5 | 3 | 4 | Zilakum(6) | 6 |
| 38 | 2 | 7 | 3 | 4 | Zilakum(5), Lu-Ningirsu(6) | 7 |
| 42 | 7 | 5 | 2 | 6 | Zilakum(3), Šū-Erra(4) | 7 |
| 43 | 2 | 3 | | | | 3 |
| 44 | 2 | 3 | 4 | 6 | Zilakum(5), Šū-Erra(7) | 7 |
| 49 | 2 | 6 | | | Lugalkuzu(3), Ennum-Ea(4), Erra-bani(5) | 6 |
| 52 | 2 | 4 | | 6 | Lugalkuzu(3), Erra-bani(5), Šū-Erra(7), Puzur-Ea(8), Abī-šarrum(9), Abum-ilī(10), Duššumum(11) | 11 |
| 53 | | 2 | | 3 | Abum-ilī(4) | 4 |
| 54 | 2 | | | | ḪA.LA-ša(3) | 3 |
| 60 | 2 | 4 | | | Lugalkuzu(3) | 4 |
| 64 | 3 | | | | 2 names broken (1-2), Erra-bani(4) | 4 |
| 65 | 2 | 3 | 5 | | Abum-ilī(4) | 5 |
| 66 | 2 | | | | | 2 |

Table III 2c: Teams III and IV of the carpenters

Team III

| text | Nadi | Erra-bani | Lugalkuzu | other workers | total # |
|---|---|---|---|---|---|
| 86 | 2 | 3 | 4 | | 4 |
| 87 | 3 | 2 | 4 | | 4 |
| 88 | 2 | 3 | 4 | | 4 |
| 89 | 2 | 3 | 4 | | 4 |
| 90 | 2 | 3 | 4 | | 4 |
| 94 | 2 | 3 | 4 | | 4 |
| 97 | 2 | | 4 | Šullulu(3) | 4 |
| 99 | 3 | 2 | | | 3 |
| 101 | 2 | 3 | | | 3 |
| 106 | 2 | 3 | | | 3 |

Team IV

| text | Uršaga | Ursig | Šullulu | Šū-Eštar | total # |
|---|---|---|---|---|---|
| 79 | 2 | | 3 | | 3 |
| 80 | 2 | | 4 | 3 | 4 |
| 81 | 2 | | 3 | 4 | 4 |
| 82 | 2 | | 3 | 4 | 4 |
| 83 | 2 | | 3 | 4 | 4 |
| 84 | 2 | | 3 | 4 | 4 |
| 85 | | 2 | 3 | [4] | 4 |
| 91 | | 2 | 3 | 4 | 4 |
| 92 | | 2 | 3 | 4 | 4 |
| 93 | | 2 | 4 | 3 | 4 |
| 95 | | 2 | 3 | 4 | 4 |
| 96 | | 2 | 3 | 4 | 4 |
| 98 | | 2 | 3 | 4 | 4 |
| 100 | | | 2 | 3 | 3 |
| 102 | | 2 | 3 | 4 | 4 |
| 103 | | 2 | 3 | 4 | 4 |
| 104 | | 2 | 4 | 3 | 4 |
| 105 | | 2 | 4 | 3 | 4 |
| 107 | | 2 | 4 | 3 | 4 |
| 108 | | 2 | 3 | | 3 |
| 109 | 2 | | 3 | 4 | 4 |
| 110 | | 2 | 3 | 4 | 4 |

the composition of team II remained constant through almost all texts, and that team I remained constant until text 41 (V/23/I.E. 11). From I.E. 12 on the assignment of teams appears less regular. The position of Šū-Eštar is taken over by Lugal-kuzu who is also often found with team II. Ennum-Ea appears more frequently; he replaces Erra-bani who is now found with team II, and becomes overseer after Ur-Lisina.

In the undated texts (79-111) the teams are somewhat different (see table III.2c). Here three members of team I, Nadi, Erra-bani and Lugalkuzu, form a separate group (team III), and team IV consists of Ursig/Uršaga[56], Šullulu and Šū-Ěstar, who consistently belonged to team I in the dated texts.

Hence, the team ties appear to be flexible. A member of one team can join the other for one day, though this is more likely to happen among lower rank workers. Nadi is never found with team II or Ursig with team I, but Šullulu and Erra-bani sometimes exchange places (text 97), or sometimes appear together (texts 28, 29, 30, 45, 49 and 52). Lugal-kuzu and Baga appear together in texts 48, 49, 50, 51 and 52. Ḫalala seems to belong to team I until text 26 (–/–/I.E. 8), then he joins team II.

From text 73 (X/7/I.E. 16) on, Ennum-Ea becomes overseer and the teams are regrouped: text 75 gives Nadi, Ursig, Erra-bani, Lugal-kuzu and Šullulu together.

Texts with broken year dates can be incorporated into this system: texts 112 and 114 record team I, and text 113, with eighteen carpenters, combines members of both teams. In *BIN* 10: no 314 Šullulu and Nadi are recorded to have been absent for one day each, Uršaga two days and Lugal-kuzu four. At the end of that text it is mentioned that Munanum, probably the carpenter of that name was absent for fifteen days. In the rest of the archive these carpenters are rarely mentioned, while work of the carpenters (kin-nagar), is mentioned eleven times[57]. Only in *BIN* 10: no 82 a conveyor of this work is mentioned; it is Galzunalulu, probably the leatherworker of that name (cf. below).

b) Leatherworkers (ašgab)

In the leatherworker section the composition of teams is more variable. Again a distinction must be made between the dated and the undated texts. In the dated texts (1-78, 112-114) two teams can be

[56] Uršaga is a writing variant for Ursig, cf. H. Limet, *Anthroponymie*: p. 300-305, for the variation $sig_5$/$ša_6$-ga in Ur III personal names.

[57] *BIN* 9: nos 191, 192, 193, 199, 341, 349, 368, 389, *BIN* 10: no 82, *JAOS* 98: p. 256 no 12.

distinguished. Team I (see table III.3a) consists of Šū-Ea, Šū-Ninšubur, Adad-rabi, Šū-Šamaš (replaced by Adda-kalla), Nūr-Ea, Adda-gina, and perhaps Adad-ellatī and Aḫūa-ṭāb. Team II (see table III.3b) is formed by Adad-bani, Nūr-Ea, Ur-Sîn, Lugal-isa, Akuma, and perhaps Šullanum[58] and Adallal. A Nūr-Ea seems to be a member of both teams. There are two different Nūr-Ea's attested among the leatherworkers (texts 51 and 52, *BIN* 9: no 130), and so it seems that each man belonged to one team. When they appear in their respective teams, they normally are not distinguished from one another, but when Nūr-Ea of team II joins team I his name is followed by the notation min. In texts 49 and 50 Nūr-Ea tur probably refers to the Nūr-Ea of team I. A small group of texts perhaps shows a third team headed by Aḫūa-ṭāb (see table III.3b).

In the undated texts (79-109) four teams can be distinguished: two in the earlier group of texts and two in the later (for the chronology of these texts, cf. below s.v. 8). The earlier two teams, IV and V (see table III.3c), are formed by Adad-ellatī, Adad-rabi and Ur-Sîn on the one hand, and Šū-Ea, Šū-Ninšubur, Nūr-Ea and Adad-bani on the other. These teams can be followed in texts 79-87 and in text 108. Later, in texts 88-107, team VI consists of Šū-Ninšubur, Adad-rabi and Ur-Sîn, and team VII includes Šū-Ea, Nūr-Ea and Adad-bani (see table III.3d). Adad-ellatī is recorded with both teams when he is "on the road" (kaskal; texts 88-96).

In the leatherworker section the order of workmen varies more than in the carpenter section, and no hierarchy seems to be indicated. Here too, the members of one team can join another, although less frequently than do the carpenters. Only two members of team I appear with team II: Adda-gina (text 39) and Adad-rabi (texts 38, 42, 44 and 45). Aḫūa-ṭāb, a member of team I, seems to head team III. Three members of team II appear with team I: Ur-Sîn (text 1), Akuma (texts 25, 26), and Šullanum (texts 31, 63).

In the undated texts the interchange of teams seems to occur even less frequently. Adad-bani twice replaces Adad-rabi (texts 95 and 99) or vice versa (text 108), and Ur-Sîn of team VI once joins team VII (text 90). In text 79 a combination of the two teams appears: Šū-Ea, Šū-Ninšubur, Adad-rabi and Nūr-Sîn.

Other texts in the archive in addition to the worker lists record groups

[58] For the name Šullanum, see W.W. Hallo, *RA* 74 (1980): p. 94. The name should be read *Šu-la-núm*, against V. Crawford, *BIN* 9: p. 33, *Šu-la-lum*, because of the variant *Šu-la-nu-um* in *BIN* 10: no 240: 16.

Table III 3a: Team I of the leatherworkers

| Šū-Ea | Šū-Ninšubur | Adad-rabi | Šū-Šamaš | Adda-kalla | Nūr-Ea | Adda-gina | Adad-ellatī | Aḫūa-ṭāb | other workers | total # |
|---|---|---|---|---|---|---|---|---|---|---|
| 2 | 3 | 4 | | | | | | | Ur-Sîn(5) | 5 |
| 2 | 4 | 3 | | | | | | | | 4 |
| 2 | 4 | 3 | | | | | | | | 4 |
| 3 | 2 | 4 | | | | | | | | 4 |
| 2 | 3 | 4 | | | 5 | | | | | 5 |
| 2 | 3 | 4 | | | 5 | | | | | 5 |
| 3 | 2 | 4 | | | 5 | | | | | 5 |
| 2 | 3 | 4 | | | 5 | | | | | 5 |
| 2 | 3 | 4 | | | 5 | | | | | 5 |
| 2 | 3 | 6 | 5 | | 4 | | | | | 6 |
| 2 | 3 | 6 | 5 | | 4 | | | | | 6 |
| 2 | 3 | 4 | 5 | | 6 | | | | | 6 |
| 2 | 3 | 6 | 5 | | 4 | | | | | 6 |
| 3 | 2 | 6 | 5 | | 4 | | | | | 6 |
| 2 | 3 | 6 | 4 | | 5 | | | | | 6 |
| 3 | 2 | 5 | | | 4 | | | | Akuma(6), Išdum-kīn(7) | 7 |
| 3 | 6 | 8 | | | 2 | | 7 | | Akuma(4), Išdum-kīn(5) | 8 |
| 3 | 2 | | | 7 | 5 | | 4 | | Šēlibum(6) | 7 |
| 3 | 2 | | | 4 | 8 | | 6 | | Šullanum(5), Šēlibum(7) | 8 |
| 3 | 2 | | | 6 | 5 | | 4 | | Šēlibum(7) | 7 |
| 3 | 2 | | | 6 | 5 | | 4 | | Šēlibum(7) | 7 |
| 3 | 2 | 5 | | 7 | 6 | | 4 | | Šēlibum(8) | 8 |
| 3 | 2 | 4 | | 5 | | 6 | | | | 6 |
| | | | | 2 | | 3 | | | | 3 |
| 1 | 8 | | | 4 | 2 | 5 | 7 | | Išdum-kīn(3), Lu-Inanna(6) | 8 |
| 2 | 5 | | | 3 | 4 | 7 | | | Išdum-kīn(6) | 7 |
| 2 | 4 | 3 | | | | | | | | 4 |
| 3 | 2 | | | | | 5 | | 6 | Nūr-Ea tur(4) | 6 |
| 3 | 2 | | | | | 5 | | | Nūr-Ea tur(4) | 5 |
| 6 | 2 | | | | 3 | 5 | | 4 | Nūr-Ea bis(7), Išdum-kīn(8) | 8 |
| 3 | 2 | | | | 4 | 7 | | 6 | Nūr-Ea bis(5) | 7 |
| 3 | | | | | 2 | | | | | 3 |
| | 2 | | | | | | | 3 | | 3 |
| | 2 | | | | | | | 3 | | 3 |
| 4 | 2 | | | | 3 | 6 | | 5 | | 6 |
| 4 | | | | | 2 | | | | Šēlibum(3), Galzululu(5) | 5 |
| 2 | | | | | | | | | Galzululu(3) | 3 |
| 5 | 4 | 6 | | 3 | 8 | 2 | 7 | | Išdum-kīn(9) | 9 |

## Table III 3b: Teams II and III? of the leatherworkers

### Team II

| text | Adad-bani | Nūr-Ea | Ur-Sîn | Lugal-isa | Akum(a) | Šulla-num | Adallal | other workers | total # |
|---|---|---|---|---|---|---|---|---|---|
| 2 | 2 | 4 | 5 | 3 | | | | | 5 |
| 6 | 4 | 2 | 3 | 5 | | | | | 5 |
| 7 | 3 | 2 | 4 | 5 | | | | | 5 |
| 8 | 3 | 2 | 4 | 5 | | | | | 5 |
| 9 | 3 | 2 | 4 | 5 | | | | | 5 |
| 11 | 2 | 3 | 4 | 5 | | | | | 5 |
| 12 | 3 | 2 | 4 | 5 | | | | | 5 |
| 13 | 2 | 3 | 4 | 5 | | | | | 5 |
| 18 | | 4 | 5 | 6 | 2 | 7 | 3 | | 7 |
| 27 | 3 | 4 | | | | | 2 | | 4 |
| 28 | 5 | 7 | 2 | 3 | 6 | | 4 | Išdum-kîn(8) | 8 |
| 37 | | 2 | 3 | | | | | several names broken | 3+ |
| 38 | 3 | | 2 | | 4 | 8 | | Adad-rabi(5), Nūr-Erra(6), Šēlibum(7) | 8 |
| 39 | 2 | 3 | | | | | 4 | Adda-gina(5) | 5 |
| 42 | 3 | | 4 | | 2 | 5 | | Adad-rabi(6), several names broken(?) | 6+ |
| 44 | 2 | 4 | 7 | | 3 | 5 | | Adad-rabi(6) | 7 |
| 45 | | | 3 | | 2 | | | Adad-rabi(4), Šēlibum(5), Galzululu(6), Lugal-isa(7) | 7 |
| 53 | 3 | | 5 | | 2 | 8 | | Lugal-isa(4), Galzululu(8), Šēlibum(7) | 8 |
| 61 | | | 2 | | | | | | 2 |
| 66 | 2 | | | | 3 | | | | 3 |
| 76 | 2 | | 6 | | | | | Lu-Bau(3), Išdum-kīn(4), Šēlibum(5) | 6 |
| 113 | 2 | 3 | | | | | | Lu-Bau(4), Šū-Ea(5), Ur-TIR(6) | 6 |
| 114 | 4 | 6 | 2 | 3 | 5 | | | 2 names broken(7-8) | 8 |

### Team III?

| text | Aḫūa-ṭāb | Lu-Ninḫursag | Galzululu | other workers | total # |
|---|---|---|---|---|---|
| 58 | 2 | 3 | | | 3 |
| 60 | | 2 | 3 | | 3 |
| 62 | 2 | | | | 2 |
| 63 | 2 | | | Šullanum(3) | 3 |
| 67 | 2 | | | | 2 |
| 69 | 1 | | | | 1 |

Table III 3c: Teams IV and V of the leatherworkers

Team IV

| text | Adad-ellatī | Adad-rabi | Ur-Sîn | total # |
|---|---|---|---|---|
| 80 | 2 | 3 | 4 | 4 |
| 84 | 3 | 4 | 2 | 4 |
| 86 | 3 | 2 | 4 | 4 |
| 87 | 2 | 3 | 4 | 4 |

Team V

| text | Šū-Ea | Šū-Ninšubur | Nūr-Ea | Adad-bani | other workers | total # |
|---|---|---|---|---|---|---|
| 81 | 2 | 3 | 5 | 4 | | 5 |
| 82 | 3 | 5 | 2 | 4 | | 5 |
| 83 | 3 | 5 | 4 | 2 | | 5 |
| 85 | | | 4 | 2 | Ur-Sîn(3), Lugal-isa(5) | 5 |
| 108 | 2 | 3 | 5 | | Adad-rabi(4) | 5 |

Table III 3d: Teams VI and VII of the leatherworkers

Team VI

| text | Šū-Ninšubur | Adad-rabi | Ur-Sîn | Adad-ellatī | other workers | total # |
|---|---|---|---|---|---|---|
| 89 | 3 | 4 | 2 | 5 | | 5 |
| 94 | 2 | 4 | 3 | 5 | | 5 |
| 95 | 2 | | 4 | 5 | Adad-bani(3) | 5 |
| 98 | 2 | 4 | 3 | | | 4 |
| 99 | 2 | 4 | 3 | | | 4 |
| 100 | 3 | 4 | 2 | | | 4 |
| 107 | 3 | | 2 | | Adad-bani(4) | 4 |
| 111 | 4 | 3 | 2 | | | 4 |

Team VII

| text | Šū-Ea | Nūr-Ea | Adab-bani | Adad-ellatī | other workers | total # |
|---|---|---|---|---|---|---|
| 88 | 2 | 3 | 4 | 5 | | 5 |
| 90 | | 2 | 4 | | Lugal-kuzu(3), Ur-Sîn(5) | 5 |
| 91 | 4 | 2 | 3 | 5 | | 5 |
| 92 | 4 | 2 | 3 | 5 | | 5 |
| 93 | 4 | 3 | 2 | 5 | | 5 |
| 96 | 2 | 3 | 4 | 5 | | 5 |
| 97 | 3 | 2 | 4 | | | 4 |
| 101 | 3 | | 2 | | Nūr-Adad(4) | 4 |
| 102 | 4 | 2 | 3 | | | 4 |
| 103 | 4 | 3 | 2 | | | 4 |
| 104 | 2 | 3 | 4 | | | 4 |
| 105 | 2 | 3 | 4 | | | 4 |
| 106 | 2 | 5 | 4? | | Lugal-isa(3) | 5 |
| 108 | 4 | 2 | 3 | 5 | | 5 |
| 110 | 2 | 3 | 4 | | | 4 |

of leatherworkers: *BIN* 9: no 130 (–/–/I.E. 7) is a record of glue deliveries with the amount in arrears. Members of teams I and II are combined; Lu-Inanna, the overseer, is mentioned first, followed by Adad-ellatī, Šū-Ninšubur, Adad-bani, Šū-Ea, Adad-rabi, Nūr-Ea, Nūr-Ea bis, Lugal-isa and Ur-Sîn. Of these only Adad-ellatī is not mentioned in the worker lists of I.E. 7. This text indicates that two Nūr-Ea's were active among the leatherworkers from I.E. 7 on. *BIN* 9: no 132 lists deliveries of glue in X/–/I.E. 9 by four members of team II who appear together in text 28 of the worker lists (VII/10/I.E. 9): Adad-bani, Lugal-isa, Ur-Sîn and Adallal. *BIN* 9: no 145 records deliveries of glue in VIII/–/I.E. 5, thus before the earliest dated worker list. Mentioned are Lu-Nanna, Nūr-Eštar, Nūr-Ea, Adad-bani, Šū-Ea, and Šū-Ninšubur; the last four form team V of the undated worker lists, and Lu-Nanna is the overseer of the leatherworkers in *BIN* 10: no 314. In *BIN* 10: no 314 Šū-Ninšubur, Šū-Ea, Nūr-Ea and Adad-ellatī are each recorded absent for one day, Adad-rabi for four.

In the Isin archive, leatherworkers appear more frequently than do carpenters, perhaps by virtue of the fact that most of the preserved texts deal with leather. Work of the leatherworkers (kin-ašgab) is also referred to several times (*BIN* 9: nos 193, 198, 232, 349, 433, 489, and *BIN* 10: no 130).

c) Reedworkers (ad-KID)

For the reedworker section, too, it is necessary to distinguish between the dated and the undated texts. The teams are larger here than in any other section of the workshop, for the average number of employed workmen per day is the highest. Team I is formed by Lugal-abba, Puzur-Eštar, Ku-Nanna, Šū-Adad, Nūr-Adad, Puzur-Sîn (succeeded by Iddin-ilī), Āmur-Ea and Lu-Inanna, team II by Ilī-rabi, Ilī-TAB.BA[59], Šū-Eštar, Išar-dajjān, Kubbulum, Šū-Eštar šu, Šū-Eštar bis, Šū-Adad (replaced by Ur-Ninmug), and Urmes (see tables III.4a and 4b). The name Šū-Adad appears in each team and probably refers to two different workers, each member of one team, since in *BIN* 10: no 80 (no date) two different Šū-Adad's are recorded as delivering reed trays. As with the two leatherworkers named Nūr-Ea there is no need to distinguish them as long as they work with their own teams. Several Šū-

[59] Sometimes written Ilī-TAB.BA-ì. For the reading of this name, see I.J. Gelb, *JNES* 20 (1961): p. 132.

Table III 4a: Team I of the reedworkers

| text | Lugal-abba | Puzur-Eštar | Ku-Nanna | Šū-Adad | Nūr-Adad | Puzur-Sîn | Iddin-ilī | Āmur-Ea | Lu-Inanna | other workers | total # |
|---|---|---|---|---|---|---|---|---|---|---|---|
| 1 | 8 | 5 |  | 2 | 7 |  |  | 9 | 3 | Šū-Eštar(4), Puzur-Enlil(6) | 9 |
| 3 | 8 | 4 | 9 | 7 | 6 | 3 |  | 2 | 5 |  | 9 |
| 4 | 3 | 9 |  | 6 | 5 | 4 |  | 2 |  | Ku-Adad(7), Dalal-ilī(8) | 9 |
| 5 | 8 | 7 | 3 | 4 | 5 | 6 |  | 2 |  |  | 8 |
| 10 | 2 | 7 | 9 | 4 |  | 6 |  | 3 | 8 | Nūr-Ea(5) | 9 |
| 14 | 2 | 4 | 8 | 6 | 5 | 3 |  | 9 | 7 |  | 9 |
| 15 | 2 | 3 | 7 | 5 | 4 |  |  | 8 | 6 |  | 8 |
| 16 | 2 | 3 | 8 | 5 | 4 | 6 |  | 9 | 7 |  | 9 |
| 17 |  | 3 | 8 | 5 | 4 | 6 |  | 9 | 7 | Lugal-isa(2) | 9 |
| 18 |  | 3 | 5 | 7 | 4 |  | 6 | 2 |  |  | 7 |
| 28 | 4 | 5 | 3 | 2 | 6 |  | 8 | 7 |  |  | 8 |
| 34 |  | 2 | 7 | 4 | 3 |  | 6 | 8 |  | Puzur-Enlil(5) | 8 |
| 38 | 3 | 8 | 2 | 5 | 6 |  | 7 | 4 |  |  | 8 |
| 39 | 3 | 4 | 2 | 6 | 7 |  | 8 | 5 |  |  | 8 |
| 40 | 4 | 7 | 2 | 5 | 6 |  | 9 | 3 |  | Puzur-Enlil(8) | 9 |
| 42 | 2' | 1' | 3' | 5' | 6' |  | 4' |  |  | several names broken | 6+ |
| 43 |  | 2' |  | 4' | 5' |  |  |  | 6' | several names broken | 6+ |
| 46 | 2 |  | 3 |  | 4 |  |  |  |  |  | 4 |
| 53 |  | 2 |  |  | 3 |  | 4 |  |  | Puzur-Ninkarak(5) | 5 |
| 54 |  | 2 |  |  | 3 |  |  |  |  |  | 3 |
| 57 | 2 |  |  |  | 3 |  |  |  |  |  | 3 |
| 75 |  | 2 |  |  | 3 |  |  |  |  |  | 3 |
| 77 |  |  |  |  | 4 |  |  | 2 |  | Ilī-TAB.BA-ì(3), Puzur-Ninkarak(5) | 5 |
| 113 |  | 2 |  |  | 7 | 6 |  |  |  | Aḫanišu(3), Ibni-Adad(4), Ilī-TAB.BA-ì(5), Puzur-Ninkarak(8) | 8 |
| 114 |  | 2 | 8 | 6 | 3 |  |  |  |  | 2 names broken(4-5) | 8 |

Eštar's belong to team II. To avoid confusion they were differentiated by the notations šu and min.

The composition of team I remains constant until text 43 (VII/14/I.E. 11), although Puzur-Sîn is replaced by Iddin-ilī. After text 43 a number of members disappear: Āmur-Ea reappears in the worker lists only in I.E. 17 (text 73), and Iddin-ilī later appears sporadically in text 45 with team II and in text 52 with team I. Lu-Inanna seems to disappear altogether, while Lugal-abba reappears only sporadically. Šū-Adad appears only once after text 43 in text 45, with team II[60].

The composition of team II remains constant until text 45 (X/26/I.E. 12). Ur-Ninmug replaces Šū-Adad after text 30 and Šū-Eštar šu and Šū-Eštar bis disappear after texts 20 and 24 respectively[61]. After text 45 Išar-dajjān and Kubbulum disappear and others appear only sporadically. As with the leatherworkers, the order in which the reedworkers are listed is not fixed and does not seem to indicate a hierarchy. Awilumma, for instance, appears in the second, the ninth and again in the second place in consecutive texts (25-27). Members of team I can be found with team II, especially in text 30, where a total of twelve reedworkers is recorded; Lugal-abba in texts 30 and 64, Puzur-Eštar in texts 30 and 76, Ku-Nanna in 30 and 45, Nūr-Adad in 30, Iddin-ilī in 45, and Āmur-Ea in 30. Fewer members of team II appear with team I: Ilī-TAB.BA in texts 78 and 113, Šū-Eštar in text 1.

The undated texts record the same teams as the early dated texts, but Ilī-TAB.BA and Āmur-Ea exchange places most of the time (see table III.4c). Ilī-TAB.BA appears with Lugal-abba and other members of team I, except in text 108 where Āmur-Ea replaces him. The latter is now found with Ilī-rabi and team II, except in texts 85 and 90 where Ilī-TAB.BA takes his place. There are two workmen, not known from the dated texts, Aa and Bēlī-amar, who occasionally join both teams, and Ku-Nanna is also found with both teams. It is not clear whether there are two Ku-Nanna's or if the same worker works for both groups.

*BIN* 10: no 313[62] lists the days of attendance of five reedworkers, all members of team IV: they are four days for Āmur-Ea, three for Šū-Eštar, Ilī-rabi and Šū-Adad, and ten for Kubbulum. The text serves the same purpose as the worker lists, but records only one section of the

[60] The Šū-Adad in text 45 is not the original member of team II, by the same name, since that worker is replaced by Ur-Ninmug after text 24 (VII/8/I.E. 8).

[61] Possibly Šū-Eštar bis also appears in text 30, but the reading is uncertain.

[62] The text is dated iti síg-ᵈIn[anna] without a year name.

Table III 4b: Team II of the reedworkers

| text | Ilī-rabi | Ilī-TAB.BA | Šū-Eštar | Išar-dajjān | Kubbu-lum | Šū-Eštar šu | Šū-Eštar bis | Šū-Adad | Ur-Nin-mug | Ur-mes | other workers | total # |
|---|---|---|---|---|---|---|---|---|---|---|---|---|
| 2 | 3 | 8 | | 4 | 5 | 6 | 7 | 2 | | | | 8 |
| 6 | 2 | 3 | 4 | 6 | 7 | | | 8 | | | Šū-Eštar šu bis(5) | 8 |
| 7 | 2 | 3 | 4 | 6 | 7 | | | 8 | | | Šū-Eštar šu bis(5) | 8 |
| 8 | 2 | 3 | 4 | 6 | 7 | | | 8 | | | Šū-Eštar šu bis(5) | 8 |
| 9 | 7 | 3 | 4 | 5 | 2 | | 9 | | | | 2 names broken(6, 8) | 9 |
| 11 | 2 | 6 | | 4 | 3 | 5 | 8 | 7 | | | | 8 |
| 12 | 2 | 3 | 5 | 7 | 8 | | 6 | 4 | | | | 8 |
| 13 | 7 | 2 | 3 | 8 | 6 | | 5 | 4 | | | | 8 |
| 19 | 2 | 6 | 3 | 8 | 7 | 5 | | 4 | | | | 8 |
| 20 | 2 | 6 | 3 | 7 | 8 | 5 | | 4 | | | | 8 |
| 21 | 2 | 5 | 3 | 8 | 7 | | 6 | 4 | | | | 8 |
| 22 | 2 | 6 | 4 | 3 | 7 | | 8 | 5 | | | | 8 |
| 23 | 3 | 6 | 2 | 4 | 5 | | 8 | 7 | | | | 8 |
| 24 | 3 | 6 | 2 | 4 | 5 | | 8 | 7 | | | | 8 |
| 25 | 8 | 4 | 3 | 5 | 9 | | | | 6 | 7 | Awilumma(2) | 9 |
| 26 | 4 | 5 | 3 | 2 | 8 | | | | 7 | 6 | Awilumma(9) | 9 |
| 27 | 8 | 4 | 3 | 7 | 9 | | | | 5 | 6 | Awilumma(2) | 9 |
| 29 | 7 | 3 | 2 | 5 | 8 | | | | 4 | 6 | | 8 |
| 30 | 3 | 2 | 5 | 10 | | | | | 9 | | Ku-Nanna(4), Puzur- | 12 |

| | | | | | | | | | | | | |
|---|---|---|---|---|---|---|---|---|---|---|---|---|
| | | | | | | | | | | | Eštar(6), Lugal-sa(7), Nūr-Adad(8), Lugal-abba(11), Āmur-Ea(12) | |
| 31 | 3 | 5 | 2 | 8 | 4 | | | | 7 | 6 | | 8 |
| 32 | 5 | 3 | 2 | 8 | 4 | | | | 7 | 6 | Awilumma(9) | 9 |
| 33 | 5 | 4 | 3 | 6 | 9 | | | | 8 | 7 | Awilumma(2) | 9 |
| 35 | | | | 3 | | | | | | 2 | | 3 |
| 41 | 8 | 5 | 3 | 4 | 2 | | | | 7 | 6 | | 8 |
| 44 | 2 | 3 | 6 | 4 | 8 | | | | 7 | 5 | | 8 |
| 45 | 3 | 4 | 2 | | | | | 7 | | 5 | Iddin-ilī(6), Puzur-Ù.GUR(8), Ku-Nanna(9) | 9 |
| 48 | 2 | | 3 | | | | | | 5 | | Aḫanišu(4) | 5 |
| 50 | | 2 | | | | | | | | | Aḫanišu(3) | 3 |
| 51 | 5 | 4 | 8 | | | | | | 7 | 6 | 3 names broken(1-3), Puzur-Enlil(9) | 9 |
| 52 | 8 | 2 | 3 | | | | | | 7 | 5 | Urdukuga(4), Aḫanišu(6) Puzur-Enlil(9) | 9 |
| 60 | 2 | | | | | | | | | | Puzur-Eštar(3) | 3 |
| 64 | 3 | | | | | | | | | 2 | Lugal-abba(4) | 4 |
| 66 | 2 | 3 | | | | | | | | 4 | | 4 |
| 67 | | | | | | | | | | 2 | Aḫanišu(3), Lu-Inanna(4) | 4 |
| 71 | | 2 | | | | | | | | | | 2 |
| 76 | | | | | | | | | | 2 | Puzur-Eštar(3) | 3 |
| 112 | 8 | 4 | 5 | 3 | 3 | | | | 6 | 2 | | 8 |

## Table III 4c: Teams III and IV of the reedworkers

### Team III

| text | Lugal-abba | Puzur-Eštar | Ku-Nanna | Šū-Adad | Nūr-Adad | Puzur-Sîn | Ilī-TAB.BA | other workers | total # |
|---|---|---|---|---|---|---|---|---|---|
| 79 | 9 | 7 | 2 | 4 | 5 | 8 | | Āmur-Ea(3), Lu-Inanna(6) | 9 |
| 81 | 2 | 4 | 9 | 3 | 7 | 6 | 5 | Bēlī-amar(8) | 9 |
| 82 | 2 | 4 | 7 | 3 | 8 | 5 | 9 | Bēlī-amar(6) | 9 |
| 83 | 2 | 3 | 7 | 4 | 5 | 6 | 9 | Bēlī-amar(8) | 9 |
| 88 | 5 | 6 | 3 | 7 | 2 | 4 | 8 | | 8 |
| 91 | 2 | 3 | | 7 | 5 | 4 | 6 | Aa(8) | 8 |
| 92 | 2 | 3 | | 7 | 5 | 4 | 6 | Aa(8) | 8 |
| 93 | 7 | 2 | | 5 | 4 | 3 | 6 | Aa(8) | 8 |
| 96 | 2 | 3 | | 5 | 4 | 8 | 7 | Aa(6) | 8 |
| 97 | 2 | 3 | | 5 | 6 | 8 | 4 | Aa(7) | 8 |
| 101 | 2 | 5 | 6 | 8 | 4 | 3 | 7 | | 8 |
| 102 | 2 | 3 | 6 | 8 | 5 | | 7 | Puzur-Enlil(4) | 8 |
| 103 | 2 | 4 | 5 | 7 | 8 | | 6 | Puzur-Enlil(3) | 8 |
| 104 | 2 | 4 | 7 | 6 | 5 | | 8 | Puzur-EN[ ](3) | 8 |
| 105 | 2 | 4 | 6 | 7 | 5 | 3 | 8 | | 8 |
| 106 | 2 | 3 | 5 | 6 | 4 | 8 | 7 | | 8 |
| 108 | 2 | 4 | 8 | 6 | 5 | 3 | | Lugal-TAB.BA-i(7), Āmur-Ea(9) | 9 |
| 109 | 8 | 6 | 2 | 7 | 3 | 4 | 5 | Bēlī-amar(9) | 9 |
| 110 | 2 | 3 | 6 | 5 | 8 | 4 | 7 | | 8 |

### Team IV

| text | Ilī-rabi | Āmur-Ea | Šū-Eštar | Išar-dajjān | Kubbu-lum | Šū-Eštar šu | Šū-Eštar bis | Šū-Adad | other workers | total # |
|---|---|---|---|---|---|---|---|---|---|---|
| 80 | 3 | 2 | | | 7 | 4 | 6 | 5 | Bēlī-amar(8), Ku-Nanna(9) | 9 |
| 84 | 4 | 6 | 2 | | 3 | | 5 | 7 | Aa(8), Bēlī-amar(9) | 9 |
| 85 | 2 | | 4 | 6 | 7 | 5 | | 8 | Ilī-TAB.BA(3) | 8 |
| 86 | 5 | 8 | 2 | | 3 | | 4 | 6 | Ku-Nanna(7), Bēlī-amar(9) | 9 |
| 87 | 4 | 5 | | | 3 | 2 | 6 | 7 | Ku-Nanna(8), Bēlī-amar(9) | 9 |
| 89 | 3 | 2 | | | 8 | 5 | 6 | 7 | Aa(4), Bēlī-amar(9) | 9 |
| 90 | 8 | | 2 | 6 | 7 | | | 4 | Ilī-TAB.BA(3), Šū-Eštar šu bis(5) | 8 |
| 94 | 4 | 2 | | | 8 | 5 | 6 | 7 | Aa(3), Bēlī-amar(9) | 9 |
| 95 | 3 | 2 | 6 | | 4 | 8 | | 5 | Aa(7) | 8 |
| 98 | 3 | 2 | | | 8 | 5 | 6 | 7 | Ku-Nanna(4) | 8 |
| 99 | 3 | 2 | 4 | | 8 | | | | Šū-Eštar šu bis(5), Ku-Nanna(7) | 8 |
| 100 | 8 | 7 | 2 | | 3 | 5 | | 6 | Ku-Nanna(4) | 8 |
| 107 | 3 | 2 | 4 | 7 | 8 | 5 | | 6 | | 8 |
| 111 | 3 | 2 | 5 | | 7 | 6 | | 4 | Ku-Nanna(8) | 8 |

workshop for a longer period than one day. *BIN* 10: no 80 (no date) is an account of deliveries of reed trays by members of both teams listed together: Ilī-rabi, Kubbulum, Lugal-abba, Šū-Adad, Šū-Adad bis, Ku-Nanna, Šū-Eštar, Puzur-Enlil, and Puzur-Eštar. In *BIN* 10: no 314 (no date) Šū-Eštar and Puzur-Ú[63] are said to have been absent for fifteen days, Ku-Nanna for four days and Kubbulum two; a second Šū-Eštar is also absent for two days. He is not distinguished from his namesake by the notations used in the worker lists, but his name is followed by a-rá-1-kam, "for the first time".

Work of the reedworkers (kin-ad-KID), is mentioned in a few texts only: *BIN* 9: no 349, *BIN* 10: nos 130 and 150. In *BIN* 10: no 130 Ilšu-êr acts as conveyor of this work.

d) Felters (túg-$du_8$)

In the felters section no teams can be distinguished. The dated texts show widely various combinations of workmen. Certain groupings of workmen under overseer ḪA.LA-ša are found, although they seem to have been temporary. For instance, Šū-Erra and Ilī-bani appear together in texts 1, 3, 4, 5 and 10, while Šū-PAP.PAP, Šū-Nisaba, and Ur-Lugalbanda appear in texts 6, 7, 8, 9, 11, 12, and 13. Subsequently Šū-Nisaba, Ur-Lugalbanda and Ilī-bani work together (texts 18-26, 28). Under Ur-Lugalbanda as overseer the composition of groups seems to change from day to day. In the undated texts — all with ḪA.LA-ša as overseer — the groupings seem somewhat more consistent, but not to the extent that they form discernable teams. For instance, Aḫubā'a, Šū-Nisaba, Šū-Erra and Nūr-Ea occur together in texts 81-83, Šū-Erra and Išar-ilī in texts 96, 97, 100-104, and Ur-Lugalbanda and Šū-PAP.PAP in texts 94, 95, 98, 99, 106 and 107.

In texts 50 and 51 a group of additional felters is mentioned after the usual ones: Ù.GUR-išar, Danni, Šū-Erra and Awilumma. In text 50 they are followed by the subscript túg-$du_8$-$^{kuš}$⌜súḫub⌝-me, "they are felters of boots", and in text 51 the phrase túg-$du_8$-me, "they are felters", is repeated after their names. Of them only Šū-Erra appears in other worker lists. The meaning of this special group is unclear.

*BIN* 10: no 72 (XII/–/I.E. 8) lists the deliveries or receipts of goat's wool by eight felters. The largest amount, three talents and five minas, is assigned to ḪA.LA-ša; Šū-Nisaba, Šū-PAP.PAP, Išar-ilī, Ilī-bani, Šū-Erra, Šū-Numušda and Nūr-Ea follow with one talent each. In *BIN* 10 no 60

[63] Puzur-Ú seems to stand for Puzur-Eštar or Puzur-Sîn.

(II/–/I.E. 11) Šū-Nisaba, Šū-PAP.PAP and ḪA.LA-ša receive goat's wool. In *BIN* 10: no 314 (no date) the following felters are recorded absent: Šū-Nisaba and Nūr-Ea for one day each, Ur-⟨Lugal-⟩banda for fifteen, and ḪI.LA-ša for four.

Work of the felters (kin-túg-du$_8$), is mentioned in *BIN* 10: no 130 (VII/30/I.E. 29) in connection with goat's hair thread. Surprisingly the conveyor mentioned is Ilšu-êr who is overseer of the reedworkers and appears in this function in the same text. Perhaps he replaced Ur-Lugalbanda that day. In *BIN* 9: no 341 (Š.i. 1) pieces of felt are called work of the felters (kin-túg-du$_8$)[64].

e) Royal carpenters (nagar-lugal)

In text 27 a section of royal carpenters is added after the four usual ones. It lists six names: Baga, Ur-Sîn, Aḫu-ṭāb, Lugal-isa, Ḫalala and Akuma. The names are recorded two per line, a departure from the worker lists. All the names are commonly found in other sections: Ḫalala and Baga among the carpenters; Lugal-isa, Ur-Sîn, Akuma and Aḫu-ṭāb with the leatherworkers. These men are not found in the other sections of text 27 although they are very common in texts of that period; thus these royal carpenters appear to have been recruited from the other professions. Since the term nagar-lugal does not occur in the rest of the archive, this seems to be the most likely explanation.

8) *Chronology of the texts*

The distribution of the worker lists is uneven over the time span covered by the Isin archive (see table I.1 and chapter Ic). All seventy-eight dated texts belong to the years I.E. 7-21, while the whole archive covers the years I.E. 4 — Š.i. 3, a period of thirty-three years. Most of the worker lists date from the years I.E. 7 — I.E. 15, a period from which only few other texts from the rest of the archive are known[65]. The years I.E. 12, 16, 17, 18, 20 and 21 are poorly represented and I.E. 19 not at all. This is probably due to the accident of recovery, and may indicate that the worker lists of one year were kept together.

Thirty-nine texts do not have a year date: three (texts 112-114) because that part of the tablet is broken, the others because the scribe

[64] Cf. P. Steinkeller, *OrAn.* 19 (1980): p. 86.

[65] E.g., from I.E. 7 there are seventeen worker lists and only seven other texts. Compare with table I.1.

did not record it (texts 79-111, 115-117). The main group of undated texts (79-111) appears to belong chronologically together, perhaps even to the same year. In all of them the overseer of each section remains the same, and the teams in the carpenter and the reedworker sections remain the same. In the reedworker section the variation in teams can be explained chronologically; until VIII/11/- (text 87) teams IV and V are active, then Šū-Ninšubur leaves team V to join members of team IV. Moreover, texts 88-96 are probably successive, since they all record Adad-ellatī as "on the road".

These lists cannot be dated by year with certainty. From the study of the personal names it appears, however, that the undated texts precede the dated ones. In the carpenter section the number of workmen recorded per day, three and four, agrees with most of the dated texts until VII/8/I.E. 8 (1-24). The workmen named Nadi, Erra-bani, Ursig, Šullulu and Šū-Eštar always appear in these twenty-three dated texts. Lugal-kuzu on the other hand only appears from X/26/I.E. 12 (text 45) on[66].

In the leatherworker section too, the number of workmen per day in the undated texts, four and five, coincides with that in the dated texts of I.E. 7 (1-17). The workers of the undated texts, Šū-Ninšubur, Adad-rabi, Ur-Sîn, Šū-Ea, Nūr-Ea and Adad-bani, occur in all the early texts. Adad-ellatī, who does not occur in the dated texts until text 26 (XIII/–/I.E. 8), is listed among the leatherworkers in *BIN* 9: no 130 (–/–/I.E. 7). All members of team V, Šū-Ea, Šū-Ninšubur, Nūr-Ea and Adad-bani, are recorded in I.E. 5 (*BIN* 9: no 145). The fact that neither Šū-Šamaš nor Adda-kalla, often mentioned in the dated texts after I.E. 7, occur in the undated texts, also supports the dating of these texts prior to I.E. 7.

In the reedworker section again the number of workmen in the undated texts, eight and nine, agrees with that in the early dated texts. The workmen of the undated texts, Lugal-abba, Puzur-Eštar, Ku-Nanna, Šū-Adad, Nūr-Adad, Puzur-Sîn, Ilī-TAB.BA, Ilī-rabi, Āmur-Ea, Šū-Eštar, Išar-dajjān, Kubbulum, Šū-Eštar šu, Šū-Eštar bis, and the second Šū-Adad, each occur regularly in the early dated texts. The undated texts must precede I.E. 8 because two workers are attested in them: Puzur-Sîn who is replaced by Iddin-ilī in IV/3/I.E. 8 (text 18), and Šū-Eštar šu, who disappears after V/10/I.E. 8 (text 20). Ur-Ninmug and

[66] He appears, however, in *BIN* 10: no 314 (–/–/–), which has to be dated in I.E. 5 because of the mention of Lu-Nanna, who occurs as foreman of the leatherworkers in *BIN* 9: no 145 (VIII/2?/I.E. 5).

Urmes, often present from text 25 (XIII/12/I.E. 8) on, do not appear in the undated texts, while Aa and Bēlī-amar, commonly attested in the undated texts, never occur in the dated ones.

In the felter section, the absence of teams renders the chronology more difficult to assess. In the undated texts, however, the foreman is always ḪA.LA-ša, a post taken over by Ur-Lugalbanda from I.E. 12 on.

Hence an early date for the undated texts seems most likely. The exact date of these texts remains, however, problematic. From comparison of texts 30 (VII/25/I.E. 9) and 82 (VII/25/–), 24 (VII/8/I.E. 8) and 80 (VII/8/–), and 14 (X/4/I.E. 7) and 94 (X/4/–), it becomes clear that they cannot be dated I.E. 9, 8 and 7 since the dated and undated texts record entirely different groups of workmen. An earlier date is more likely and would explain the differences in teams between the dated and the undated texts as a temporal transformation.

The consistent absence of year dates could be explained as follows: the administration may have been uncertain whether Ibbi-Sîn or Išbi-Erra would gain supremacy over the city, and preferred not to make a commitment by using year dates. When it became clear in I.E. 7 that Išbi-Erra would remain in power, the administration started to use consistently his year dates. The scribe, or the part of the administration, that wrote *BIN* 9: no 127 (XI/–/I.E. 4) and 145 (VIII/2?/I.E. 5) used Išbi-Erra year dates but Ur month names, showing similar indecision. The consistent use of Nippur month names in the undated worker lists may make an early dating of them seem unlikely, but a study of the month names used in the rest of the archive (see appendix A) shows that different calendars were in use until I.E. 8. The dating of the undated worker lists to I.E. 6 is supported by *BIN* 9: no 145 (VIII/2?/I.E. 5) which records all the members of team V of the leatherworkers; in the proposed reconstruction this team remains active until month VIII of I.E. 6.

The chronological table demonstrates that the worker lists were made up on a daily basis. Texts 92-93 (both IX/28/–) show that at times more than one copy was made[67].

9) *Further information on craftsmen in the Isin archive*

Although the archive covers a much longer period than the worker lists, only a few workers, unknown from the lists, appear with their

[67] The order of the personal names differs somewhat between the copies and in text 93 the scribe omitted the vertical wedge in front of Adad-bani.

professions specified in the account texts. Two are indicated as carpenters: Aḫam-arši receives a chariot for repair in *BIN* 9: no 228 (I.E. 33), and Galbana (?) acts as conveyor of leather in *MCS* 5: p. 120, no 6 (I.E. 26)[68]. Aḫam-arši is indicated as a leatherworker in *BIN* 9: no 246 (I.E. 28) where he is conveyor of hides. Ur-Lugalbanda appears as leatherworker on the left edge of a balanced account of hides (*BIN* 9: no 150: no date). Šū-Gunura is called reedworker when he delivers reedbaskets in *BIN* 10: no 171 (Š.i. 2), and Šū-Mama is called felter in *BIN* 9: no 246 (I.E. 28).

It is clear that these professions are specified only in texts which include workers of different professions or when two workers of identical names must be distinguished from one another.

## 10) Conclusions

Our main source of information concerning gašam, the craftsmen in the Isin workshop, is the worker lists. The texts, 117 in number, list the names of four groups of workmen active in the four sections of the workshop: carpenters (nagar), leatherworkers (ašgab), reedworkers (ad-KID), and felters (túg-du$_8$). The number of workmen per section can vary daily from none up to eighteen men. Reedworkers seem to be of the greatest number, followed by those working with leather, wood and felt. From analysis of the worker lists it is clear that each workman specialized in one craft and did not transfer from one section of the workshop to another.

The overseer (ugula), who headed each section, is accounted for daily, but the rest of the workmen are not. It seems that in each section of carpenters, leatherworkers and reedworkers, two teams of workmen, put to work on different days, were active. These teams have been outlined in detail above. The team ties are flexible and members of one team can join the other; but such transfers seldom occurred. Each team appears to have worked for approximately the same number of days. The system by which it was decided which team was to be on duty is unclear since we do not have records for each day. It is possible that a team was specialized in a type of manufacture and was put to work only when its skill was needed. The alternation of teams was not synchronized in all sections of the workshop, and thus it appears that they were rather independent. In the felting section, however, no teams can be distinguished.

[68] The copy of this text needs collation. The function of conveyor of leather is usually taken by a leatherworker, and Galzululu is a leatherworker known from the worker lists.

The composition of the workshop was most stable during its early recorded years. If the assignment of the undated worker lists to I.E. 6 is accepted, a general shift of team members must have taken place in I.E. 7. Some often attested persons, such as Lugal-kuzu, the carpenter, or Adad-ellatī, the leatherworker, seem to have been removed for a number of years and the teams were slightly reorganized. From then on, the dating system of this part of the administration is standardized so that all texts give month and year date. From I.E. 13 on, the productivity of the workshop seems to diminish, for a greater number of texts records entire sections as inactive[69].

The closest parallels to the Isin worker lists are found in the archive of the Ur workshop active under Ibbi-Sîn[70]. In these texts, too, the names of workmen active in each section of the workshop are listed[71]. A study of the dated worker lists of Ur shows that the craftsmen were not grouped into teams that worked on alternating days, but most of them were employed daily (table III.5)[72]. The workshop was divided into a

[69] Carpenters: text 76-78, leatherworkers: text 55, reedworkers: texts 63, 65, 69, 70 and 73, felters: texts 63-65, 68-71, 75 and 78.

[70] See D. Loding, *A Craft Archive from Ur,* Univ. Microfilms, Ann Arbor, 1974: p. 20-26 and 197-260.

[71] I.e., in the long form of worker lists: *UET* 3: nos 1475-1478, 1480-1481, 1486-1487, 1490-1492, 1495-1496, 1500, *UET* 9: nos 489, 512, 532-533, 539, 559-560, 562, 564-568, 571, 577-583, 585, 587-594, 597-598, 601, 608-610, *UET* 5: no 690 = fifty-two texts. The short form only gives the number of workmen per section and their overseer: *UET* 3: no 1474, 1482-1485, 1488-1489, 1497, *UET* 9: nos 542, 548, 553, 572, 586, 595 = sixteen texts.

[72] In table III.5 only the worker lists with preserved date are listed. The years of Ibbi-Sîn are dated following E. Sollberger, *AfO* 17 (1954-56): p. 43 and most recently, D. Frayne, *The Historical Correlations of the Sumerian Royal Hymns,* Univ. Microfilms, Ann Arbor, 1981: p. 288f.

| date | | | publication | | text # |
|---|---|---|---|---|---|
| Ibbi-Sîn year | month | day | | | |
| 15 | I | 6 | *UET* | 9: no 512 | 1 |
| 15 | II | 4 | | 9: no 533 | 2 |
| 15 | II | [ ] | | 3: no 1481 | 3 |
| 15 | VII | 12+? | | 3: no 1478 | 4 |
| 15 | VIII | 4 | | 3: no 1476 | 5 |
| 15 | VIII | 9 | | 9: no 532 | 6 |
| 15 | VIII | 20 | | 3: no 1477 | 7 |
| 15 | VIII | 25 | | 3: no 1475 | 8 |
| 15 | X | 27 | | 3: no 1480 | 9 |
| 15 | XI | 3 | | 9: no 539 | 10 |
| 15 | XI | 10 | | 9: no 552 | 11 |
| 16 | II | 1 | | 9: no 562 | 12 |
| 16 | II | 3 | | 3: no 1492 | 13 |
| 16 | VI | 26 | | 3: no 1487 | 14 |
| 16 | VIII | 5 | | 3: no 1491 | 15 |

greater number of sections than was the Isin workshop. Despite the fragmentary condition of most Ur worker lists, it is clear that in many sections the same craftsmen worked daily, e.g., the stonecutters, the carpenters, and the leatherworkers. Only the names of goldsmiths show variations, but they are not grouped in teams and many of them appear daily[73]. Thus, unlike in the Isin workshop, no system of alternating teams was in practice in Ur.

In the worker lists the craftsmen are called guruš[74], i.e., "grown people able to perform a full man's day of work"[75]. The worker lists are accounts of their work and their assignment — information found in other types of texts in the Sargonic and Ur III periods. For example, ration lists, often found in the preceding periods, are not preserved from Isin[76]. The worker lists only record the names of those who performed a

| | | | | |
|---|---|---|---|---|
| 16 | VIII | 20 | 9: no 578 | 16 |
| 16 | VIII | 29 | 3: no 1490 | 17 |
| 16 | VIII | 30 | 3: no 1486 | 18 |
| 16 | VIII | [ ] | 9: no 601 | 19 |
| 16 | X | [ ] | 9: no 566 | 20 |
| 16 | XI | 6 | 3: no 1496 | 21 |
| 16 | XI | 10+ | 9: no 566 | 22 |
| 16 | XI | 13 | 9: no 560 | 23 |
| 16 | XI | [ ] | 3: no 1495 | 24 |
| 17 | V | [ ] | 9: no 571 | 25 |

The Craftsmen are listed alphabetically per section. The following symbols are used:
–: section is not recorded because of break in the tablet,
x: craftsman is mentioned in the text,
0: section is mentioned in the text without personal names.

Because of the fragmentary state of many of the tablets several names of craftsmen in recorded sections may have been lost, but this is not indicated in the chart. Many other indications in the text, such as illness or activity outside the workshop are also not recorded in the chart.

[73] The texts list the goldsmiths in two groups, called kù-dím I and II sections by D. Loding, but these groups always appear together when the tablet is entirely preserved.

[74] The term guruš occurs only once in the rest of the Isin texts in *BIN* 10: no 53: níg-ga é-du$_6$-la *Puzur$_4$*-$^d$Šul[ ] / guruš-guruš-e-ne, "possessions of the guruš of the storage house of Puzur-Šul[ ]", which does not provide any additional information.

For the term guruš, see I.J. Gelb, "The Ancient Mesopotamian Ration System", *JNES* 24 (1965): p. 230-243, *id.*, "From Freedom to Slavery", *CRRA* 18 (1970): p. 81-92, *id.*, "Prisoners of War in Early Mesopotamia", *JNES* 32 (1973): p. 70-98, esp. p. 83f., I.M. Diakonoff, "Slaves, Helots and Serfs in Early Antiquity", *Wirtschaft und Gesellschaft im alten Vorderasien*, (eds. Harmatta and Komoroczy), Budapest, 1976: p. 45-78, B.R. Foster, "Dependent Labor in the Sargonic Period", forthcoming.

[75] I.J. Gelb, *JNES* 24: p. 239.

[76] V. Crawford, *BIN* 9: p. 65 and L. Matouš, *BiOr.* 13 (1956): p. 139 call *BIN* 9: no 520 a paylist. Since no commodity is mentioned which would have been used as payment, this interpretation has little foundation. Moreover, the occurrence of officials such as the énsi and šabra excludes any relationship with the worker lists.

Table III 5: Attendance of the craftsmen in the Ur workshop.

| Text | 1 | 2 | 3 | 4 | 5 | 6 | 7 | 8 | 9 | 10 | 11 | 12 | 13 | 14 | 15 | 16 | 17 | 18 | 19 | 20 | 21 | 22 | 23 | 24 | 25 |
|---|---|---|---|---|---|---|---|---|---|---|---|---|---|---|---|---|---|---|---|---|---|---|---|---|---|
| Craftsmen | | | | | | | | | | | | | | | | | | | | | | | | | |
| -Coppersmiths | – | | | | | | | | – | – | | – | | | | | | | | | | | – | | |
| Amar'sîn-mālik | | | | | | | | | | | | | | x | x | | x | x | | | x | | | x | |
| Banzige | | x | x | x | x | x | x | x | | | x | | x | x | x | x | x | x | x | x | x | x | | x | x |
| Kiag | | | | | | | | | | | | | | x | x | | x | x | | | x | | | x | |
| -Goldsmiths | | | | | | | | | | | | | | | | | | | | | | | | | |
| Adad-bani | | | | | | | | | | | | | | x | x | | x | x | | | x | | | x | |
| Ḫabat | x | x | x | x | x | x | x | x | x | x | x | x | x | x | x | x | x | x | x | x | x | x | x | x | x |
| Ilī-andul | | | | | x | | | x | | | x | | | x | x | | x | x | | | x | | | x | |
| Irmu | | | | | x | x | | | | x | x | | | | | | | | | | | | | | x |
| Ir-Nanna | | | | | x | x | x | x | x | | x | | | | x | | x | | | | x | | | x | |
| Itti-ilī | | | | | | | | | | | | | | | x | | x | | | x | x | x | x | | |
| Lamara-iša | | x | x | | x | | x | x | | x | x | x | x | x | x | | x | x | | x | x | x | x | x | x |
| Lu-Amar'sîn | | | | x | | | | | | | | | | | x | x | x | | | | x | x | | | x |
| Lu-Bau | | | | | | | | | | | x | | | | | | | | | | | | | | |
| Lu-dingira | | | | | | | | | | | | | | | | | | x | | | | | | | |
| Lu-Dumuzida | x | x | x | | x | x | x | x | x | | x | | x | x | | | | x | x | | | | | | |
| Lugal-ḫegal | x | | | x | x | | x | x | x | x | x | x | x | x | x | | x | x | | x | x | x | x | x | x |
| Lugal-murube | | | | x | | | | | | | | | | | x | x | x | | | | x | x | x | x | |
| Lu-Nanna | x | x | x | | x | x | x | x | x | | x | | x | x | | | | x | x. | | | | | | |
| Lu-Utu | | | | x | | | | | | | | | x | x | | | | x | | | | | | | x |
| Mašum | | | | x | x | ? | x | | | | x | | | | x | x | x | | | | x | x | | x | |
| Puzur-Mama | | | | x | | | | | | | | | | | x | x | x | | | | x | x | x | x | x |
| Šeškalla | x | x | x | | x | x | | x | x | | | | x | x | | | | x | x | x | | | | | |

| | | | | | | | | | | | | | | | | | | | | | | | | | |
|---|---|---|---|---|---|---|---|---|---|---|---|---|---|---|---|---|---|---|---|---|---|---|---|---|---|
| Šeštabba | | | | | | x | | | | | | | | | | | | | | | | | | | |
| Šukubum | x | x | x | | | x | | x | x | | | | | | | | | | | | | | | | |
| Ur-Šulpa'e | | | | | | x | | x | x | | | | x | x | | | | x | x | x | | | | x | |
| -lú-sa-sum$_4$-ma | | – | | – | | – | – | | | – | – | – | – | | | – | | | – | – | | | – | | – |
| Puzur-Enlil | x | | x | | | | | x | x | | | | | x | x | | x | x | | | x | x | | x | |
| -Stonecutters | | – | | – | | – | – | | – | – | – | – | – | | | – | | | – | – | | | – | | – |
| Lu-Ningirsu | x | | x | | x | | | x | | | | | | x | x | | x | x | | | x | x | | x | |
| Utu-bane | x | | x | | x | | | x | | | | | | x | x | | x | x | | | x | x | | x | |
| -Carpenters | | – | – | – | | – | – | | – | – | – | – | – | | | – | | | – | – | | – | – | | – |
| Šeškalla | x | | | | x | | | x | | | | | | x | x | | x | x | | | x | | | x | |
| Ur-Bau | x | | | | x | | | x | | | | | | x | x | | x | x | | | x | | | x | |
| -Blacksmiths | – | – | – | – | | – | – | | | – | – | – | – | | | – | | | – | – | | – | – | | – |
| Ibni-Adad | | | | | | | | | | | | | | x | x | | x | x | | | x | | | | |
| Lugal-kuzu | | | | | x | | | x | | | | | | x | x | | x | x | | | x | | | x | |
| Šešduga | | | | | | | | x | | | | | | x | x | | x | x | | | x | | | x | |
| Utu-bane | | | | | | | | x | | | | | | x | | | | | | | | | | | |
| -Leatherworkers | – | – | – | – | 0 | – | – | 0 | – | – | – | – | – | | | – | | | – | – | | 0 | – | | – |
| A'abbamu | | | | | | | | | | | | | | x | x | | x | x | | | x | | | x | |
| Lu-Inanna | | | | | | | | | | | | | | x | x | | x | | | | x | | | x | |
| Mannum-kī-Amar'sîn | | | | | | | | | | | | | | x | x | | x | x | | | x | | | x | |
| -Reedworkers | | – | | – | | – | – | | – | – | | | – | | | – | | | – | – | | | – | | – |
| Lu-Ašnan | x | | x | | x | | | x | | | x | x | | x | x | | x | x | | | x | x | | | |
| Una | x | | x | | x | | | x | | | | x | | x | x | | x | x | | | x | x | | x | |
| -lú-sa-ḫi-ra | | – | | – | | – | | | | – | | | | | | – | | | – | | | | | | |
| Enimad | | | | | x | | x | x | x | | x | x | x | x | x | | x | x | | x | x | x | | x | x |
| Geme-Nanna | x | | x | | | | | | | | | | | | | | | | | | | | | | |
| Uznenuš | | | | | | | | | | | | | | x | x | | x | x | | x | x | x | x | x | |

man day of work, their station, and at times their particular assignment. Also recorded were illnesses[77], and days of absence which brought the work of the guruš in arrears. Although they were skilled craftsmen (gašam) they were sometimes obliged to participate in agricultural labor.

In the preceding periods the semi-free guruš form the major source of labor in Southern Mesopotamia[78]. The state distributed year-round rations of food and cloth[79] to the workers and their families, even when they were ill or had become old[80]. Concerning the duration of service of the guruš, I.J. Gelb thinks they were employed part-time[81], while I.M. Diakonoff argues for full-time employment, allowing some time for producing food[82]. It is clear that the guruš did not rely solely on rations for their sustenance[83], but the rations seem to have been sufficient to support them during the entire year[84].

The system of alternating teams of laborers seems to be attested in the Ur III period. K. Maekawa has convincingly shown that varying groups of erín were used in agricultural labor in Lagaš[85]. There the alternating teams of erín do corvée duty for one month. When they do extra work in the following month, they are given pay (á) instead of rations. A similar system probably existed for the šub-lugal in pre-Sargonic Lagaš. This system is thus not entirely the same as the one attested in the Isin workshop, where skilled craftsmen worked on alternate days.

It is clear from a comparison of two account texts that the system of teams working on alternate days for craftsmen in Isin was an actual practice[86]. This system refutes the often stated opinion that craftsmen

[77] For records of illness in the Ur III Period, see e.g., A.L. Oppenheim, *Eames Coll*: p. 87f. s.v. H33.

[78] I.J. Gelb, *JNES* 24: p. 241. Many ideas expressed here are found in B.R. Foster, "Dependent Labor in the Sargonic Period", forthcoming.

[79] I.M. Diakonoff, *op. cit.*: p. 61.

[80] I.J. Gelb, *JNES* 24: p. 230-243.

[81] *CCRA* 18: p. 87 n. 15. He considers the possibility, however, that the guruš worked full-time for the state.

[82] *Op. cit.*: p. 58 n. 6, and p. 61.

[83] Cf. the law-case where guruš state that they did not receive rations for two years, A. Falkenstein, *Gerichtsurkunden* II: p. 356, no 209: 30-47.

[84] Cf. J.W. Turner, *op. cit.*: p. 432-5. He concludes that a ration of 2 sila barley a day provided sufficient calories for a man to do all but the most strenuous agricultural tasks.

[85] *RA* 70 (1976): p. 9-44.

[86] In *BIN* 9: no 249 (XI/6/I.E. 19) and *BIN* 9: no 250 (XI/16/I.E. 19) deliveries of products by three craftsmen are listed. Hides are delivered by Adad-bani in 249 and by Šū-Ea in 250. The first is member of team II of the leatherworkers while the second is member of team I. Bitumen and gypsum are delivered by Ilī-TAB.BA-ì (249) and Ku-Nanna (250), respectively members of teams II and I of the reedworkers sections. Goat's hair thread is delivered by Ur-Lugalbanda and Iddin-ilī, both felters known from the worker lists.

are bound to the state or the temple which provides them with everything they need[87]. This leads us to consider the activity of the workmen when they were not engaged. It is very unlikely that they were active and accounted for outside the workshop, since such activities are also recorded in the worker lists. Moreover, the days of absence cannot all have been days of rest, since in Ur III Umma only six or seven days per month were days of rest, and since the overseer is recorded to have been present each day. It is possible that they were working independently as craftmen, but many unanswerable questions arise in that context. Did they, for instance, work with the tools they used in the workshop, or did they use other ones. It is possible that they owned their tools, and that they even brought those to the workshop when they had to do work there, as we do not have account texts that mention tools from the Isin crafts archive (cf. chapter II, p. 27). Since no private archive of a craftsman is known presently, it is impossible to give a conclusive answer to these questions[88].

The Isin craftsman's assignment to the workshop for only fifty percent of his time thus marks a departure from the practices attested in the slightly earlier workshop from Ur. This probably allowed the craftsmen time to do work for themselves, and may indicate the origins of free enterprise that became the major source of labor in the Old Babylonian period[89].

## B. Supervisory personnel

The transactions in the workshop were supervised by a few individuals whose careers can be followed in the account texts. As described above (chapter Ib), there were five steps which have to be supervised: (1) receipt of raw materials from other institutions or individuals; (2) distribution of these materials to the craftsmen; (3) manufacture of the finished products; (4) their receipt, and (5) disbursement of the finished products. Steps 1, 2 and 5 are documented extensively in the account

[87] Cf. most recently, C. Zaccagnini, *JNES* 42 (1983): p. 245.

[88] It is, however, interesting that the much later Seleucid text, D. Weisberg, *YNER* 1: text 1, mentions explicitly that the craftsmen connected to the Eanna temple were not allowed to do work elsewhere. This indicates that private work of craftsmen existed in that period.

[89] Cf. I.J. Gelb, *JNES* 24: p. 243: "the growing urbanization of the country brought about a rise of industry and an increased number of artisans who were free to work for wages".

texts. Step 4 is only sparsely documented; step 3 is documented only in the worker lists and not at all in the account texts. In the following section each step and its supervising officials will be described. Finally, the exact meaning of the terms ugula, gìr, kišib, šà-tam, maškim, and dub-sar will be discussed.

## I. *Supervision of transactions with materials and products*

### 1) Step 1: Receipt of raw material

The workshop was provided with all types of raw materials by several institutions and individuals. The receipt of all these products was accounted for by two officials: one receives them (šu ba-an-ti), and another certifies the receipt with his seal (kišib). The latter function is always performed by Nanna-kiag; he is attested as sealing official from I.E. 10 — Š.i. 3[90]. From I.E. 33 on, he is sometimes accompanied by Adad-bani (*BIN* 9: no 76, *BIN* 10: no 49, LB 1948), whose seal is preserved on an undated tablet recording the expenditure of sandals by Nanna-kiag (*BIN* 9: no 88): $^{d}$*Adad-ba-ni* / dumu *Ku-lí-lí*. Although the phrase "sealed by Nanna-kiag" occurs very often, there are no receipt texts where his seal is actually preserved[91].

Several successive officials received the raw material: attested for the longest duration is Šū-Ninkarak (XIII/–/I.E. 10 - III/–/I.E. 25)[92], succeeded by Lu-Enki (IV/–/I.E. 25 - XII/–/I.E. 26)[93]. From I.E. 27 on the situation is not entirely clear: Ur-Lugalbanda, the overseer of the felters, receives wool[94], while Nanna-kiag and Adad-bani šu receive oil[95]. It seems that Nanna-kiag as sealing official takes over part of the duty to receive goods, a responsibility he may already have had during Šū-Ninkarak's tenure of office[96]. A comparison of the succession of officials in step 1 with that of step 5, where Lu-Enki is succeeded by Išbi'erra-zikalama, may lead to the conclusion that the latter was responsible for

[90] Prior to I.E. 10 no such receipts are attested. For examples of this type of texts where Nanna-kiag occurs, cf. *BIN* 9: nos 40-87, 89-103.

[91] The only text where his seal occurs is *BIN* 9: no 146, a delivery of glue by the leatherworker Lugal-isa acknowledged by Nanna-kiag, a record of step 4.

[92] E.g., *BIN* 9: nos 41-64, 66-80, 89-99.

[93] E.g., *BIN* 9: nos 65, 84, 102, 112.

[94] *BIN* 9: nos 517, 524, *BIN* 10: nos 42, 43.

[95] *BIN* 10: no 44.

[96] A group of texts records receipts of raw material with only the phrase "sealed by Nanna-kiag", e.g. *BIN* 9: nos 1-12, 13-14, 17-24, and some texts record Nanna-kiag as recipient ($^{d}$Nanna-ki-ág šu ba-an-ti), *BIN* 9: nos 113, 115, 117, 120.

receipts as well as disbursements after that period. No text explicitly records him as receiving raw materials, but one text suggests that he was involved in this step as well: "3 talents of wool, as material for the workshop, from the storage house on behalf of Ur-Lugalbanda. Sealed by Nanna-kiag. Išbi'erra-zikalama (was) overseer" (*BIN* 9: no 500 [I.E. 28])[97].

It has been stated that all references to Nanna-kiag are to the šà-tam of that name, and that he presided over the issue and receipt of items from the storage house (é-kišib-ba)[98]. L. Matouš seems to think that the often mentioned é-kišib-ba is part of the workshop, and that the texts with the phrase "sealed by Nanna-kiag" have the formal character of a document because the receiver (Šū-Ninkarak) and the sealer (Nanna-kiag) are not the same. All deliveries from individuals such as Šū-Eštar that contain the phrase "sealed by Nanna-kiag" supposedly originate from the é-kišib-ba. M. Gallery thinks that Nanna-kiag and the other šà-tam's have close interactions with both the é-kišib-ba and the workshop (giš-kin-ti). The name Nanna-kiag was, however, not uncommon in the Isin archive[99], and the šà-tam and the sealing official were two different men. Attested most frequently is Nanna-kiag, the aforementioned sealing official, who is never called šà-tam[100]. Nanna-kiag the šà-tam, however, cannot be an official of the workshop because he is recorded as receiving products of the workshop[101]. In all the texts where Nanna-kiag the šà-tam is attested he acts as conveyor for foreign cities and the palace[102], the usual function of the šà-tam in Isin (cf. below).

[97] 3 gú síg-ud$_5$ / níg-gù-dé / giš-kin-ti-šè / é-kišib-ba-ta / mu-Ur-$^d$Lugal-bàn-da-šè / kišib $^d$Nanna-ki-ág / $^d$Iš-bi-Èr-ra-zi-kalam-ma ugula / date.

[98] L. Matouš, *BiOr.* 13 (1956): p. 139, M. Gallery, *AfO*, 27 (1980): p. 8.

[99] Also occurring are Nanna-kiag agrig, *BIN* 9: nos 33, 463, and gu-za-lá, *BIN* 9: nos 263, 425, 429, 433, *BIN* 10: nos 156, 161.

[100] It is true that the title šà-tam is not always recorded, cf. *BIN* 10: no 107 where Kurrub-Erra šà-tam, and its duplicate Lindblom High School 1 where this title is omitted, but the consistent absence of the title with Nanna-kiag as sealing official cannot be accidental.

[101] *BIN* 10: 145, and *JAOS* 93: p. 255 no 11.

[102] He is attested as conveyor for Nippur (*BIN* 9: no 304), Karzida (the harbor of Ur, *BIN* 10: no 106), the Amorites (*BIN* 9: nos 293, 419), the palace (*BIN* 9: nos 237, 368), and for Dagan (*BIN* 9: no 258). L. Matouš's suggestion that every receipt sealed by Nanna-kiag deals with a delivery from the é-kišib-ba is mistaken, for there are several texts which indicate other places of origin, cf. chapter IV. Moreover, the central storage house (é-kišib-ba) must be distinguished from that of the workshop (é-kišib-ba giš-kin-ti), attested in *BIN* 9: nos 88, 109, 507, and *BIN* 10: no 170. Nanna-kiag and Šū-Ninkarak are active in the storage house of the workshop, cf. *BIN* 9: no 88: é-kišib-ba giš-kin-ti $^d$Nanna-ki-ág-ta, "(from the) storage house of the workshop, from Nanna-kiag", and

2) Step 2: Distribution of the materials to the craftsmen

Once the materials entered the workshop, they were distributed to the craftsmen by the same officials who received them: Šū-Ninkarak (e.g., *BIN* 9: nos 147-149) and Lu-Enki (e.g., *BIN* 10: no 69). Nanna-kiag also seems to have distributed material during Šū-Ninkarak's tenure (e.g., *BIN* 9: no 13, *BIN* 10: nos 60, 66).

In combined records of steps 1 and 2, Nanna-kiag appears as sealing official (e.g., *BIN* 9: nos 19-26). In those texts where the verb šu...ti is used, Šū-Ninkarak or Lu-Enki are the subject, while the coveyor is the craftsman for whom the material is intended (e.g., *BIN* 9: no 104).

3) Step 3: Manufacture

Since this step is barely documented in the account texts, we have little information concerning the supervisory personnel. From the study of the worker lists we know that each type of craftsmen — carpenters, leatherworkers, reedworkers, and felters — was supervised by an overseer (ugula). Although the extent of his power is difficult to assess, it appears that he was able to determine the composition of the teams working under him (cf. above).

L. Matouš suggested that the craftsmen were supervised by a general overseer (ugula), Išbi'erra-zikalama, based on *BIN* 9: no 500[103]. He acts there, however, as the supervisor of the receipt of material, in the same function as Šū-Ninkarak and Lu-Enki (cf. above).

4) Step 4: Receipt of finished products

This step, too, is poorly documented and only a few accounts of deliveries of finished products by craftsmen are extant. In these the name of the official receiving the material is often missing. The overseer of the felters, ḪA.LA-ša, is recorded once as receiving the finished products of his workmen (*BIN* 10: no 72). In *BIN* 9: no 106 (VIII/–/I.E. 25) Lu-Enki is said to receive products from the craftsmen (giš-kin-ti-ta). Thus it seems that this step is supervised by the same persons who supervise steps 1, 2, and 5: Šū-Ninkarak, Lu-Enki and Išbi'erra-zikalama.

The products of the felters were often weighed before they left the

*BIN* 9: no 109: é-kišib-ba giš-kin-ti ki *Šu-dNin-kar-ak*-ta, "(from the) storage house of the workshop, from Šū-Ninkarak".

103 *BiOr.* 13 (1956): p. 139.

workshop. In several texts this function was performed by Ur-Lugalbanda, their overseer[104], or by a šà-tam[105].

5) Step 5: Disbursement of finished products

This step is recorded in abundance by documents that are mostly lists of finished products and the materials used in them. After each item comes the phrase gìr PN, "PN (was) conveyor", indicating a person who represents the receiving institution. The end of the list records the official who issues (ba-zi) the products; he is the same as the one who receives the raw material (step 1): Šū-Ninkarak from VII/–/I.E. 6 to III/–/I.E. 25, Lu-Enki from II/–/I.E. 25 to IV/–/I.E. 27 and Išbi'erra-zikalama from V/–/I.E. 33 to V/–/Š.i. 3[106]. At the very end of the text a general conveyor is named: Buqqušum from I.E. 19 to 33, and he and Lušaga from I.E. 23-27. Sometimes one — mostly Buqqušum — or both of them seal the tablet instead of being named. In some cases both the phrase (gìr PN1 [and PN2]) and the seal-impression are recorded[107]. It is unclear whether Buqqušum and Lušaga are officials of the workshop or represent a higher supervisory institution. The sealing of the tablets cannot be an acknowledgement of receipt, as in the texts discussed below, since many of the tablets they seal indicate a variety of recipients. Since their seals are found on tablets preserved in the archive of the workshop, it seems likely that their office was located there as well. Smaller disbursements out of the workshop often do not have a supervisor, and only a conveyor of the receiving party or in some cases no conveyor is recorded[108].

Some texts are written from the perspective of the recipient, where he is the subject of the verb šu...ti: for instance, in *BIN* 9: no 118 leather bags are received by Lu-Ninšubur. In such texts the receiver often seals the tablet[109].

Sometimes the products go directly from the craftsmen to the outside destination: for instance, in *BIN* 9: no 385 ḪA.LA-ša, the overseer of the felters, delivers felt for the lining of the boots of the prince.

104 E.g., *BIN* 9: nos 257, 453, *BIN* 10: nos 76, 84.
105 E.g., *BIN* 9: nos 397, 417, 429.
106 From the period I.E. 27 - I.E. 33 no such texts are preserved.
107 E.g., *BIN* 9: nos 370, 421, *BIN* 10: no 137.
108 E.g., *BIN* 9: nos 454-457.
109 E.g., *BIN* 9: nos 108-109, 118, 123-125, 129.

### 6) Conclusions

The supervision of the products which enter and leave the workshop thus appears to have been in the hands of a few persons (see figure 2). Šū-Ninkarak, Lu-Enki, and Išbi'erra-zikalama receive the raw material and distribute the finished products, brough into and taken away from the workshop by a number of outsiders. The incoming material is certified by Nanna-kiag, the outgoing by Buqqušum and Lušaga. Within the workshop, the raw materials are distributed and the finished products received by the same officials. Therefore they act as intermediaries between the outside world and the craftsmen and control the exchange of material between them.

## II. *Study of specific titles*

### 1) Overseer (ugula)

The title "ugula" is rare in the Isin texts. We only know of the existence of an overseer in each section from *BIN* 10: no 314 and the fact that certain persons appear each day in the worker lists and are more prominent in the account texts. They are guruš for they are accounted for in the same way as their men. Sometimes the overseers, especially of the felters, perform important functions such as weighing or sealing. The fact that they seem to have been àble to change the composition of their teams suggests that they had considerable authority. The function of ugula in Isin may have been in the hands of a limited number of families[110]. There was no general overseer of the production part of the workshop, unlike in Ur, where Ir-Nanna is attested in this function at the end of each worker list.

In the rest of the Isin archive the term ugula seems to refer to an overseer of a transaction, not of people[111]. One text, however, seems to refer to the supervision of workers, a function familiar from the Ur III material: in *BIN* 10: no 183 Šū-Eštar the overseer of the weavers (ugula

[110] The only evidence for this hypothesis can be found in the case of Aḫubā'a and Ur-Lugalbanda, the felters. Ur-Lugalbanda calls himself the son of Aḫubā'a in his seal inscription and Aḫubā'a appears as leading felter in worker list 79, possibly as overseer. The succession of overseers may thus have been: Aḫubā'a, ḪA.LA-ša and Ur-Lugalbanda. For the hereditary character of crafts in the O.B. period, cf. F.R. Kraus, *Vom mesopotamischen Menschen der altbabylonischen Zeit und seiner Welt,* Amsterdam, 1973: p. 71.

[111] *BIN* 9: nos 494, 500, *BIN* 10: no 48, LB 1104. This is an unusual function for the ugula who in the Sargonic and Ur III periods seems to supervise people, not transactions.

uš-bar) receives fir(?) trees. The other reference is from a text of an unusual type: in *BIN* 9: no 520, a list of issues (?), Sîn-bani is called ugula[112].

2) Conveyor (gìr)

The function of the gìr official is a matter of controversy among Assyriologists, and two schools of thought can be distinguished[113]. One group thinks the gìr official was "conveyor" of goods and represented their place of origin or destination[114]. The other group considers the gìr to be responsible for the verification of transactions and the correctness of accounts[115]. From research of the Isin material it seems that both opinions are valid.

There are many examples where the gìr represents the receiving institution[116], e.g.:
2$^{\text{giš}}$ig mi-rí-za ésir / ... / abul $^{\text{d}}$*Da-mu*-šè / gìr *I-šar-be-lí* ì-du$_8$, "two doors made of small boards and bitumen, ..., for the gate of Damu, Išar-bēlī the doorman (was) conveyor" (*BIN* 9: no 347),
2$^{\text{giš}}$zà-mi / ... / gìr Lú-$^{\text{d}}$Ba-ú nar, "two zami-instruments, ..., Lu-Bau the singer was conveyor" (*BIN* 9: no 353).
In the disbursement records (step 5) the gìr officials named after each item all seem to represent the receiving institution, e.g., *BIN* 9: no 396:

| | | |
|---|---|---|
| Obv | 4 $^{\text{kuš}}$ummu(d) | 4 waterskins, |
| | ka-tab-dug-nag-lugal-šè | lids of drinking vessels for the king |
| | gìr Lú-$^{\text{d}}$Nin-šubur | Lu-Ninšubur (was) conveyor; |
| | 4 kuš-udu-babbar ka-tab/dug-ì | 4 white sheepskins for lids for oil jars, |
| | gìr *Li-bur-be-lí* | Libūr-bēlī (was) conveyor; |
| | 7 $^{\text{gi}}$gíd níg-dab$_5$/é-$^{\text{d}}$En-líl-lá | 7 flutes, offerings for the temple of Enlil, |
| Rev | esír-é-a-bi 2 1/3 sìla | their bitumen is 2 1/3 sila, |
| | gìr Ur-$^{\text{d}}$Šul-pa-è/gudu$_4$ | Ur-Šulpa'e, the gudu$_4$-priest (was) conveyor; |
| | ki *Šu-$^{d}$Nin-kar-ak-*/ta | Issued by Šū-Ninkarak: |
| | ba-zi | |
| | iti du$_6$-kù | Month VII, |
| | mu Nin-zi-/an-na | I.E. 22, |
| LE | u$_4$ 7-kam | day 7. |

[112] Note that the PA sign occurs both before and after the name.

[113] For recent surveys of opinions, cf. P. Steinkeller, *BiM* 6: no 42, M. Tanret, *Akkadica* 25 (1981): p. 10f.

[114] E.g., G. Buccellati, *The Amorites in the Ur III period*, Naples, 1966: p. 278 n. 25, P. Steinkeller, *loc. cit.*

[115] E.g., A. Falkenstein, *Gerichtsurkunden* I: p. 46, S.T. Kang, *SACT* I: p. 257-260.

[116] Cf. also G. Buccellati, *loc. cit.*

Lu-Ninšubur appears very often in connection with the king or palace: in *BIN* 9: no 188 he receives drinking vessels for the king from Šū-Ninkarak, and in other texts he is most frequently conveyor for the king or palace[117]. Libūr-bēlī appears most often as conveyor of jars or bags for oil[118], and at times as deliverer of oil to the workshop[119]; thus it appears that he was representing an institution working with oil. Ur-Šulpa'e is gudu$_4$-priest of the temple of Enlil; he is conveyor of flutes for Enlil in many texts[120], and in *BIN* 9: no 376 he is conveyor of material for the repair of the temple door of Enlil. Thus the three conveyors in *BIN* 9: no 396 represent the institutions for which the materials are intended. The texts recording deliveries to the workshop also show the same function of the gìr, now a representative of that part of the workshop that uses the material: for instance, in *BIN* 9: no 22 Ku-Nanna, the leatherworker, is conveyor of leather, and in *BIN* 10: no 3 ḪA.LA-ša, the felter, is conveyor of wool.

The gìr functionary can also be a representative of the delivering institution: for instance, in *BIN* 9: nos 141-143 Ur-Lugalbanda, the overseer of the felters, is conveyor of their products for a leather bag, and in *BIN* 9: no 246 the felter Šū-Mama and the leatherworker Aḫam-arši are conveyors of wool and leather for the throne of Enlil. We may thus conclude that both receiving and expending parties can be represented by a gìr official.

The second hypothesis concerning the function of the gìr functionary, that he is responsible for the verification of transactions and the correctness of accounts, also finds support in the Isin material. Buqqu-šum and Lušaga, often mentioned as gìr at the end of disbursement texts, seem to have no function in the transportation of the goods, taken care of by outside conveyors, but appear to have been responsible for the certification of delivery. In this capacity they often seal the tablet; this corresponds to the phrase "sealed by Nanna-kiag" in the records of deliveries for the workshop. Similarly, Nanna-kiag appears as conveyor in the receipt texts[121]. The act of sealing and the gìr function both indicate thus the supervision of a transaction. In every case where a high official such as the šà-tam is recorded as gìr we can assume that he oversaw the delivery rather than transporting it.

[117] E.g., *BIN* 9: nos 36, 118, 311, 344, 395, 399, *BIN* 10: nos 133, 175.
[118] E.g., *BIN* 9: nos 320, 345, 361, 365, 393, 397.
[119] *BIN* 9: no 505, *BIN* 10: nos 38, 44.
[120] E.g., *BIN* 9: nos 359, 393-395, 397, 399, *BIN* 10: no 133.
[121] E.g., *BIN* 9: nos 27, 37, 102.

3) Sealing officials

Sealing of Sumerian economic documents has not been conclusively analyzed due to the sheer abundance of material, although P. Steinkeller recently provided a limited survey, mainly based on Ur III material[122]. The Isin material can shed some additional light on this practice. Most of the texts which contain a seal impression are records of receipts and disbursements. In receipt texts the recipient, the subject of the verb šu...ti in the text, sometimes sealed the tablet[123]. The term kišib PN occurs twice with PN's seal impression on the tablet: in *BIN* 9: nos 13 and 146, where the sealers are certainly the recipients.

It is remarkable that none of the tablets with the phrase "sealed by Nanna-kiag", have his seal impression. But of the more than one hundred texts with this phrase only seven do not contain the phrase gaba-ri or gaba-ri DUB-ba, "copy (of a tablet)"[124]. A comparison of four pairs of duplicate texts[125] shows that copies were not sealed; the four originals contain the seal impression of Buqqušum[126], while the four copies do not. It seems thus likely that the texts with the phrases "sealed by Nanna-kiag" and "copy" (gaba-ri) are copies of sealed originals. In the seven texts without gaba-ri, this term was probably erroneously omitted. Therefore, we must read gaba-ri dub-ba, "copy of a tablet", and not "sealed copy", gaba-ri kišib-ba[127].

On disbursement records the seal impression of Buqqušum is often found without mention of his name in the text[128]. When he does appear in the text, alone[129] or with Lušaga[130] he is called conveyor. Since it is unlikely that he was the person who actually transported the products, as pointed out above, it is probably that he certified the disbursement with his seal[131].

[122] *BiM* 6: p. 41-53.

[123] E.g., Išbi'erra-mālik in *BIN* 9: nos 108-109, 111, 507, Lu-Enki in *BIN* 9: no 116, Ur-Lugalbanda in *BIN* 9: nos 484, 501, *BIN* 10: no 69.

[124] *BIN* 9: nos 12, 46, 55, 59, 63, 95, and *MCS* 5: p. 117 no 3.

[125] *BIN* 9: no 344 = no 345, *BIN* 9: no 356 = no 357, *BIN* 9: no 448 = no 449, and *BIN* 9: no 363 = *ASJ* 5 (1983): p. 57, no 9.

[126] *BIN* 9: nos 345, 357, 448, and 363.

[127] Against M. Gallery, *AfO* 27 (1980): p. 8 n. 40. Note also that kišib is not a verb. The verb used for "to seal" is kišib-ra(-ra), cf. *CAD* K: p. 136, *AHw*: p. 434, s.v. *kanāku*.

[128] *BIN* 9: nos 6, 345-347, 350, 357, 362-363, 365, 382-384, 401, 430, 443, 448, *BIN* 10: nos 128, 129, 133, 177, 202.

[129] *BIN* 9: no 421, *BIN* 10: no 137.

[130] *BIN* 9: nos 370, 373.

[131] Note also *BIN* 10: no 130 col. IV 9'-11': gìr *Bu-qú-šum* / ù $^{d}$Nanna-ki-ág / kišib-a-ne-ne íb-ra, "Buqqušum and Nanna-kiag (were) conveyors, they rolled their seals".

Seal impressions are also found on five of the texts which state that there were no transactions on a certain day[132], most likely to make the document official. Only three worker lists are sealed, 53, 77 and 78 (*BIN* 10: nos 253, 274 and 275), but unfortunately the seal impressions are illegible.

The seal was thus probably applied to make official a receipt or disbursement. In the workshop receipts were sealed by Nanna-kiag and expenditures by Buqqušum and Lušaga. Seals of recipients are sometimes found on the tablets, probably as proof to the workshop that the material was indeed delivered. Since many tablets are copies, and thus unsealed, only a small percentage of the tablets have a seal impression.

4) šà-tam

The function of šà-tam has been discussed extensively by M. Gallery[133]. For the early Isin material she comes to the conclusion that they have close connections with both the storage house (é-kišib-ba) and the workshop (giš-kin-ti). They act often as conveyors for the storage house (é-kišib-ba)[134], with which the šà-tam's have close relations as is suggested by *BIN* 9: no 114: níg-gál-la šà é-kišib-ba / ki šà-tam-e-ne, "provisions in the storage house, of the šà-tam's". They were, however, *ex officio* involved with other institutions as well, especially the é-kù-dím, "the house of the goldsmiths"[135]. They also served the gods: Enlil[136], Dagan[137], Nergal of Apiak[138], and ᵈNA[ ][139]. They were also involved in deliveries to other cities — Nippur[140] and Karzida[141], to the Amorites[142] and to the palace[143]. They act as weighing officials of goods leaving the workshop, probably representing the destinations

[132] *BIN* 9: no 528 and *JAOS* 98: p. 254 no 8: seals of Buqqušum and Warad-Erra; *BIN* 10 nos 200 and 202: seal of Buqqušum; *BIN* 10: no 203: seal of Warad-Erra.

[133] *AfO* 27 (1980): p. 1-36.

[134] *BIN* 9: nos 395, 421, 525, *BIN* 10: no 143.

[135] *BIN* 9: nos 28, 260, 264, 378-381, 418, 467. They also act as conveyors of metals: gold: *BIN* 9: nos 31, 472, silver: *MCS* 5: p. 121 no 7, *ASJ* 5: p. 56 no 6, and copper: *BIN* 10: no 124.

[136] *BIN* 9: nos 246, 255, 429. In *BIN* 9: no 254, dated one day before no 255, Ur-Šubula and Lu-Amar'sîn known from other texts as šà-tam's, act as conveyors for Enlil.

[137] *BIN* 9: no 258.

[138] *BIN* 9: no 453.

[139] *BIN* 9: no 247.

[140] *BIN* 9: no 304, *BIN* 10: no 118.

[141] *BIN* 10: no 106.

[142] *BIN* 9: nos 286, 293, 419.

[143] *BIN* 9: nos 237, 459.

which are also the institutions for which the šà-tam act as conveyors: the palace[144], the temples[145], the Amorites[146], and some other important institutions in the city such as the é-uz-ga[147], and the house of the female singers (é-nar-SAL)[148]. They appear only in two texts in connection with the workshop (giš-kin-ti), and both references suggest close ties: *BIN* 9: no 37 has, in a parallel position to níg nam-šà-tam-kam, "property of the office of šà-tam", níg-gál-la šà giš-kin-ti, "supplies for the workshop"[149] and *BIN* 10: no 130 has, following a list of products called kin-ašgab, kin-ad-KID, and kin-túg-du$_8$, nam-šà-tam-kam, "work of the leatherworkers, work of the reedworkers, and work of the felters, of (the office of) the šà-tam".

The following šà-tam's are attested:

Ališunu, *BIN* 10: no 118, I.E. 14.
Ilšu-muballiṭ, *BIN* 9: no 366, Š.i. 3.
Ipquša, *BIN* 9: nos 378, 459, *BIN* 10: no 143, I.E. 21-23.
Išar-aḫi, *BIN* 9: nos 274, 378, *BIN* 10: no 143, I.E. 22-23.
Kurrub-Erra, *BIN* 10: nos 62, 107, I.E. 12-13.
Lu-Amar'sîn, *BIN* 9: nos 246, 265, 395, I.E. 26-28.
Nanna-kiag, *BIN* 9: nos 237, 258, 286, 293, 304, 367, 368, 419, 421, *BIN* 10: nos 106, 164, *JAOS* 98: p. 255 no 11, *ASJ* 5 (1983): p. 56 no 6, I.E. 13-Š.i. 3.
Nūr-Eštar, *BIN* 9: nos 256, 525, LB 1112, I.E. 13-15.
Ur-Bau, *BIN* 9: nos 28, 246, 255, 265, I.E. 28.
Ur-Šubula, *BIN* 9: nos 31, 453, I.E. 12-13.
Ur-Šulpa'e, *BIN* 9: nos 265, 453, I.E. 12-15.

Thus from the Isin material it seems that the šà-tam's were responsible for the supervision of transactions with important institutions such as the palace, temples, the workshop of the goldsmith, and the central storage house of the city. They also supervised contacts with other cities and countries. Their function within the workshop is sparsely attested, however.

### 5) Comptroller (maškim)

The function of the maškim in the Ur III period is still not fully

[144] *BIN* 9: no 397, *BIN* 10: no 136.
[145] *BIN* 9: no 429, *ASJ* 5 (1983): p. 57 no 8.
[146] *BIN* 9: no 430.
[147] *BIN* 9: no 436. The term may refer to a part of the temple here, cf. J. van Dijk, *Götterlieder* II: p. 125.
[148] *BIN* 9: no 417.
[149] Cf. M. Gallery, *AfO* 27 (1980): p. 8.

understood, but from the Drehem texts it seems that the specific authority of maškim was given to an official to expend governmental property[150], as representative of the king[151]. He requested important transactions such as the distribution of ingots from the "Treasury of Drehem" or the receiving of goods by a *šakkanakku* or énsi[152]. Similar functions are assigned to the maškim in Isin. Most often a maškim is present when goods are issued to foreigners, mostly Amorites.

Puzur-Enlil, for instance, is present when sandals and bags are given to Amorite messengers[153], or to messengers from Mari[154], or when bags are sent to Borsippa and Dilmun[155]. A maškim is involved when goods are sent to a temple or a deity: for instance, Išbi'erra-zikalama presides when a door is sent to the temple of Dagan[156], and Libūr-bēlī when offerings are made for the boat of Inanna[157]. They were also supervisors of issues to the palace[158], and to the house of the goldsmiths (é-kù-dím)[159]. Transactions of metal also involve a maškim: for instance, Šū-ilī was maškim when bags were issued to hold seven silver vessels[160], and Lu-Ninšubur when copper was leaving Uruk[161].

The function of maškim was assigned to people who hold other offices: most prominent of these is the sukkal-maḫ, who seems to have been the most powerful non-royal official in the government[162]. He most often controls transactions with foreigners: for instance, deliveries to Amorites[163], men of Kiš[164], Karaḫar[165], and Borsippa[166]. He

[150] S.T. Kang, *SACT* I: p. 255.

[151] S. Oh'e, *ASJ* 5 (1983): p. 113-126.

[152] M. Sigrist, *Or.* NS 48 (1979): p. 42. For maškim as "supervisor of a transaction" in the Sargonic period, see B.R. Foster, *Mesopotamia* 9: p. 79.

[153] *BIN* 9: nos 39, 325, 326, 382, 395, 421.

[154] *BIN* 9: no 384.

[155] *BIN* 9: no 391.

[156] *BIN* 9: no 443.

[157] *BIN* 9: no 387.

[158] *BIN* 9: nos 199, 366.

[159] *BIN* 9: no 260.

[160] *BIN* 9: no 308.

[161] *BIN* 10: no 124.

[162] E. Sollberger, *AfO* 17 (1954-56): p. 136-8 and n. 143, W.W. Hallo, *Early Mesopotamian Royal Titles* (*AOS* 43), New Haven, 1957: p. 128, Dsch. M. Scharaschenidze, *Wirtschaft und Gesellschaft im alten Vorderasien* (eds. Harmatta-Komoroczy), Budapest, 1976: p. 103-112.

[163] *BIN* 9: no 365 = *ASJ* 5 (1983): p. 57 no 9, *BIN* 9: nos 383, 388, 390, 392, 422.

[164] *BIN* 10: no 149.

[165] *BIN* 9: no 424.

[166] *BIN* 9: no 415.

supervises a delivery to the temple of Nininsina[167], and for the wall of the city[168]. A sukkal, Puzur-Sîn, is maškim when a slave girl is given to Emezum the Amorite[169]. Other professions that are attested as maškim are the sagi, "cupbearer"[170], the šu-i, "barber"[171], and the rá-gaba, "rider"[172]. Although these professions seem rather menial, they may have represented high offices[173]. Some names of the maškim are well known as officials in other contexts: for instance, Buqqušum[174] and Išbi'erra-zikalama[175], officials of the workshop, appear as maškim.

6) Scribe (dub-sar)

The few persons called dub-sar, "scribe", in the Isin texts mostly do not belong to the workshop, but represent other institutions as conveyors: Aḫam-arši and Erra-gāšer, for instance, represent the storage house (é-kišib-ba)[176], Ibni-Adad and Nūr-Adad the Amorites[177]. In the workshop only two persons are called dub-sar: Buqqušum in his seal inscription and in *BIN* 9: no 497, and Lušaga in *BIN* 9: no 107. Since the title seems to have been an honorific rather than a true professional name[178], it probably does not refer to the function these people performed in the workshop but to the fact that they were graduates of the scribal school.

This survey shows that the five steps of transactions in the workshop were supervised by a limited number of officials (see figure 2). Although they most often do not possess specific titles, they were assigned well-defined functions.

The first step involves the delivery of raw materials to the workshop.

[167] *BIN* 10: no 159.

[168] *BIN* 9: no 448 = 449.

[169] *BIN* 10: no 146.

[170] *BIN* 90: no 445, *BIN* 10: no 137.

[171] *BIN* 9: no 366.

[172] *BIN* 9: no 448-449.

[173] Lu-Ninšubur the barber, for instance, is often attested in connection with the palace or the king (*BIN* 9: nos 35, 36, 118, 335, 354, 427, *BIN* 10: no 4) and has a seal (*BIN* 9: no 118).

[174] *BIN* 9: no 352.

[175] *BIN* 9: nos 356 = 357, 382, 430, 443.

[176] *BIN* 9: nos 413, 421, *JAOS* 98: p. 255 no 10. For Aḫam-arši in a Nippur text, see F.R. Steele, *BASOR* 122 (1951): p. 46.

[177] *BIN* 9: nos 244, 271, 410.

[178] W.W. Hallo *apud* B. Buchanan, *Early Mesopotamian Seals in the Yale Babylonian Collection*, New Haven-London, 1981: p. 441.

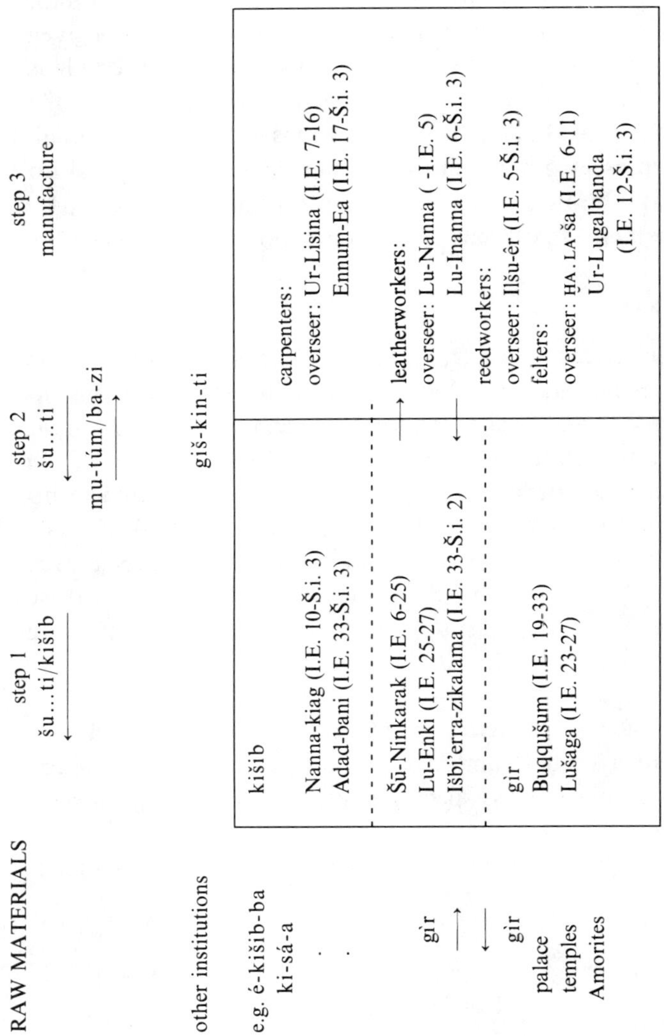


Figure 2: Schematic reconstruction of the workshop

They are brought in most frequently by representatives of the delivering institutions who act as conveyors (gìr). In the workshop two officials account for the delivery. The first official receives it (šu ba-an-ti). Several persons in succession are attested in this function: Šū-Ninkarak (XIII/–/I.E. 10 until III/–/I.E. 25), Lu-Enki (IV/–/I.E. 25 until XII/–/I.E. 26), and probably Išbi'erra-zikalama (V/–/I.E. 33 until V/–/Š.i. 3). A second official is present to certify the receipt with his seal (kišib). For the entire period covered by the archive this function is performed by Nanna-kiag, in later years assisted by Adad-bani. Although the phrase "sealed by Nanna-kiag" occurs very often, his seal is not preserved on any of these tablets, for they all seem to be unsealed copies of originals (gaba-ri dub-ba).

The second step, the distribution of the raw materials to the craftsmen, is supervised by the same officials who received them: Šū-Ninkarak and Lu-Enki, and sometimes Nanna-kiag.

The third step, the manufacture, is scarcely documented. The type of craftsmen involved in the manufacture of a specific part of a product is sometimes mentioned in the records of deliveries of finished products. Four types of craftsmen are attested: carpenters (nagar), leatherworkers (ašgab), reedworkers (ad-KID), and felters (túg-du$_8$). Our main source of information about them is the worker lists, which primarily record presence or absence of the workmen, but which sometimes indicate what type of work they performed. Each section of the workshop has an overseer (ugula): for the carpenters this is Ur-Lisina from I.E. 7 until I.E. 16 and then Ennum-Ea who is attested until Š.i. 3; for the leatherworkers Lu-Nanna is attested until I.E. 5, succeeded by Lu-Inanna from I.E. 6 until Š.i. 3; Ilšu-êr appears as overseer of the reedworkers for the entire period covered by the archive; ḪA.LA-ša is overseer of the felters from I.E. 6 - I.E. 11, succeeded by Ur-Lugalbanda from I.E. 12 on.

The finished products are then delivered by the craftsmen in step 4, which is also sparsely documented. The craftsmen were responsible for a certain quota and some texts list how much they had finished and how much they were in arrears.

The final step is the disbursement of the finished products (step 5). The same persons who received the raw materials are responsible for this step: Šū-Ninkarak (VII/–/I.E. 6 - III/–/I.E. 25), Lu-Enki (II/–/I.E. 25 - IV/–/I.E. 27) and Išbi'erra-zikalama (V/–/I.E. 33 - V/–/Š.i. 3). The products were picked up by a representative of the receiving institution, acting as conveyor (gìr). The workshop is also represented by a conveyor (gìr) who is mentioned at the end of the text: Buqqušum from I.E. 19 - I.E. 33, and he and Lušaga from I.E. 23 - I.E. 27. These are the only two people in the workshop who bear the title scribe (dub-sar). They seem to certify the disbursements, sometimes by sealing the tablet. Some texts record receipts (šu...ti) of the finished products by other institutions, often sealed by the recipient.

CHAPTER IV

# ECONOMIC RELATIONS OF THE WORKSHOP

Since the workshop manufactures specialized products, it is in contact with many other institutions and individuals in acquiring materials and in disbursing finished products. These connections show the importance of this workshop in the economic life of the city Isin.

## A. ISSUING

Only a few deliverers seem to provide the workshop with its raw materials; they include a number of institutions, known by name, and a number of individuals, probably representing an institution whose name is not mentioned.

The main provider of products is the storage house, é-kišib-ba. Virtually everything used by the workshop is issued by it: leather (e.g., *BIN* 9: nos 54, 69-79) and the products to process it — alum (e.g., *BIN* 9: nos 80, 83, 104), madder (e.g., *BIN* 9: nos 80, 84, 105), im-KÙ.GI (e.g., *BIN* 9: nos 81, 82, *BIN* 10: 5), and alkali (e.g., *BIN* 9: nos 81, 82). The storage house also provides bitumen (e.g., *BIN* 9: nos 493, 498, *BIN* 10: no 19), and wool (e.g., *BIN* 9: nos 81, 82, 500). One text records the delivery of gypsum (*BIN* 9: no 80). The large variety of products delivered from the storage house, and the fact that some of them are also delivered by other institutions and individuals (cf. below), suggests that the é-kišib-ba was a central storage house where products, derived from several sources, were kept[1]. This storage house was supervised by the šà-tam[2]. Although L. Matouš stated that it was part of the workshop[3], he is mistaken, since this hypothesis is based on his erroneous identification of Nanna-kiag the šà-tam with his namesake who acts as sealing official for the workshop (cf. chapter III).

Another office delivering to the workshop is the ki-sá-a, mentioned

[1] Cf. W.F. Leemans, *RA* 48 (1954): p. 57-66, for a similar function of the é-kišib-ba in Ur III and O.B. periods.

[2] M. Gallery, *AfO* 27 (1980): p. 7f.

[3] *BiOr*. 13 (1956): p. 139.

in this capacity in only two texts: in *BIN* 9: no 7 leather is delivered from it, and in *ASJ* 5: p. 57 no 8 a couch. The nature of this office is unknown, but it could have derived its name from its location near the wall.

The workshop of Lu-Damu, the gardener (é-du$_6$-la Lú-$^d$Da-mu nu-kiri$_6$) provides the crafts workshop with wool and chairs in two texts, both dated in XI/–/I.E. 14 (*BIN* 10: no 9, *JAOS* 98: p. 252 no 2).

Other workshops deliver only one type of product: three texts record the delivery of wool from the house of the weavers (é-uš-bar, *BIN* 9: no 524, *BIN* 10: nos 42, 43), and leather is delivered by the skinflayers (su-si-ig, *BIN* 9: no 476, é-su-si-ig, *BIN* 9: no 303). In *BIN* 9: no 511 a delivery of bitumen is said to be from the gá-nun-kišib-ba, which is probably the sealed storage house. These are the only institutions known by name which deliver to the workshop. Otherwise a number of individuals, without clear affiliation to an institution, delivers specific products.

Leather is often delivered by a small group of people. Most prominent is Šū-Eštar, who is attested from I.E. 10-26 in numerous texts (e.g., *BIN* 9: nos 40-53). From I.E. 20 on, four other men deliver leather, or act as conveyors for Šū-Eštar: Ku-Nanna (I.E. 20-30)[4], Nanna-maba (I.E. 20-25)[5], Šū-Mamitum (I.E. 21-30)[6], and Šū-Šamaš (I.E. 21-30)[7]. It is clear that these four man are subordinates of Šū-Eštar, for, whenever they act as conveyor the leather is said to be from Šū-Eštar, and three deliveries of leather from Šū-Šamaš, Šū-Mamitum, and Nanna-maba respectively, are summed up as being from Šū-Eštar (*BIN* 9: no 50, IX/–/I.E. 24). Moreover, on the left edge of two tablets deliveries of leather are said to be from Šū-Mamitum (*BIN* 9: no 47) and Šū-Šamaš (*BIN* 9: no 61), while in the text they are said to be from Šū-Eštar. It is unclear to which profession these men belonged. Ku-Nanna is once called leatherworker when he acts as conveyor for Šū-Eštar (*BIN* 9: no 20, XI/–/I.E. 22), and in the worker lists Šū-Šamaš appears in the leatherworker section (worker lists 19-24, all I.E. 8). Since the latter name is common and its occurrence in the worker lists predates the activity as conveyor by several years, it may refer to another man, or if he is indeed the

[4] Delivering: e.g., *BIN* 9: nos 3, 8, 11, 14, as conveyor: e.g., *BIN* 9: nos 22, 90, 93, 96. The Ku-Nanna delivering leather in I.E. 7 (*BIN* 9: no 110) is given the difference in time probably another person.

[5] Delivering: e.g., *BIN* 9: nos 4, 5, 15, conveyor: e.g., *BIN* 9: nos 18, 57, 91, 92.

[6] Delivering: e.g., *BIN* 9: nos 7, 10, 23, conveyor: e.g., *BIN* 9: nos 94, 95, 97, 99.

[7] Delivering: e.g., *BIN* 9: nos 9, 24, 50, 113, conveyor: e.g., *BIN* 9: nos 20, 98, 101.

conveyor, he may have worked occasionally, or originally, as a leather-worker. Šū-Eštar may have been an oxslaughterer ($gu_4$-gaz, *BIN* 10: no 102: X/–/I.E. 12)[8], although the reference may be to another man with that name. Nor do the texts give the name of any institution which they might have represented. They were probably specialists in skinning animals and preparing the hides for tanning. Since the hides in that state could not be stored for a long period of time in the storage house, they were directly delivered to the workshop. Šū-Eštar was the principal person, assisted by four subordinates from I.E. 20 on.

Other products are also delivered to the workshop by individuals: two men deliver oil — Adda-kalla, the oilpresser (ì-šur)[9], and Libūr-bēlī[10]. Both men appear elsewhere as conveyors of oil or of container for oils and fats[11]. Glue (še-gín and a-še-gín) is delivered by Aḫu-ṭāb, the lú-še-gín[12] (I.E. 16-28)[13], and wool is delivered by Lu-šālim[14]. Ea-mālik delivers date-palm products[15], and Erra-dan, the gardener (nu-$kiri_6$) delivers pomegranate hearts (peš-nu-úr-ma)[16].

Individuals can thus deliver directly to the workshop, especially where leather is concerned, but otherwise deliveries normally were first stored in the é-kišib-ba. One additional text records a delivery direct from the source: 90 sila bitumen is delivered from the city Kiritab (*BIN* 9: no 478), although this product is usually brought in from the é-kišib-ba.

## B. Receiving

The products of the workshop have many destinations; they were delivered to other administrative and industrial institutions for use or for completion of manufacture, to religious and royal institutions, and to other cities. The expenditures are not always directly to their recipients,

[8] This is not entirely certain since the text reads gìr *Šu-Eš₄-tár ù ᵈIš-bi-Èr/-ra/-ba-ni* $gu_4$-gaz, "Šū-Eštar and Išbi'erra-bani, the oxslaughterer(s) (were) conveyors". The profession may refer to the second name only.

[9] *BIN* 10: nos 49, 50; both times sesame oil (i-giš).

[10] *BIN* 9: no 505, *BIN* 10: nos 32, 38, 44 and *ASJ* 5: p. 54 no 3; all sesame oil except *BIN* 10: nos 32 and 44.

[11] Libūr-bēlī: e.g., *BIN* 9: nos 241, 242, 491 (I.E. 8-33), Adda-kalla: e.g., *BIN* 9: nos 236, 351, *BIN* 10: no 163 (I.E. 16 - Š.i. 1).

[12] Cf. *MSL* 12: p. 238, col. ii line 1.

[13] E.g., *BIN* 9: nos 12, 164, 165.

[14] *BIN* 10: no 4, VII/–/I.E. 11 and *BIN* 9: no 32, IV/–/I.E. 16.

[15] *BIN* 9: no 490, IX/11/I.E. 33, *JAOS* 98: p. 255 no 9, IX/18/I.E. 33.

[16] *BIN* 10: nos 24, 25, both II/–/I.E. 22.

for in many texts it is clear that the workshop contributed only partly to the product which was ultimately intended for the institution mentioned in its records.

1) *Other administrative and industrial institutions*

A number of institutions receives finished products from the workshop. The house of the goldsmiths (é-kù-dím), however, receives products to be used in manufacture as well. Several texts record the delivery of glue (e.g., *BIN* 9: nos 260, 380, 381), gypsum (*BIN* 9: no 260), bitumen (*BIN* 9: no 206), thread (*BIN* 9: nos 206, 264), and leather (*BIN* 9: nos 206, 467, 470). Their use is sometimes mentioned, for instance, in *BIN* 9: no 28 where glue and leather are delivered to the house of the goldsmiths for the thrones of Nanna and Ningal. Some of the products, such as glue and bitumen, were delivered to the workshop from the é-kišib-ba and it is unclear why they were again disbursed. From the preserved texts it seems that in the house of the goldsmiths two types of workmen were active — the blacksmith (simug, *BIN* 9: no 381) and the metalworker (tibira, e.g. *BIN* 9: nos 366, 380, 381). The profession of goldsmith (kù-dím) itself is not attested in the Isin archive, except in a seal impression (seal H)[17] on a receipt for shields (*BIN* 9: no 123). The šà-tam's seem to be closely connected with the house of the goldsmiths, since they often act as conveyors for it (e.g., *BIN* 9: nos 260, 264, 378, 379).

Other institutions, including workshops and storage houses, receive finished products. The house of the oilpressers (é-ì-rá-rá) receives oil jars and bags (*BIN* 9: nos 235, 289, 366), and in three worker lists carpenters are recorded active there (worker lists 37, 45, and 56). The kitchen (é-muḫaldim) receives vessels (*BIN* 10: no 168), baskets (*BIN* 9: no 362, *BIN* 10: no 154) and tables (*BIN* 9: no 238), and the house of the milling women (é-SAL-níg-àr-ra, *BIN* 10: no 98) receives sieves. The fattening shed (é-uz-ga) often receives baskets (e.g., *BIN* 9: nos 361, 390, 395), sieves (*BIN* 9: no 433, *BIN* 10: no 154), and trays (*BIN* 9: no 234), and in one text the house of fattened oxen and sheep (é-gu$_4$-udu-niga, *BIN* 9: no 429) receives beervats.

Several storage houses are mentioned in the archive: the gá-nun receives baskets for flour (*BIN* 9: no 530), the new wool storage house (é-kišib-ba-gibil-síg, *BIN* 9: no 525) receives matting for doors, and

[17] Cf. V. Crawford, *BIN* 9: pl. 93.

the door of the granary (gur$_7$, *BIN* 9: no 447) is produced in the workshop. The central storage house, é-kišib-ba, also receives products of the workshop; most texts mention the expenditure of tablet baskets ($^{gi}$pisan-im-sar-ra, *BIN* 9: nos 395, 399, 413, 523, *BIN* 10: no 158) or bags to hold sealed tablets ($^{kuš}$dùg-gan-ti-bala kišib-ra-a ba-an-gar, *BIN* 10: no 159) to the é-kišib-ba. Hence it becomes clear that this institution was, in addition to a storage house for goods, a place where tablets were stored, as it was in the Ur III period[18].

2) *Religious institutions*

Since many religious institutions are recipients of products of the workshop, the texts give us a good idea of the pantheon in the early Isin period. D.O. Edzard has collected all the relevant material from the texts published in *BIN* 9[19], but a few additions can be made from the unpublished texts. Some gods not mentioned by Edzard appear in the new material: Adad (*BIN* 10: no 83, his throne), Lugal-AM (*BIN* 10: no 155, door for new temple of Lugal-AM, Inanna and Išbi-erra)[20], Meslamtaea (*BIN* 10: no 160, his nin-dingir), and Ninḫursag (*BIN* 10: no 188, her temple). Two new temples have also been attested, one of Damu (*BIN* 10: no 92) and one of Pabilsag (é-gal-DN, *MCS* 5: p. 121 no 7).

The workshop delivers either directly to the temples and gods (e.g., *BIN* 9: no 320, *BIN* 10: no 108) or provides its specialized labor for their thrones (e.g., *BIN* 9: no 28), beds (e.g., *BIN* 10: no 90), or cloth (e.g., *BIN* 9: no 84). Work by craftsmen in certain temples is also recorded in the worker lists (e.g., worker lists 48, 49, 50: carpenters in the temple of Dagan). Temple personnel are also provided for by the workshop: the devotees (*sekrū*) receive boots (*BIN* 9: no 328) and lyres (*BIN* 9: no 444), the singers beds (*BIN* 9: no 348) and lyres (*BIN* 9: no 441). The *giparu*, the official residence of the *enu* priest and the *entu* priestess[21], receives vessels in *BIN* 10: no 167. It is unclear whether the *giparu* in Ur is intended, or that of another city. Products were delivered

[18] Cf. W.F. Leemans, *RA* 48 (1954): p. 57-66.

[19] *Zwischenzeit*: p. 65f.

[20] The line reads ká-é-gibil $^{d}$Lu[gal]-AM / $^{d}$Inanna $^{d}$*Iš-bi-Èr-ra*. Lugal-AM is, so far, unknown. The reading of lugal is not entirely certain but likely. It is peculiar that the conjunction ù is not used, and that the temple is devoted to three gods. Moreover, it is unusual that the deified Išbi-Erra has a temple already in his twenty-fifth year (date of this text).

[21] R. Harris, *RlA* 3 (1957-71): p. 377-9, P.N. Weadock, *Iraq* 37 (1975): p. 101-128.

for certain religious festivities: for instance, jars for the ezen-maḫ (*BIN* 9: no 322).

3) *Royal family*

Many texts refer to products delivered to the king and the palace. They include chairs (e.g., *BIN* 9: nos 342, 434), bags (e.g., *BIN* 9: nos 237, 310), shields (e.g., *BIN* 9: no 330), and numerous other objects. Many products of the workshop are described as "royal" (lugal), another indication that the king is one of its main recipients. The family of the king also receives products: the queen (nin) receives baskets as a present in her place in Larak (LB 1108, cf. below), and her house (é-nin-a) is mentioned in several texts (*BIN* 9: no 382, *BIN* 10: nos 96, 151). Several children of the king receive goods: both his sons Išbi'erra-narām-Kakka[22] (*BIN* 9: no 432) and Nūr-Dagan (*SET* no 291) receive thrones inlaid with silver. The house of Šū-ilišu, probably Išbi-Erra's successor, receives reed mats (*BIN* 9: no 480), while the house of unnamed sons of the king (é-dumu-lugal) is provided with doors (*BIN* 10: no 77, 97)[23]. A unique text describes the furniture given as wedding gifts to Libūr-nīrum, the daughter of the king (*BIN* 9: no 438):

| | | |
|---|---|---|
| Obv | 1 $^{\text{giš}}$gu-za-SAL $^{\text{giš}}$dúr / kù-babbar-gar-ra | 1 woman's chair, (its) seat inlaid with silver, |
| | 10 gín še-gín-bi | its glue is 10 shekels; |
| | 5 gín kuš-gu$_4$ ku-ša-nu-um | 5 shekels oxhide (for the) cushion, |
| | 2/3 kuš-udu-babbar 1 kuš-udu-ú-ḫáb / ba-a-si | with 2/3 white sheepskin (and) 1 red sheepskin it is covered, |
| | 2/3 kuš-udu-babbar šà-ra-bi-šè | 2/3 white sheepskin for its lining. |
| | 1 giš-nú-mes | 1 bed of mes-wood, |
| | 10 gín še-gín ba-an-gar | 10 shekels glue have been applied to it, |
| | $^{\text{giš}}$gu-za giš-nú / é-du$_6$-la-ta | the chair and the bed are from the workshop. |
| | 1 $^{\text{kuš}}$AB kuš-e-rí-na | 1 waterproofed(?) covering, |
| | 10 kuš-udu-*a-lum*-e-rí-na-bi | its waterproofed(?) *alum*-sheepskins are 10, |
| | 7 gín níg-U.NU-a síg-gin-bi | its thread of ordinary wool is 7 shekels. |

[22] Cf. P. Steinkeller, *JNES* 41 (1982): p. 291.

[23] One more name of a royal son is known: Ada. He acts as conveyor of bags in *BIN* 9: no 284.

| | | |
|---|---|---|
| | 1 $^{\text{kuš}}$Á.SI-$^{\text{kuš}}$AB | 1 hinge(?) of a cover, |
| | 6 gín kuš-gu$_4$-ú-ḫáb-bi | its red oxhide is 6 shekels: |
| | gìr Lú-$^{\text{d}}$Nin-šubur | Lu-Ninšubur (was) conveyor. |
| Rev | 1 $^{\text{dug}}$šáman-ì-du$_{10}$-ga / 5 sìla | 1 jar of 5-sila for good oil. |
| | 4 $^{\text{dug}}$dal-ì | 4 large oil-jars, |
| | ésir-bi 1 1/2 sìla | their bitumen is 1 1/2 sila, |
| | kuš-udu-bi 70 gín | their sheepskin is 70 shekels, |
| | ka-tab-šè | for their lids: |
| | gìr *Li-bur-be-lí* | Libūr-bēlī (was) conveyor. |
| | níg-ba *Li-bur-ni-rum* dumu-SAL / lugal | Presents for Libūr-nīrum, the daughter of the king, |
| | u$_4$ *Išdum-ki-in* | the day she was married |
| | dumu *Ḫu-ba-sí-im-ti* sukkal | by Išdum-kīn, the son of |
| | ba-an-tuk-a | of Ḫuba-simti, the sukkal. |
| | ki *Šu-$^{d}$Nin-kar-a[k*-ta] | Issued by |
| | ba-[zi] | Šū-Ninkarak, |
| | u$_4$-3-[kam] | day 3, |
| | iti gu$_4$-si-[su] | month II, |
| | mu-ús-sa bàd l[i-bur] / $^{\text{d}}$*Iš-bi-* [*Èr-ra* ba-dù] | I.E. 15. |
| Le | gaba-ri šà dùg-gan | Copy of (the tablet) in a bag. |

This text, which records the wedding of a princess, possibly with the son of the sukkal of Elam[24], shows how the furniture of the household was provided by the workshop.

The workshop also provides objects for the cult of deceased kings. In

[24] D.O. Edzard, *Zwischenzeit*: p. 62 n. 290, D. Frayne, *AfO* Beiheft 19 (1982): p. 27. The name Ḫuba-simti is perhaps Elamite with the elements *huban-* and *simti*. W. Hinz, *The lost world of Elam*, London, 1972: p. 94 reads Ḫumban-shimiti, whom he calls the son of Ḫutran-tempt, who was at that time "regent" (sukkal) of Susiana. However, in *BIN* 9: no 438 the name of the sukkal, and not of his son, is Ḫuba-simti. Since the text records the wedding of a princess, the term sukkal probably does not refer to a common messenger, but to an important person, conceivably the king of Susa (cf. W.W. Hallo, *Early Mesopotamian Royal Titles* [*AOS* 43], New Haven, 1957: p. 119-121, for sukkal as title of the king of Susa). The name Ḫuba-simti may contain the Elamite theophoric element *Humban* and *simti* may be an attempt to assimilate Elamite *temti* or the like in Akkadian. It is, however, peculiar that this text dates from the same month from which we have two texts recording the day that Elam was defeated (*BIN* 9: no 152, *BIN* 10: no 124, both dated II/–/I.E. 15). It is unlikely that an important diplomatic wedding, on the third day, would coincide with a battle. So possibly the name Ḫuba-simti is not Elamite but Akkadian, cf. *simtu*, "belonging to", *AHw*: pp. 1045f., "ornament", J. Stamm, *Namengebung*: p. 81. The person who marries Libūr-nīrum is Išdum-kīn, who has clearly an Akkadian name. He may occur elsewhere in the Isin archive: from the same month as *BIN* 9: no 438 (II/–/I.E. 15) there is a text that mentions Išdum-kīn as conveyor of *zamirītum* for Uruk (*BIN* 10: no 124). The text dates from the day that Elam was smitten (u$_4$ *Elam* ba-ab-ra-a), and it is rather unlikely that a prince of Susa would act as official on that day. The sukkal mentioned may thus be a high official of the administration in Isin (cf. W.W. Hallo, *ibid.*: p. 121).

*BIN* 9: no 440 chairs are issued for the "libation place of the ghost and kings" (ki-a-nag *ma-al-ku-um* lugal-lugal-e-ne)[25]. Royal servants also receive products from the workshop: the cupbearers (sagi, e.g., *BIN* 9: nos 360, 398, *BIN* 10: no 168), the barbers (šu-i, *BIN* 9: no 417), and the messengers. The last group mostly receives waterbags ($^{\text{kuš}}$ummu(d)) and sandals ($^{\text{kuš}}$e-sír) needed for their profession (e.g., *BIN* 9: nos 233, 390)[26].

4) *Other cities*

The recipients of the products of the workshop also include other cities, or persons from other cities who may have been in Isin at the moment of the transaction. With the information from these texts some idea can be obtained about the geographical horizon of the workshop, and of the city Isin itself.

Not far north of Isin is a group of cities which seem related to it early in the reign of Išbi-Erra: Apiak, Mur and Kiritab[27]. Early year dates (I.E. 4 and 5) mention the destruction of Kiritab by Išbi-Erra, and in I.E. 9 a carpenter of the workshop is said to be active in Mur (worker list 31). By I.E. 12 the workshop receives bitumen from Kiritab (*BIN* 9: no 478) and it produces rope for the bed of Nergal of Apiak (*BIN* 9: no 453). A citizen of Marad, Puzur-ŠU.NI, seems to act as conveyor for the Amorites in one text (*BIN* 9: no 414).

Somewhat farther northwest lies Borsippa, the goal of several trips recorded in the Isin texts (kaskal Barsipa, *BIN* 9: nos 391, 415, 479). The people who go on these trips receive bags from the workshop, and in one text bags are the official present for this city (níg-šu-tag$_4$-a šà Bar-sí-pa$^{\text{ki}}$-šè, *BIN* 9: no 414). Two soldiers from Kiš (aga-uš dumu Kiš$^{\text{ki}}$ 2-a-bi) receive bags(?) and sandals on their way to Karaḫar (*BIN* 10: no 149).

Relations between Isin and Nippur in the early part of the Isin dynasty are clear from texts from both sites[28]. In the Isin texts the first

[25] For *malkum* as "ghost", a god or chthonic deity, cf. *CAD* M/1: p. 168. The grammar of the phrase is unclear, since *malkum* is in the nominative singular. Perhaps the Akkadian word was borrowed into the Sumerian without declining it.

[26] Cf. M. Stol, *RlA* 6 (1980-83): p. 542, on the issuing of sandals and waterbags to messengers.

[27] Mur, which is only once attested in the Ur III period, seems to be close to Marad for its troops are dependent on the énsi of that city, cf. *Répertoire Géographique* 2: p. 134. For the relative locations of Apiak, Marad and Kiritab, see F.R. Kraus, *ZA* 51 (1955): p. 56f.

[28] For later contacts between Isin and Nippur, see F.R. Kraus, *JCS* 3 (1951).

mention of Nippur appears in I.E. 6 (*BIN* 9: no 502), when wooden parts ($^{giš}$ge-en) are sent to that city. If the dating of the undated worker lists proposed in chapter III is accurate, already in I.E. 6 a felter from the Isin workshop is recorded to be in Nippur (worker list 87). From I.E. 13 on, mention of Nippur in the Isin texts becomes more frequent. In the seal impression on *BIN* 10: no 110, dated VIII/–/I.E. 13, Išbi-Erra is called the beloved of Enlil and Nininsina (ki-ág $^{d}$En líl-[lá] / ù $^{d}$Ni[n]/-in-si-[na]) which indicates his dominance over both Nippur and Isin. In month XI of I.E. 13, the day that the boat of the queen went to Nippur is specially recorded (*BIN* 9: no 267, XI/5/I.E. 13), and in the same year a reed basket is sent to that city (*BIN* 9: no 502, *BIN* 10: no 112). A later text records that the énsi of Nippur receives bags for the gu$_4$-si-su festival (*BIN* 9: no 216), and in a text with broken date (Ash 1932-280) jars are sent to the king who is in Nippur (níg-šu-tag$_4$-a lugal šà Nibru$^{ki}$-šè).

In the Nippur material two groups of texts contain documents dated in the first reigns of the Isin dynasty: the Inanna temple archive and the texts excavated in the area TB of the Scribal Quarter. The Inanna temple archive covers most of the Ur III period and is extremely well attested in the year I.S. 5 (information, courtesy R.L. Zettler). From I.S. 7 six texts are preserved, the last probably dated in month V (6 NT 378). The two last texts of this archive are dated with Išbi-Erra year names: 5 NT 77 in I.E. 4, and 5 NT 656 in I.E. 6[28a].

A small group of texts dated in the first three reigns of the Isin dynasty was excavated in the Scribal Quarter of Nippur, area TB[29]. Many correspondences between this group and the Isin material are found in the personal names. The texts deal with loaves of bread and flour delivered, for instance, as food for the king (*BASOR* 122: p. 47) or for a festival (2 NT 555). The food seems to be provided by the temple of Enlil (*BASOR* 122: p. 47, *JCS* 24: p. 17-18). This famous temple is also attested in the Isin archive[30]. *BASOR* 122: p. 47 is a summary of the expenditures for the years Š.i. 1-9. Its subscript reads:

Col. IV

| | |
|---|---|
| 15) šuku lugal | Food allotments for the king. |
| é-$^{d}$En-líl-lá-ta | From the temple of Enlil |
| gìr $^{d}$Utu-ba-an-è | via Utu-bane. |
| dub lú-níg-dab$_5$-ba-ke$_4$-/ne-bi | These tablets of its *nindabû* officials |

[28a] See now, R.L. Zettler, *AfO* 31 (1984): p. 9 and note 53.

[29] Cf. Mc. Cown, *Nippur* I: p. 74f.

[30] *BIN* 9: nos 304 (šà Nibru$^{ki}$), 344, 345, 368, 396, 441.

| | |
|---|---|
| é-kišib-ba-šè ba-gíd | were transferred to the storage house. |
| 20) kišib šà-tam-e-ne | Sealed by the šà-tam's[31]. |

Of the three seals on the tablet, two contain personal names known from the Isin texts[32]:

| | | | |
|---|---|---|---|
| 1) *A-ḫa-am-ar-ši* | | Aḫam-arši | |
| dub-sar | | the scribe[33]. | |
| 2) ᵈ*Šu-ì-lí-šu* | ᵈŠára-mu-túm | Šū-ilišu | Šara-mutum |
| lugal-kal-ga | dub-sar | mighty king | the scribe |
| [ ] | dumu Ur-ᵈŠul-/pa-è | [ ] | son of Ur-Šulpa'e. |

Utu-bane, mentioned as conveyor in the subscript, is attested in several other of the Nippur texts as conveyor or deliverer of the foodstuff. In the Isin archive, he is attested as conveyor on behalf of Nippur (*BIN* 9: no 412, XI/6/I.E. 21). Aḫam-arši, the scribe appears three times in texts from I.E. 25 as conveyor of leather bags to hold sealed tablets[34] for the storage house, é-kišib-ba. The two other sealers are probably the šà-tam's mentioned in the subscript. The father of one of them, Ur-Šulpa'e, is often mentioned from I.E. 19 - Š.i. 2 as the gudu$_4$-priest of Enlil[35]. It is probable that the same man is attested in texts from both cities.

*BASOR* 122: p. 47 also mentions the é-kišib-ba to which Aḫam-arši is connected. The same connection is clear from the Isin texts[36] where no special indication of the location of the storage house is given. This may indicate that the é-kišib-ba with close connections to the Isin workshop was located in Nippur, although it seems more likely that Isin itself had also an é-kišib-ba. The earliest record of delivery from the é-kišib-ba is XI/–/I.E. 4 (*BIN* 9: no 127), coinciding with the use of Išbi-Erra's year names in Nippur (5 NT 77). There is thus a slight possibility that the é-kišib-ba was located in Nippur.

From these texts it is thus clear that Išbi-Erra conquered Nippur early

[31] lú-níg-dab$_5$-ba = "person in charge of *nindabû* offerings", *CAD* N/2: p. 238. For this function, see A. Falkenstein, *Gerichtsurkunden* II: p. 345 note to line 52. gíd = *šadādum* "to transfer", *AHw*: p. 1121.

[32] The third seal is of the son of Lu-bala-šaga. A boatsman with that name is known from the Isin texts (*BIN* 9: no 26, *BIN* 10: nos 129, 137, I.E. 16-19), but is probably a different person.

[33] As copied, *Aḫam-arši* dub-sar seems to be part of the subscript, but collation shows that it is a seal impression found all over the tablet.

[34] ᵏᵘˢdùg-gan-ti-bala kišib-ra-a ba-an-gar, *BIN* 9: no 413, *BIN* 10: no 159, *BIN* 9: no 421 (without kišib-ra-a ba-an-gar).

[35] *BIN* 9: nos 359, 365, 368, 376, 377, 393-397, 399, 402, *BIN* 10: no 133.

[36] *BIN* 9: nos 413, 421, *BIN* 10: no 159.

in his reign, at least in his fourth year. Since Isin and Nippur are in close proximity to each other, it is possible that the conquest took place in his first regnal year[37]. This is also suggested by the fact that in the Inanna temple archive year names of Ibbi-Sîn are abandonned in I.S. 7. The last Nippur text dated in Ibbi-Sîn's reign is *NRVN* 1: no 118, dated I.S. 8, thus in the first year of Išbi-Erra. Perhaps neither king had continuous control over Nippur in these year, and only in I.E. 4 the new king's rule was firmly established. Once this took place, it seems that the contacts between Isin and Nippur were very close.

Contacts furter northeast are also attested in the Isin archive: sandals and bags are given to messengers of Karaḫar (*BIN* 9: no 424), and to the king of Simmurum and his messengers (*BIN* 9: no 421).

Contacts with Anšan, east of the Tigris, are also documented; *BIN* 9: no 302 records bags to hold sealed tablets from Anšan. Elam is attested as an adversary in the year dates I.E. 16, 26 and 27. The day of Elam's earlier defeat is mentioned in two texts from I.E. 15 (*BIN* 9: no 152, *BIN* 10: no 124). It is possible that *BIN* 9: no 438 (cf. above) records the wedding of Libūr-nīrum, the daughter of Išbi-Erra, with Išdum-kīn, the son of the king (sukkal) of Susa, Ḫuba-simti. Since this text dates from the same month as the two texts which record the day that Elam was defeated (II/–/I.E. 15), the wedding was probably not with the prince of Susa, and this text does not illustrate diplomatic relations between Susa and Isin. Peaceful contacts are, however, clear from other texts: in *BIN* 9: no 332 (XI/–/I.E. 9) Zinnum, known to be from Elam from the correspondence between Puzur-Numušda and Ibbi-Sîn, receives official presents[38]. In *BIN* 9: no 382 (VII/16/I.E. 19) messengers and escorts of Kindattu and possibly of Idadu, succcessive kings of Elam, receive bags and sandals[39].

Relations with Sumer are better documented and seven cities are attested in the Isin texts: Ur, the former capital, is mentioned in late year dates of Išbi-Erra, when the Elamites are expelled from that city (years 26, 27 and 31). Two earlier texts mention the sending of bags and leather to wrap silver from Ur (*BIN* 9: no 332, XI/–/I.E. 9 and *BIN* 9:

[37] Cf. D. Frayne, *Historical Correlations*: p. 311-318.

[38] This text mentions the transport of silver from Ur, which is probably tribute from this city, cf. L. Matouš, *BiOr*. 13 (1956): p. 136 n. 2. It is remarkable that in the same text official presents are sent to the Amorites and to Zinnum, the Elamite. This may indicate that Elamites and Amorites helped Išbi-Erra in his struggle against Ur.

The same Zinnum may appear in *BIN* 10: no 188 (no date).

[39] Cf. M. Stolper, *ZA* 72 (1982): p. 47f., D. Frayne, *AfO* Beiheft 19 (1982): p. 28.

no 386, III/–/I.E. 10). L. Matouš relates these to *UET* 3: nos 702 and 704, which record the delivery of gold, silver, copper and bronze to acquire merchandise of Isin[40]. According to L. Legrain's reconstruction, both texts are dated in Ibbi-Sîn 16, which would correspond with I.E. 9 (cf. appendix A). But the redating of the Ibbi-Sîn year names by E. Sollberger[41], would date these texts not in Ibbi-Sîn 16, but in Ibbi-Sîn 13, and thus L. Matouš' correlation of them no longer holds[42]. In the Ur texts Isin is rarely mentioned: only in *UET* 3: no 1421 (I.S. 14) a messenger of Išbi-Erra and men from Isin are provided with beer and bread[43].

Other cities of Sumer are mentioned in earlier texts. A man of Karzida, the harbor of Ur[44], receives bitumen and wool in I.E. 13 (*BIN* 10: no 106); *zamirītum* and shields are sent to Larsa (*BIN* 9: no 338, IV/–/I.E. 13) and Uruk receives(?) *zamirītum* and vessels (*BIN* 10: no 124, –/–/I.E. 15, *JCS* 20: p. 40 no 5, VII/–/I.E. 33). BÀD.A, probably Dūrum close to Uruk[45], receives oxhides and rope (*BIN* 9: nos 78, 526, both in I.E. 16) and GARšana, in the Umma region[46], is mentioned in one text as the destination of Ribum, the Amorite (*BIN* 9: no 266). Interesting is the mention in LB 1108 (XI/–/I.E. 13) of Larak, the third antediluvian city[47], which is otherwise rarely attested in economic texts antedating the first millennium[48]. The location of this city is not certain: possibilities are near Isin[49], and in eastern Sumer, north of Umma[50]. In this Isin text it is said that official presents are sent to the place of the queen in Larak (níg-šu-tag$_4$-a k[i] nin-a-šè / šà La-ra-ak-šè).

Dilmun, farther south, in the Persian Gulf, is also in contact with Isin: leather bags are sent to it as an official present from I.E. 19 on[51]. These

[40] *BiOr.* 13 (1956): p. 136 and n. 2.

[41] *AfO* 17 (1954-56): p. 43.

[42] Note that L. Matouš accepts E. Sollberger's synchronism between Ibbi-Sîn and Išbi-Erra, but does not take into account Sollberger's redating of Ibbi-Sîn's year names.

[43] For an historical interpretation of these three texts from Ur, cf. P. Michalowski, *The Royal Correspondence of Ur,* Univ. Microfilms, Ann Arbor, 1976: p. 89-92.

[44] W.W.Hallo-J. van Dijk, *YNER* 3: p. 8 n. 56.

[45] P. Michalowski, *Mesopotamia* 12 (1977): p. 83-96. See B. Groneberg, *Répertoire Géographique* 3: p. 33 for other possible identifications.

[46] *Répertoire Géographique* 2: p. 52. Cf. E. Sollberger, *AfO* 18 (1957-8): p. 104-108.

[47] Cf. Th. Jacobsen, *AS* 11: p. 74 n. 24, W.W. Hallo, *JCS* 23 (1970): p. 63.

[48] D.O. Edzard, *RlA* 6 (1983): p. 494f.

[49] J. Krecher, *SK*: p. 86f. and n. 215.

[50] R. Mc. Adams, *Heartland of Cities*, Chicago, 1981: p. 348 n. 3. N. Postgate, *Sumer* 32 (1976): p. 82, suggests an identification with Tell al-Wilayah in Northern Sumer.

[51] *BIN* 9: nos 403 = 404, VI/20/I.E. 19, *BIN* 9: no 381, III/24/I.E. 27, *BIN* 9: no 405, II/14/Š.i. 2.

contacts were established through merchants and sailors, who acted as conveyors[52]. The large Dilmun boat is provided with bitumen by the workshop (*BIN* 10: 129, VI/7/I.E. 19). Hence this Dilmun trade, which used Ur as mainland base[53], started before the Elamites were driven out of that city. One text shows a puzzling connection between Dilmun and the Amorites, since both receive official presents on the same occasion (*BIN* 9: no 405, II/14/Š.i. 2). A similar connection is also found in texts from Drehem, Bahrein, and Tell Asmar[54].

The Amorites, usually located in the west of Mesopotamia[55], are often attested in the Isin texts. The earliest mention of them is in *BIN* 10: no 90 (VI/–/I.E. 6) and they are regularly attested until Š.i. 3. Bags, vessels or sandals are often given to them as official presents (e.g., *BIN* 9: nos 383, 395, 400), and Amorite messengers often receive sandals and bags (e.g., *BIN* 9: nos 39, 325, 326). Many Amorite names appear in the Isin texts[56]. Three among them seem to be most prominent: Usi(um)[57], whose messengers are often provided with bags and sandals (e.g., *BIN* 9: nos 324, 325, 326, Ash 1932-280, I.E. 13-26), Šamamum[58], who often receives bags (e.g., *BIN* 9: nos 224, 316), and to whom royal messengers are sent (*BIN* 9: no 390)[59] (I.E. 14 - Š.i. 3), and Gaušum who is less often attested, (I.E. 17 - Š.i. 1), but whose chariot is repaired three times by the workshop (*BIN* 9: nos 187, 191, *BIN* 10: no 86). These frequent contacts with the Amorites are understandable since Išbi-Erra was a "man from Mari"[60] a city with close relations to this group of people. Mari itself is also mentioned in the Isin texts: official presents are sent to it (*BIN* 9: nos 324, 384), and presents are given to citizens of that city, for Ilī-bani receives furniture (*BIN* 10: no 113), and Lu-kiag-Anum, an Amorite, chairs and a lustration bowl (*JAOS* 98: p. 254 no 7). Bags are

[52] *BIN* 9: no 403: gìr Lugal-iti-da dam-gàr, *BIN* 9: no 391: gír Ab-ḫé-gál lú-má-gal-gal.

[53] A.L. Oppenheim, *JAOS* 74 (1954): p. 6-17.

[54] Cf. G. Buccellati, *The Amorites in the Ur III period,* Naples, 1966: p. 149f., I.J. Gelb, *AS* 21: p. 1f.

[55] See, however, S. Lieberman, *JCS* 22 (1969): p. 61f. for a location north, and P. Michalowski, *The Royal Correspondence of Ur,* Univ. Microfilms, Ann Arbor, 1976: p. 101-132, for the location of kur Mardu in the Jebel Hamrin in the northeast.

[56] G. Buccellati, *op. cit.*: p. 23-34.

[57] Written Ú-si-i or Ú-si-um.

[58] Written Ša/Ša$_{10}$-ma-mu-um.

[59] lú-kin-gi$_4$-a-lugal / ḫur-sag ki Ša-ma-mu-um Mar-tu-šè / gin-na-me "royal mesengers who go to the mountain, the place of Šamamum, the Amorite".

[60] D.O. Edzard, *Zwischenzeit*: p. 59.

also issued to hold tablets from Mari and Ebla, farther west (*BIN* 9: no 417, II/21/I.E. 24).

This review of institutions, individuals and cities with which the workshop is in contact, shows the workshop's importance in the economy of the city Isin. Numerous religious and royal institutions are among its customers, and the workshop provides them with important objects, such as the emblem of a god or royal furniture. The military is provided with shields, and parts of the fortification of the city are manufactured in the workshop. Other cities and countries are in direct contact with the workshop, and official presents sent to them are often manufactured there.

# CONCLUSIONS

The aim of this study was to describe the activities and organization of the crafts workshop active in Isin in the reigns of Išbi-Erra and Šū-ilišu (2017-1975 B.C.), on the basis of the surviving documents of its archive. These texts, 920 in number, record mainly the transactions of the workshop with the outside; the largest group of texts records expenditures of finished products, and many other texts account for the receipt of raw materials. Records of internal activities are less numerous; they include account texts recording deliveries to craftsmen and receipts of their products, and a group of worker lists giving a daily register of the names of active workmen. From these documents we derive the following picture of the activities of the workshop.

The materials used in the workshop are mostly delivered from the é-kišib-ba, the central storage house in the city. This institution seems to store materials from different sources and distribute them to the workshop when needed. Sometimes, however, the workshop receives materials — in most cases leather — directly from their source. At the receipt of the materials two officials of the workshop are present: one receiving, and the other certifying the original record of delivery with his seal. In the files of the workshop a copy of the record of receipt is kept, and it is these copies that are now preserved.

The same two officials distribute the materials to the workmen who use them. Four groups of craftsmen, each working under an overseer, are attested in this workshop: carpenters, leatherworkers, reedworkers, and felters. The workmen must have been specialized in their craft since no transfers from one section of the workshop to another occur. They are organized in teams which are put to work on alternating days. The number of workmen varies from day to day, but mostly a total of between fifteen and twenty are active. Most of them are reedworkers, followed by leatherworkers, carpenters and felters. On some days, when the demand is great, a larger number of one or more types of craftsmen is employed. After I.E. 12, however, the worker lists indicate that some sections of the workshop are inactive on certain days. Each craftsman works with a specific group of materials: the carpenter with wood and glue; the leatherworker with leather and catgut, tanning materials, dyes, and oils; the reedworker with reed, bitumen and gypsum; and the felter with wool. Many products of the workshop are the combined effort of different types of craftsmen; thus leather boots are sometimes lined with felt, or beds are made of wood, leather and rope. This can explain why these crafts are located in the same building.

The greatest amount of information is available about leatherwork. The leatherworkers do not process leather from the raw hide to a finished product, but rather begin with hides already prepared for tanning. From wool the felters produce felt, rope, and thread, which are then applied to other products. The work of the carpenters and the reedworkers is less well documented, but many of the products of the workshop, such as doors, furniture and vehicles, require their skill. The work of these craftsmen is thereby limited to particular aspects of their craft. Some of their products are sent to another workshop for completion, especially to the house of the goldsmiths where precious metals are applied.

When products are sent out of the workshop two officials are again present; one issues the product, and the other acts as conveyor, in this instance indicating that he supervises the transaction. The latter official seals the document drawn up on that occasion, which is kept in the archives of the workshop. The products are destined for a large number of institutions both in the city Isin and in other cities. Many are for use by the palace, the temples, and the military, or are sent to other countries as official presents. This indicates that the workshop caters to the higher levels of society.

From this information it seems that this workshop was only one of many in Isin, and performed only specific tasks; the materials delivered have already been treated by other craftsmen and certain products are brought to other workshops for completion. There is no clear information as to what authority supervised this activity. None of the persons in the workshop has an official title which links him to the palace or a temple with certainty. It seems, however, that this workshop was under the control of the palace, especially since many of its products are destined for the palace and are used as official presents for other countries. The many connections between the date formulae and the records of the workshop also suggest royal control. Moreover, the fact that labor is provided by guruš, and that officials such as the sukkal-maḫ act as comptroller of transactions, indicate that the government had control over the workshop.

The documents of the Isin archive show a continuation of the traditions of the Ur III period; the language and the format of the texts are the same as in the preceding period. Only in the organization of the labor in the workshop a change seems to have taken place: whereas in the craft archive from Ur under Ibbi-Sîn the craftsmen are recorded active every day, in the Isin archive the records indicate that they were only present fifty percent of the time. This may be an indication of the growing role of private enterprise in the early second millennium.

The analysis of one single archive allows us to reconstruct several aspects of craftswork at one point in Mesopotamian history in great detail. It leads, of course, not to a history of crafts without analysis of other sources with the same detail. A study of the craft related Neo-Sumerian texts from Ur would probably yield similar information about the crafts studied here — carpentry, leatherwork, reedwork, and felting — and about the work of other craftsmen — coppersmiths, goldsmiths, blacksmiths, and stonecutters. Unfortunately, no other archives of workshops are known at the moment. The study of isolated texts from other archives throughout Mesopotamian history will illuminate other aspects of crafts. The archaeological record has revealed very limited information about the crafts studied here, but the pictorial record may give us quite some information unavailable through the texts. A detailed analysis of all these sources should be undertaken before a history of Mesopotamian crafts can be written.

## APPENDIX A

# CHRONOLOGICAL PROBLEMS

### 1. The chronology of Išbi-Erra's reign

The chronology of the thirty-three year reign of Išbi-Erra is not firmly established. Since certain aspects of the study of the archive, such as the term of office of certain officials, and the chronology of the texts, depend on the chronology of Išbi-Erra's reign, it seems useful to reconsider the entire problem here. Moreover, the study of the Early Isin craft archive shows that certain aspects of Išbi-Erra's chronology have to be revaluated.

Our major source of information on the chronology of Išbi-Erra's reign is a date list[1] which give the succession of twenty-three year names. V. Crawford discusses twenty-one of these plus twelve additional names (years A-L) which are found in the economic texts only[2]. B. Kienast proposes a reconstructed succession of twenty-eight years[3]. The evidence will be entirely reexamined here to derive the chronology which was used throughout the study of this archive.

The date list published by T. Baqir is broken at the top, and the year names of the beginning and the end of Išbi-Erra's reign are lost. Twenty-one names are preserved in their entirety, and of the two following these only the verb is legible. Baqir estimated that two or three lines are missing at the beginning of the tablet, but a careful reexamination by J. Black established that this number could easily be higher[4].

[1] T. Baqir, "A Date-List of Ishbi-Erra", *Sumer* 4 (1948): p. 103-113. Note that B. Kienast, *JCS* 19 (1965): p. 45, erroneously calls this a date list from Tell Harmal. Baqir, p. 103, states that he found the tablet while he was searching in the Iraq Museum for material relevant to the Harmal texts, and that the tablet is of unknown origin.

In this appendix the year names will be assigned the numbers they have in this date list, i.e. x+1 - x+23, cf. *JCS* 19 (1965): p. 53. A concordance with the numbers used throughout this study will be given at the end of this section. The letters used are those assigned by V. Crawford in *BIN* 9.

[2] *BIN* 9: p. 6-21.

[3] "Zu einigen Datenformeln aus der frühen Isinzeit", *JCS* 19 (1965): p. 45-55.

[4] Letter of November 12, 1983. The thickest point of the tablet is about where the third preserved line of the observe is written, c. 8 cm from the lower left corner of the tablet.

A second list containing some of the year names of Išbi-Erra is *UET* 1: no 292, a date list covering the reigns of Ibbi-Sîn to Iddin-Dagan. In Col. II lines 4-21 the years I.E. x+12 through x+18 are listed[5]. This list is important since it provides a way to establish the temporal relationship between Ibbi-Sîn and Išbi-Erra.

The following year names are attested only in the economic texts: Year A, mu bàd-gal Ì-si-in-na$^{ki}$mu-dù, is only attested in *BIN* 9: no 85. D.O. Edzard[6] and B. Kienast[7] consider the building of the wall as a formal declaration of independence by Išbi-Erra and the start of his independent rule. This formula would thus be the first year name of Išbi-Erra. F. Schmidtke[8] assumes that year A commemorates the building of the wall of Isin in year 1 of Išbi-Erra, and is thus the name of his second year. W.W. Hallo[9] accepts Schmidtke's assumption that year A is year 2 but suggests that it may be a variant reading of another year name commemorating the building of a wall. S.N. Kramer[10] points out that the wall of Isin is called Itilpāšunu in a letter from Puzur-Numušda, énsi of Kazallu, to Ibbi-Sîn, and the building of that wall is commemorated in the year name x+6: mu-bàd-gal *I-ti-il-pá-šu-nu* ba-dù. D. Frayne restates this argument and adds that the use of a Nippur month name in *BIN* 9: no 85 (year A) suggests a date later than years I and J which use Drehem month names[11]. The argument of Kramer and Frayne seems most convincing to me, and it seems that year A is a variant of year x+6. Moreover, Nanna-kiag, who is an important official of the workshop and appears in *BIN* 9: no 85, is only attested from the year x+4 on. An early date for *BIN* 9: no 85 seems thus unlikely.

Year B, mu giš-nú $^{d}$Inanna ba-dím, is attested in nine Isin texts[12], and in one or two[13] texts from Nippur. B. Kienast was unable to place

Eleven more lines are written on the obverse after that point. Since it is expected that the point of maximum thickness is about in the middle of the tablet, a larger part seems to have been broken off than was suggested by Baqir. Dr. Black estimates that the tablet may have been some 14.5 cm long, and that there was room for up to five or six lines before line 1' of the obverse.

[5] Cf. E. Sollberger, *AfO* 17 (1954-56): p. 41.

[6] *Zwischenzeit*: p. 61f. and note 287.

[7] *JCS* 19 (1965): p. 45.

[8] *ZDMG* 106 (1956): p. 55.

[9] *JNES* 18 (1959): p. 55.

[10] *JAOS* 75 (1955): p. 129.

[11] *The Historical Correlations of the Sumerian Royal Hymns* (2400-1900), Univ. Microfilms, Ann Arbor, 1981: p. 308.

[12] Cf. *BIN* 9: p. 17, add *BIN* 10: no 93.

[13] 2 NT 686 is dated mu giš-nú-$^{d}$Nanna, which seems to be a variant of year B, since

the year name[14], while D. Frayne suggested it to be a variant of the year x+7, mu en-GABA $^{d}$Inanna máš-e ì-pà[15]. Since a Nippur text from the Inanna temple archive, 5 NT 656 (= A307784, courtesy R. Zettler), dated in this year, mentions Sag-Enlila, who was the chief administrator of the temple by Ibbi-Sîn 5, the text is probably from early in I.E.'s reign[15a]. Only two texts from the Inanna temple archive are dated with Išbi-Erra year names, which indicates that the archive ends early in his reign. D.O. Edzard[16] suggested that year B is I.E. 2 or 3 because of the absence of the divine determinative before Išbi-Erra in seal impression P on *BIN* 9: no 502, dated year B. The divine determinative with Išbi-Erra is indeed only found from year x+6 on in the date formula of that year and in the personal name $^{d}$*Iš-bi-Èr-ra-ba-ni* (*BIN* 10: no 102), but a seal cut before that date could easily have been impressed on a tablet of later date. Similarly, the seal of Libūr-bēlī mentioning Išbi-Erra without divine determinative, is impressed on a tablet dated in I.E. x+18 (*BIN* 10: no 152).

The years C, mu nin-dingir $^{d}$Lugal-ír-ra ba-íl, and D, mu-ús-sa ..., are often attested[17]. Based on the personal names in the texts, B. Kienast has convincingly shown that they belong in the last third of Išbi-Erra's reign[18]. That they have to be placed very late in the reign is clear from the occurrence of Išbi'erra-zikalama as supervisor of disbursements of finished products in *BIN* 9: nos 37 and 367 (year D). In texts other then these he is attested in this function only in the years Š.i. 1-3.

Years E, mu Elam šà Urí$^{ki}$-ma durun-a im-ta-e$_{11}$, and F, mu-ús-sa ...[19], are to be equated to the years x+20, mu Elam šà Urí$^{ki}$-ma durun-a ba-dab$_{5}$, and x+21, mu-ús-sa ...[20]

The common year name G, mu nin $^{d}$Nin-urta ba-ḫun[21], is beyond

this name is otherwise not attested in the Ur III and E.O.B. periods. A similar confusion between Inanna and Nanna appears in the year name of Ibbi-Sîn 10, where in the date list *UET* 1: no 292 Inanna is replaced by Nanna, cf. E. Sollberger, *AfO* 17 (1954-56): p. 41 and p. 24 notes 70 and 76.

[14] *JCS* 19 (1965): p. 53.

[15] *Correlations*: p. 300, *AfO* Beiheft 19 (1982): p. 25f.

[15a] See now, R.L. Zettler, *AfO* 31 (1984): p. 9 and note 53.

[16] *Zwischenzeit*: p. 60 note 277 (misprint for 279).

[17] C: cf. *BIN* 9: p. 17, add LB 1101. NBC 6467 does not belong to the Isin craft archive. D: cf. *BIN* 9: p. 18, add *BIN* 10: no 198, *MCS* 5: p. 121 no 7, *JAOS* 98: p. 254 no 8, 255 no 9, *SET* no 291, LB 1109, 1125, 1988.

[18] *JCS* 19 (1965): p. 52f., tables 4-8.

[19] E: cf. *BIN* 9: p. 18, add *BIN* 10: no 40, F: cf. *BIN* 9: p. 19.

[20] Cf. B. Kienast, *JCS* 19 (1965): p. 49f.

[21] Cf. *BIN* 9: p. 19, omit NBC 7463 and add *JAOS* 98: p. 252 no 1.

doubt equal to year x+1, mu nin ᵈNin-urta ba-íl[22], especially since the verb is often omitted[23].

Year H, mu nin-dingir ᵈNin-gi$_4$-lí-in ba-íl[24], seems to belong in the last part of Išbi-Erra's reign, based on the study of the personal names:

| texts | personal name | period attested |
|---|---|---|
| *BIN* 9: no 19 | Ku-Nanna | I.E. x+14 - x+18 |
| *BIN* 9: nos 21, 24 | Šū-Šamaš | I.E. x+15 - x+18 |
| *BIN* 9: no 23 | Šū-Mamitum | I.E. x+15 - x+19 |
| *BIN* 9: nos 19, 21, 23, 24 | Lu-Inanna (gìr) | I.E. x+1 - x+14, Š.i. 1 |
| | Nanna-kiag (kišib) | I.E. x+4 - x+22, Š.i. 1-3 |

The year I, mu Kiri$_8$-tab$^{ki}$ba-ḫul, and J, mu-ús-sa ...[25], seem to belong in the beginning of Išbi-Erra's reign, based on historical and prosopographic evidence[26]. One text from the Inanna temple archive in Nippur, 5 NT 77 (= IM 58670, courtesy R. Zettler), is dated in year I, which suggests a date early in Išbi-Erra's reign (cf. year B). The only Isin texts dated in these years are *BIN* 9: no 127 (year I) and no 145 (year J). Due to the use of Drehem month names, it has been disputed[27] that these texts belong to the Isin archive, but a study of the personal names shows that they belong in this corpus (see chapter I).

Year K, mu Urí$^{ki}$ ki-dúr-ba bí-in-⟨ge-⟩en is attested in one text only[28]. The only attested proper name is that of Lu-Amar'sîn who is otherwise found from I.E. x+20 - x+22. The content of the year name, "year that he established Ur firmly in its place of living", is similar to that of year x+20 and hence year K is probably chronologically proximate to x+20[29].

Year L, mu $^{giš}$gu-za ᵈNanna ᵈNin-gal ba-dím, is probably the last name of T. Baqir's date list, of which only the verb is preserved[30].

22 Cf. the equation in meaning of íl and ḫun by F.R. Kraus, *JCS* 3 (1951): p. 9. See B. Kienast, *JCS* 19 (1965): p. 49.

23 *BIN* 9: p. 19.

24 Cf. *BIN* 9: p. 20. All texts are dated in month II.

25 Cf. *BIN* 9: p. 20f.

26 Cf. B. Kienast, *JCS* 19 (1965): p. 45-49.

27 L. Matouš, *BiOr*. 13 (1956): p. 137, I.J. Gelb, *JNES* 20 (1061): p. 131.

28 *BIN* 9: no 523. For the reading of the year name, see D.O. Edzard, *Zwischenzeit*: p. 58.

29 Cf. B. Kienast, *JCS* 19: p. 54. See now, C. Wilcke, *Or*. NS 54 (1985): p. 308, who suggests that this year name may be Š.i. "2". The name Lu-Amar'sîn indicates an earlier date for this year name, however.

30 B. Kienast, *JCS* 19 (1965): p. 50-52.

In synopsis, the following can thus be said about the unassigned date formulae:

A = x + 6
B = early in I.E.'s reign
C = late in I.E.'s reign
D = year following C
E = x + 20
F = x + 21
G = x + 1
H = late in I.E.'s reign
I = early in I.E.'s reign
J = year following I
K = proximate to x + 20
L = last year in T. Baqir's date list.

The relative position of these years remains a problem. In the beginning of Išbi-Erra's reign, year B seems to precede year x + 1 immediately, since *BIN* 10: no 90 (VI/–/B) mentions an issue of glue for the bed of the nin-priestess of Ninurta, which probably coincides with the inauguration of this office commemorated in year x + 1: mu nin-dingir ᵈNinurta ba-ḫun/íl. The sequence of years seems thus to be I, J, and B. The two Nippur texts from the Inanna temple archive are both dated in these years (5 NT 77 = year I, 5 NT 656 = year B). This reconstruction is supported by 2 NT 686, which lists food allotments for two years. The traces of the year name on the observe can be read as mu-ús-sa K[iri$_8$-tab$^{ki}$]/ba-ḫ[ul], thus year J, and the date on the reverse is year B.

In the last part of Išbi-Erra's reign years C, D, H, and K are to be placed. Their exact chronology is unknown, except that year D follows year C. In *BIN* 9: no 470 (XI/15/D) there is mention of oxleather used to wrap the emblem of Nanna, an object referred to in the year name of Š.i. 2: mu ᵈ*Šū-ilišu* lugal-e $^{giš}$šu-nir ᵈNanna mu-dím "year that Šū-ilišu the king fashioned the emblem of Nanna". This suggests that year D immediately precedes Š.i. 2. The fashioning of the emblem of Nanna may very well have been ordered by Šū-ilišu acting as king, since *BIN* 9: no 470 is dated in month XI, and the accession probably took place sometime in the final year of Išbi-Erra. The occasion was, however, only commemorated in the name of the second year of his reign, since his first year name proclaimed his accession. Moreover, the similarity between the names of years x + 20 and K suggests that year K precedes C and D. In divergence from B. Kienast's scheme[31], years C

[31] *JCS* 19 (1965): p. 53.

and D will thus be placed at the end of Išbi-Erra's reign (years 32 and 33), preceded by H and K (years 30 and 31).

A sequence of thirty years is thus established. B. Kienast assumes that three years were missing at the beginning of T. Baqir's date list, and reconstructs a sequence of I.E. 1-28 with two unassigned years. This proposed reconstruction is problematic, however, for it assumes a gap of three years in the Isin archive at the end of Išbi-Erra's reign of thirty-three years. The archive would then resume in the years Š.i. 1-3. It is unlikely that Išbi-Erra ruled only for thirty years, since most historical sources agree on thirty-three years: of the five relevant examplars of the Sumerian King List, four assign thirty-three years to his reign and one thirty-two[32]. Two subsequently published lists of kings of Ur and Isin also assign thirty-three years to Išbi-Erra[33].

The sequence of thirty years established above seems to end with I.E. 33. The first year of that sequence would thus be I.E. 4, and the first date preserved on T. Baqir's date list I.E. 7. The latter is possible since the re-examination of the texts has determined that up to six lines may be broken from the top of the tablet (cf. above).

This reconstruction requires some revision of the chronology of the beginning of the second millennium B.C., and of the end of the Ur III period. T. Baqir's date list and *UET* 1: no 292 have been used to establish the synchronism between Ibbi-Sîn and Išbi-Erra, always with the assumption that the preserved part of Baqir's list starts with I.E. 4[34]. Since in *UET* 1: no 292 the year name of I.E. x + 12 — reconstructed as I.E. 15 — follows that of Ibbi-Sîn 24 (in Sollberger's table), a synchronism between Ibbi-Sîn 11 and Išbi-Erra 1 is established. However, if the preserved portion of Baqir's date list begins with I.E. 7, this synchronism would have to be revised to Ibbi-Sîn 8 = Išbi-Erra 1. After Ibbi-Sîn 7, Išbi-Erra would have assumed independence. In his first year he seems also to have controlled Nippur[35], where the last attested Ur III tablet is dated in the second month of Ibbi-Sîn 8[36].

[32] Th. Jacobsen, *AS* 11 (1939): p. 124. See also, P. Michalowski, *JAOS* 103 (1983): p. 246, for a new exemplar of the King List. F.R. Kraus, *JCS* 3 (1951): p. 15 n. 14, calculates that thirty-three is more likely than thirty-two.

[33] E. Sollberger, *JCS* 8 (1954): p. 135f.

[34] Th. Jacobsen, *JCS* 7 (1953): p. 43, E. Sollberger, *AfO* 17 (1954-56): p. 43f.

[35] D. Frayne, *Historical Correlations*: p. 314.

[36] *NRVN* 1: no 118. Cf. W.W. Hallo - W.K. Simpson, *The Ancient Near East, A History*, New York, 1971: p. 86. The Inanna temple archive also indicates that Ibbi-Sîn lost Nippur in his seventh or eighth year. The last texts in this archive dated in his reign are from the early months of Ibbi-Sîn 7 (R. Zettler, letter Feb. 13, 1984). The later texts are both dated in the early years of Išbi-Erra (cf. above).

The newly established synchronism would also agree with the date of the Išbi-Erra — Ibbi-Sîn correspondence proposed by Th. Jacobsen[37]. Because the letter of Išbi-Erra to Ibbi-Sîn mentions the invasion of the Amorites who endanger the heart of the empire, it must be dated in Ibbi-Sîn 6 since the name of that year commemorates the construction of walls around Ur and Nippur. In that letter Išbi-Erra asks to be put in charge of the defense of Nippur and Isin. This request was granted and he was able to assume independence in Ibbi-Sîn 8[38]. A synchronism Ibbi-Sîn 8 = Išbi-Erra 1 would thus correspond with the historical sources.

The following list gives a concordance of the year dates used in this study compared with those of B. Kienast[39] and V. Crawford[40] and those of T. Baqir's date list:

| I.E. year | Kienast | Crawford | Baqir |
|---|---|---|---|
| 4 | 2 | I | |
| 5 | 3 | J | |
| 6 | B | B | |
| 7 | 4 | 1 and G | x+1 |
| 8 | 5 | 2 | x+2 |
| 9 | 6 | 3 | x+3 |
| 10 | 7 | 4 | x+4 |
| 11 | 8 | 5 | x+5 |
| 12 | 9 and 1 | 6 and A | x+6 |
| 13 | 10 | 7 | x+7 |
| 14 | 11 | 8 | x+8 |
| 15 | 12 | 9 | x+9 |
| 16 | 13 | 10 | x+10 |
| 17 | 14 | 11 | x+11 |
| 18 | 15 | 12 | x+12 |
| 19 | 16 | 13 | x+13 |
| 20 | 17 | 14 | x+14 |
| 21 | 18 | 15 | x+15 |
| 22 | 19 | 16 | x+16 |
| 23 | 20 | 17 | x+17 |
| 24 | 21 | 18 | x+18 |

[37] *JCS* 7 (1953): p. 421.

[38] C. Wilcke, *ZA* 60 (1970): p. 54 dates the correspondence in Ibbi-Sîn 9 for this year relates battle against Elam. Išbi-Erra mentions battles with the Elamites in his letter (lines 24-5, cf. P. Michalowski, *The Royal Correspondence of Ur*, Univ. Microfilms, Ann Arbor, 1976: p. 243-51) but only in a cursory manner. The main subject matter of the letter is, however, the invasion of the Amorites.

[39] *JCS* 19 (1965): p. 53.

[40] *BIN* 9: p. 6-21.

| | | | |
|---|---|---|---|
| 25 | 22 | 19 | x+19 |
| 26 | 23 | 20 and E | x+20 |
| 27 | 24 | 21 and F | x+21 |
| 28 | 25 | 22 | x+22 |
| 29 | 26 | L | x+23 |
| 30 | H | H | |
| 31 | K | K | |
| 32 | 27 | C | |
| 33 | 28 | D | |

For the year dates of Šū-ilišu the sequence is firmly established from a text found at Nippur[41]. The system used by V. Crawford in *BIN* 9 is followed here.

The following list of date formulae was used in this study:

I.E. 4 : mu Kiri$_8$-tab$^{ki}$ ba-ḫul
I.E. 5 : mu-ús-sa Kiri$_8$-tab$^{ki}$ ba-ḫul
I.E. 6 : mu giš-nú $^{d}$Inanna ba-dím
I.E. 7 : mu nin-dingir $^{d}$Nin-urta ba-ḫun / ba-íl
I.E. 8 : mu uru$^{ki}$ Mar-tu ba-ḫul
I.E. 9 : mu-ús-sa uru$^{ki}$ Mar-tu ba-ḫul
I.E. 10: mu a-šà-gibil a-ta im-ta(?)-DU-a
I.E. 11: mu nin-dingir $^{d}$Iškur ba-íl
I.E. 12: mu $^{d}$*Iš-bi-Èr-ra* lugal ma-da-na-ke$_4$ bàd-gal *I-ti-il-pá-šu-nu* mu-dù / mu bàd-gal Ì-si-in-na$^{ki}$ mu-dù
I.E. 13: me en-GABA $^{d}$Inanna $^{d}$*Iš-bi-Èr-ra* máš-e in-pà
I.E. 14: mu bàd *Li-bur-$^{d}$Iš-bi-Èr-ra* ba-dù
I.E. 15: mu-ús-sa bàd *Li-bur-$^{d}$Iš-bi-Èr-ra* ba-dù
I.E. 16: mu-ús-sa bàd *Li-bur-$^{d}$Iš-bi-Èr-ra* ba-dù mu-ús-sa-bi / mu $^{d}$*Iš-bi-Èr-ra* lugal-e ugnim lú SU.A ù Elam bi-in-ra
I.E. 17: mu bàd *Eš$_4$-tár-tá-ra-am-$^{d}$Iš-bi-Èr-ra* ba-dù
I.E. 18: mu-ús-sa bàd *Eš$_4$-tár-tá-ra-am-$^{d}$Iš-bi-Èr-ra* ba-dù / mu $^{d}$*Iš-bi-Èr-ra* lugal-e $^{d/giš}$šu-nir-gal $^{d}$En-líl ù $^{d}$Nin-urta mu-ne-dím
I.E. 19: mu bàd $^{d}$*Iš-bi-Èr-ra-ri-im-*$^{d}$En-líl ba-dù
I.E. 20: mu-ús-sa bàd $^{d}$*Iš-bi-Èr-ra-ri-im-*$^{d}$En-líl ba-dù / mu $^{d}$*Iš-bi-Èr-ra* lugal-e $^{d}$Nin-me-an-ki $^{giš}$šu-nir-gal $^{d}$Inanna mu-ne-dím
I.E. 21: mu-ús-sa $^{d}$*Iš-bi-Èr-ra* lugal-e $^{giš}$šu-nir-gal $^{d}$Inanna mu-dím
I.E. 22: mu Nin-zi-an-na dumu-SAL-lugal máš-e in-pà
I.E. 23: mu-ús-sa Nin-zi-an-na dumu-SAL-lugal máš-e in-pà / mu nin-dingir $^{d}$Lugal-már-da ba-íl
I.E. 24: mu-ús-sa nin-dingir $^{d}$Lugal-már-da ba-íl / mu en $^{d}$En-líl-lá ba-íl
I.E. 25: mu $^{d}$*Iš-bi-Èr-ra* lugal-e $^{giš}$gu-za bára $^{d}$Nin-urta mu-ne-dím
I.E. 26: mu-ús-sa $^{d}$*Iš-bi-Èr-ra* lugal-e $^{giš}$gu-za bára $^{d}$Nin-urta mu-ne-dím / mu Elam šà Urí$^{ki}$-ma durun-a ba-dab$_5$ / im-ta-e$_{11}$

[41] F.R. Steele, "The Date Formulae of Shu-ilishu of Isin", *BASOR* 122 (1951): p. 45-49. See, however, now some reservations made by C. Wilcke, *Or.* NS 54 (1985): p. 304-308.

I.E. 27: mu-ús-sa Elam šà Urí$^{ki}$-ma durun-a ba-dab$_5$ / im-ta-e$_{11}$
I.E. 28: mu $^{giš}$gu-za $^{d}$Nin-líl-lá (ba-dím)
I.E. 29: mu $^{giš}$gu-za $^{d}$Nanna $^{d}$Nin-gal ba-dím
I.E. 30: mu nin-dingir $^{d}$Nin-gi$_4$-lí-in ba-íl
I.E. 31: mu Urí$^{ki}$ ki-dúr-ba bi-in!-⟨ge-⟩en
I.E. 32: mu nin-dingir $^{d}$Lugal-ír-ra ba-íl
I.E. 33: mu-ús-sa nin-dingir $^{d}$Lugal-ír-ra ba-íl
Š.i. 1 : mu $^{d}$*Šu-ì-lí-šu* lugal-àm
Š.i. 2 : mu $^{d}$*Šu-ì-lí-šu* lugal-e $^{giš}$šu-nir-gal $^{d}$Nanna mu-ne-dím
Š.1. 3 : mu-ús-sa $^{d}$*Šu-ì-lí-šu* lugal-e $^{giš}$šu-nir-gal $^{d}$Nanna mu-ne-dím / mu $^{d}$*Šu-ì-lí-šu* lugal-e nin $^{d}$Nin-urta mu-un-íl

## 2. Month names in the early Isin texts

The Isin texts are usually dated following the Nippur calendar[42] which became standard in Babylonia in the early Old Babylonian period. During the first years of the archive, however, there are a number of other month names attested, some borrowed from Drehem/Ur, some otherwise unknown. These are used simultaneously with Nippur months until I.E. 8.

In the first five years of the archive the following months are attested:

| | | | | |
|---|---|---|---|---|
| I.E. 4 | iti diri ezen me-ki-gál | = Drehem XII | *BIN* 9: no | 127 |
| I.E. 5 | iti šu-eš-ša | = Drehem VIII | *BIN* 9: no | 145 |
| I.E. 6 | iti bára-zag-gar | = Nippur I | *BIN* 10: no | 87 |
| | iti sig$_4$-a | = Nippur III | | 88 |
| | | | | 89 |
| | iti kin-$^{d}$Inanna | = Nippur VI | | 90 |
| | iti apin-du$_8$-a | = Nippur VIII | | 91 |
| | iti ab-è | = Nippur X | | 92 |
| | | | | 93 |
| I.E. 7 | iti ne-ne-gar | = Nippur V | | 95 |
| | iti du$_6$-kù-ga | = Nippur VII | *JAOS* 98: p. | 252 no 1 |
| | | | *BIN* 10: no | 209 |
| | | | | 210 |
| | | | | 211 |
| | | | | 212 |
| | | | | 213 |
| | | | | 214 |
| | iti apin-du$_8$-a | = Nippur VIII | *BIN* 9: no | 110 |
| | | | *BIN* 10: no | 216 |
| | | | | 217 |
| | | | | 218 |

42 Cf. Hunger, *RlA* 5 (1976-80): p. 300.

| | | | | | |
|---|---|---|---|---|---|
| | iti gan-gan-è | = | Nippur IX | | 219 |
| | iti ab-è | = | Nippur X | *BIN* 9: no | 513 |
| | | | | | 514 |
| | | | | *BIN* 10: no | 220 |
| | | | | | 221 |
| | iti kin $^{d}$Nanna | = | ? | *BIN* 9: no | 515 |
| | | | | *BIN* 10: no | 96 |
| | | | | | 208 |
| | iti gu$_4$-zag-gar | = | ? | *BIN* 9: no | 516 |
| I.E. 8 | iti šu-numun-a | = | Nippur IV | *BIN* 10: no | 98 |
| | | | | | 222 |
| | iti ne-ne-gar | = | Nippur V | | 223 |
| | | | | | 224 |
| | | | | | 225 |
| | iti kin-$^{d}$Inanna | = | Nippur VI | *BIN* 9: no | 522 |
| | iti du$_6$-kù-ga | = | Nippur VII | *BIN* 10: no | 226 |
| | | | | | 227 |
| | iti zíz-a | = | Nippur XI | | 1 |
| | iti še-kin-kud | = | Nippur XII | *BIN* 9 no | 369 |
| | | | | *BIN* 10: no | 72 |
| | iti diri še-kin-kud | = | Nippur XIII | | 228 |
| | iti [ ] $^{d}$Nin-a-zu | = | Drehem IV/V | | 99 |
| no date | iti gu$_4$-zag-a | = | ? | | 181 |
| | iti síg-$^{d}$Ina[nna] | = | ? | | 313 |

The month names not belonging to the Nippur calendar can be divided into two groups: those belonging to the Drehem/Ur calendar[43], and those not otherwise attested. The texts in which months from the Ur calendar are found, can be assigned to the Isin archive based on the study of the personal names. *BIN* 9: nos 127 and 145, dated iti diri ezen me-ki-gál (Drehem XII) and iti šu-eš-ša (Drehem VIII) respectively, were studied in chapter I. *BIN* 10: 99 is dated iti [ ] $^{d}$Nin-a-zu, which can be restored ki-síg-$^{d}$Nin-a-zu (Drehem IV) or ezen-$^{d}$Nin-a-zu (Drehem V); since the text mentions Šū-Ninkarak and Girini-ša, it certainly belongs to the archive.

Three other month names are not otherwise attested. In I.E. 7 three tablets are dated iti kin-$^{d}$Nanna (*BIN* 9: no 515, *BIN* 10: nos 96 and 208). The first two are worker lists and the names in them are all commonly found in the lists of that year. *BIN* 10: no 96 is a record of delivery of wooden poles and doors, and the names Šū-Ninkarak and Išar-lubalլiṭ indicate that the text belongs to the Isin archive[44]. The

[43] This is the so-called "Reichskalender" of the Ur III dynasty, cf. F.R. Kraus, *WO* 8 (1976): p. 198.

[44] Išar-lubalիṭ occurs, for instance, also in *BIN* 10: no 95, a text dated iti ne-ne-gar (Nippur V) in I.E. 7.

name could be an error for iti kin-$^{d}$Inanna (Nippur VI), but since it occurs three times, this seems unlikely.

Another month name is found on two tablets: iti $gu_4$-zag-gar in *BIN* 9: no 516 and iti $gu_4$-zag-a in *BIN* 10: no 181 are probably the same. What the name would mean in either variant is unclear. V. Crawford considered the $gu_4$ sign in *BIN* 9: no 516 to be mistake for bára[45], but the second attestation in *BIN* 10: no 181 makes this unlikely[46]. The personal names in *BIN* 10: no 181 — Ipquša and Adad-rabi — assure its assignment to the archive. In *BIN* 9: no 516 no names are attested.

Finally, an unusual month name occurs only in an undated text, *BIN* 10: no 313. The signs are clearly iti síg-$^{d}$Ina[nna], which does not make sense. The síg may be an error for kin, or possibly ki-síg $^{d}$Inanna was intended which is also an unattested month name. The text contains a list of reedworkers all common in the worker lists, and thus belongs certainly to the Isin archive.

In Isin three calendars were thus in use until I.E. 8. Afterwards the Nippur calendar is used consistently, and will become the standard calendar of the Old Babylonian period.

45 *BIN* 9: p. 65.

46 Note iti $bara_7$($AGAR_2$)-zag-gar in an Ur III text from Nippur, *NRVN* 1: no 299, cf. H. Sauren, *ZA* 59 (1969): p. 50. The $AGAR_2$ sign is, however, much closer to bára then $gu_4$, and a mistake seems more likely than in the case of $gu_4$.

## APPENDIX B

# COLLATIONS

*BIN* 9:

no 54: add [nít]a after máš
no 55: 9, last sign clearly udu
no 102: L.E.,  are not impressions
no 116: 5, end traces of [GA]L
no 145: 10, add separation line between l. 10 (iti šu-eš-ša) and l. 11 (mu-ús-sa Kiri$_8$-tab$^{ki}$ / ba-ḫul)
no 233: 1, second sign clearly udu
2, second sign clearly udu
8, third sign MAḪ
12, last sign clearly lugal
22, first 3/4th of line broken
no 240: add separation line between l. 6 (6 kuš-udu *a-lum* babbar) and l. 7 (ka-tab $^{dug}$dal-geštin)
no 250: add separation lines between each line except in year date
no 308: add separation line between l. 1 (1 $^{kuš}$dùg-gan-ti-bala-a) and l. 2 (im-sar-ra $^{dug}$laḫtan 7 / guškin ba-an-gar)
no 311: 4, eighth sign clearly sila$_4$
no 312: 7, add ŠA after UŠ
L.E., mostly erased
no 329: add separation line between l. 12 (8 kuš-gu$_4$) and l. 13 ($^{kuš}$*ga-ba-bu-*bi 32 / diri 2 $^{kuš}$*ga-ba-bu-um* tur / ì-gál)
no 366: 1, third sign clearly udu
no 382: 19, after lú 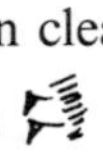
no 390: 2, third sign clearly UD
no 401: seal impression B on tablet
no 412: 9, ésir-é-bi sic!
no 427: add on Lo.E., še-gín-bi 2 gín
no 435: 13, first sign NÍG not UD
no 441: 10, erased line
no 447: add separation line between l. 11 ($^{giš}$ig-mi-rí-za) and l. 12 (ká?-gur$_7$-šè)

no 453: 3, first sign [K]A
no 491: 22, last sign clearly sun

R.D. Freedman, *JAOS* 98 (1978): pp. 251-257.

text A: no separation line between l. 14 (mu en [d]Inanna) and l. 15 (máš-e ì-pàd)
text C: 4, first sign 
10, first sign clearly preserved má
no 1: no separation line between l. 10 (*Be-lí-šar ù*) and l. 11 (Lú-ša$_6$-ga šu ba-ti)
no 4: 1, last signs clearly gu$_4$ ú-ḫáb
no 6: 1, first signs clearly 8 gú
2, first sign clearly é
no 7: the first is a tag, upper left corner is broken
15, 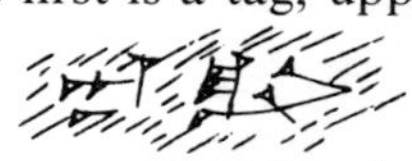
no separation line between l. 19 (ki [d]*Iš-bi-Èr-ra*-zi) and l. 20 ([kala]m-ma-ta ba-zi)

no 10: last line of rev. add: 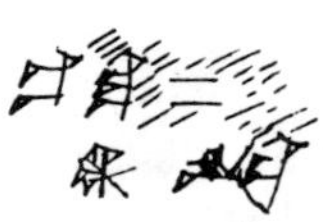
no 11: 1, second sign giš
3, add kin-ti-ta
7, second sign 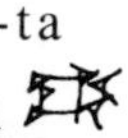
year name, add: [d]*Šu-ì* / nin-ding[ir] / íl
no 13: 2, last signs 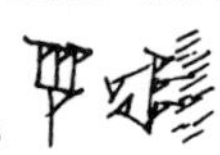
7, clearly *Šu-*[d]Nin-ka[r-ak]
no 14: 1, last sign 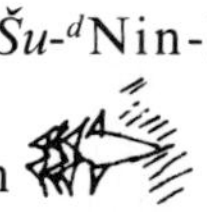
3, first sign [i]m
8, last signs: 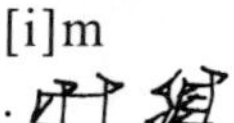
10, first sign traces of im
no 15: sealed, impression illegible
no 16: 7, first sign dum[u]

# GLOSSARY[1]

A-*allaḫarum*. The product is usually equated with *allaḫarum*, and the A considered as a phonetic complement (*CAD* A/1: p. 359, *AHw*: p. 38). But since the al-sign does not require a phonetic indicator, and A-*allaḫarum* in the Isin texts is found only in records of deliveries to the workshop, while *allaḫarum* only in records of production, it is possible that two separate products are intended; cf. a-še-gín and še-gín. Note, however, that, unlike a-še-gín and še-gín which are measured in sila and mina respectively, both A-*allaḫarum* and *allaḫarum* are measured in sila.
*BIN* 9: nos 80, 81, 82, 83, 104, 105.

A-*allaḫarum liqtum*. The product is usually read as *allaḫarum niqdum* and considered as a powdered form of the *niqdum* plant (P. Steinkeller, *OrAn.* 19 [1980]: p. 96 n. 34), or as a mineral dye (D. Snell, *YNER* 8: p. 229). Since the product cannot be both a mineral (*allaḫarum*) and a plant (*niqdum*), it is preferable to read *allaḫarum lí-iq-tum*, cf. S. Dalley, *OBT Tell Rimah*: p. 102f., where *annuḫara li-iq-tam* "collected *allaḫarum*" is requested as material for the leatherworkers. *liqtum* is also used as an adjective for gold and cloth where it indicates "a fine quality", *CAD* L: p. 207. Note that the product is measured by weight in *BIN* 9: no 83 (5 minas) and as a liquid in *BIN* 10: no 33 (1 sila), while *allaḫarum* and A-*allaḫarum* are both measured as liquids.
*BIN* 9: no 83, *BIN* 10: no 33.

a-še-gín. Probably a solution of še-gín in water, L. Matouš, *BiOr.* 13 (1956): p. 138. It is used with še-gín in the manufacture of doors and is measured as a liquid. All mentions of a-še-gín in the Isin texts are for work on the ki-sá-a, mainly for its doors (*BIN* 9: nos 153-157, 162-168, 177, *ASJ* 5: p. 50 no 7, LB 1020, 1105). I am unable to explain why this product is only used for the ki-sá-a, which is part of the city wall.
*BIN* 9: nos 12, 153, 154, 155, 156, 157, 162, 163, 164, 165, 166, 167, 168, 177, *ASJ* 5: p. 56 no 7, LB 1020, 1105.

[1] This glossary studies the Sumerian and Akkadian terms used in this study and lists their attestations throughout the Isin archive.

$^{kuš}$ Á, "a weapon", L. Matouš, *BiOr.* 13 (1956): p. 139, or maybe a leather holder for a weapon.
*BIN* 9: nos 108, 109, 507.

$^{kuš}$Á.SI = $^{kuš}$ A.SI, "hinge". For $^{urudu}$ Á.SI as "doorhinge", see H. Limet, *Métal*: p. 198 and 200. Á.SI and A.SI seem to alternate in the Isin texts. $^{kuš}$á-si as "whip", cf. M. Civil, *Iraq* 23 (1961): p. 162 *ad* l. 88, does not make sense in the Isin texts.
*BIN* 9: nos 106, 438, *ASJ* 5: p. 57 no 8.

$^{kuš}$ AB, "tarpaulin", V. Crawford, *Terminology*: p. 84. In the Isin texts this translation is the most likely since this object is used to cover boats (e.g., *BIN* 9: no 445), and can reach the size of 12 by 3.5 meters (*BIN* 9: no 37). The second sign may be $KU_7$ and the term should then be read dabašin = *dabašinnum, CAD* D: p. 14, *AHw*: p. 148 (a leather object). Its function to store fodder (*CAD* D: p. 14), or as waterbag for animals (S. Lieberman, *The Sumerian Loanwords in Old Babylonian Akkadian,* Missoula, Montana, 1977: p. 193), does not apply in the Isin texts.
*BIN* 9: nos 37, 88, 183, 378, 438, 445, *ASJ* 5: p. 57 no 8.

ad-KID = *atkuppum*, "reedworker", *CAD* A/2: p. 494f., *AHw*: p. 87. Although the Akkadian translation suggests a reading at-$kup_x$ as proposed by E. Sollberger, *TCS* 1: p. 102, the older reading ad-KID (cf. A. Goetze, *JCS* 2 (1948): p. 176) is preferred until further evidence is presented.
*BIN* 9: nos 234, 349, *BIN* 10: nos 62, 67, 170, 171, 313, *passim* in the worker lists.

$^{giš}$al-ak, "to work with the pickaxe", Salonen, *Agricultura*: p. 405f.
*BIN* 10: nos 244, 247, 308.

*allaḫarum*, "a mineral dye or mordant to produce white color", *CAD* A/1: p. 359f. s.v. *alluḫarum, AHw*: p. 38 s.v. *allu/aḫaru(m)*, cf. D. Snell, *YNER* 8: p. 216. The product is used as a tanning agent, L. Matouš, *BiOr.* 13 (1956): p. 137, M. Stol, *RlA* 6 (1980-83): p. 533. In the textile industry it is used to raise the quality of garments, cf. H. Waetzoldt, *Textilindustrie*: p. 174 and *BIN* 9: no 129, where *allaḫarum* and ú-ḫáb are used to shine (su) a guzza-garment. In the tanning process it occurs together with ú-ḫáb and is used to produce red leather. In the first millennium B.C. the equivalent of ú-ḫáb, *ḫūratu* is often found together with im-saḫar-$na_4$-kur-ra = *aban gabî* "alum", cf. F. Thureau-Dangin, *RA* 17 (1920): p. 27-

30, *CAD* H: p. 247, *AHw*: p. 358, s.v. *ḫūratu, CAD* G: p. 79, *AHw*: p. 272, s.v. *gabû*. Note also that in the Old Babylonian text S. Dalley, *OBT Tell Rimah*: no 102, *ḫūratu* and *allaḫarum* occur together (cf. s.v. ú-ḫáb). *allaḫarum* is thus probably a variant of *gabû* "alum", perhaps a liquid form of it, for *allaḫarum* is measured as a liquid and *gabû* in mina. Moreover, in Uruanna III 511 *annuḫaru* is equated with black *gabû* (*CAD* A/I: p. 359, G: p. 7, M. Sigrist, *JCS* 33 [1981]; p. 157). Although B. Landsberger stated in *JCS* 21 (1967): p. 169 that alum is still unknown in this period, in the Royal Cemetery of Ur leather decayed to white powder was found (cf. L. Woolley, *The Antiquaries Journal* 8 [1928]: p. 443), which was tanned with alum according to R.J. Forbes, SAT V: p. 40.

*BIN* 9: nos 467, 470, 489, *BIN* 10: no 130.

ašgab = *aškāpum*, "leatherworker", *CAD* A/2: p. 442, *AHw*: p. 81, A. Salonen, *Fussbekleidung*: p. 22f., 111.

*BIN* 9: nos 22, 150, 193, 199, 232, 246, 248, 250, 295, 349, 433, 489, *BIN* 10: no 130, *passim* in the worker lists.

ba-sig$_4$, "tortoise shell", W.W. Hallo, *JCS 17 (1963)*: p. 60, D. Snell, *YNER* 8: p. 231 s.v. sig$_4$-ba, and p. 73 n. 40 for variation ba-sig$_4$/sig$_4$-ba. Perhaps the signs should be read ba-mur$_7$.

*BIN* 9: no 182.

ba-zú = *suppīn ṣurrim*, "toothed knife", *AHw*: p. 1060 and 1114, cf. A. Salonen, *Hausgeräte* I: p. 33. Note that in *AHw*: p. 1060 *suppīnum* is translated as "ein Bau-Werkzeug". $^{giš}$ba-z[u] in *BIN* 10: no 120 may refer to the same object.

*BIN* 9: no 374.

$^{giš}$balag = *balangu*, "harp or lyre", *CAD* B: p. 38, *AHw*: p. 98, cf. H. Hartmann, *Musik*: p. 52-67. Note $^{giš}$balag-balag in *BIN* 9: no 441.

*BIN* 9: nos 312, 441, 445.

da-$^{giš}$gigir = *marḫaṣu*, "side(-board) of a chariot", *CAD* M/1: p. 280, *AHw*: p. 611, M. Civil, *JAOS* 88 (1968): p. 7f.

*BIN* 9: nos 192, 193.

dabin = *tappinnum*, "barley flour", *AHw*: p. 1321. For its use as glue, cf. A. Salonen, *Türen*: p. 118.

*BIN* 9: nos 172, 191, 341, 381, 433, 443, 450, 509, *BIN* 10: nos 98, 185, *JAOS* 98: p. 156 no 12.

$^{dug}$dal = *tallum*, "vessel for oil", *AHw*: p. 1311. A. Salonen, *Hausgeräte* II: p. 179-182 "large jar with wide mouth".
*BIN* 9: nos 240, 289, 322, 363, 438, *ASJ* 5: p. 57 no 9.

$^{giš}$dal = *tallum*, "traverse beam", *AHw*: p. 1311.
*BIN* 10: nos 109, 156, 188.

DU$_8$.IG = ? A. Salonen, *Türen*: p. 75, du$_8$-ig = "key" derived from du$_8$ = *petûm*, "to open". In the Isin texts the product is made of leather, which may indicate the use of a thong-like instrument.
*BIN* 9: nos 75, 463.

$^{kuš}$dùg-gan-túg, "leather bag". $^{kuš}$dùg-gan = *tukkannum*, "bag", *AHw*: p. 1367 = *naruqqu*, Hg XI: 148 (*MSL* 7: p. 149). The meaning of túg is unclear. V. Crawford, *Terminology*: p. 74-80, suggests that there is no special value to it, and indeed the texts do not seem to make a difference between $^{kuš}$dùg-gan and $^{kuš}$dùg-gan-túg. I.J. Gelb, *JNES* 20 (1961): p. 132, translates "a leather bag of boxwood (túg)" which seems very unlikely. K. Oberhuber, *Or*. NS 36 (1967): p. 426f., reads $^{kuš}$dùg-gan-zíd which is impossible since zíd and túg are clearly distinguished in third millennium cuneiform script. The túg probably refers to the fact that the bag was used primarily to hold cloths, like a "duffle" bag, cf. M. Stol, *RlA* 6 (1980-83): p. 537.
*BIN* 9: nos 87, 150, 184, 198, 215, 216, 217, 218, 219, 220, 221, 222, 223, 224, 226, 241, 268, 273, 274, 275, 276, 277, 278, 279, 280, 281, 282, 283, 284, 285, 287, 288, 289, 290, 291, 292, 294, 295, 296, 297, 298, 299, 300, 301, 310, 316, 359, 400, 403, 404, 405, 406, 407, 408, 409, 410, 411, 414, 416, 468, 491, *BIN* 10: nos 157, 160, 165. *MCS* 5: p. 123 no 9, *Or* 36: p. 426f.

dul$_4$, "to cover", variant for dul = *katāmum, AHw*: p. 464. Cf. T. Fish, *MCS* 5 (1955): p. 117, Å. Sjöberg, *ZA* 63 (1973): p. 9, dul$_4$(-dul$_4$) = "to cover". D. Loding, *JCS* 28 (1976): p. 235 n. 5 doubts that dul and dul$_4$ are variants, and suggests that dul$_4$ has a more technical meaning.
*BIN* 9: nos 37, 200, 307, 370, 371, 373, 375, 426, 451, 465, 477, 525, *BIN* 10: nos 83, 94, 105, 109, 150, *MCS* 5: p. 115 no 1, *JAOS* 98: p. 253 no 5.

$^{gi/giš}$dúr = *šubtum*, "seat", *AHw*: p. 1257f., cf. Salonen, *Möbel*: p. 78.
*BIN* 9: nos 426, 438, *BIN* 10: no 87.

dúr-gar = *durgar(r)û*, "ornate chair, throne", *CAD* D: p. 191, *AHw*: p. 177, A. Salonen, *Möbel*: p. 75.
*BIN* 9: nos 32, 334, 336, *BIN* 10: no 77.

$^{kuš}$e-sír = *šēnum*, "sandal", *AHw*: p. 1213, cf. Salonen, *Fussbekleidung*: p. 15-30.

*BIN* 9: nos 39, 88, 107, 129, 185, 226, 231, 232, 233, 238, 323, 324, 325, 326, 327, 369, 382, 383, 384, 388, 395, 397, 415, 420, 421, 422, 423, 424, 425, 426, 431, 432, 440, 460, *BIN* 10: nos 33, 83, 117, 128, 149, 181, *TLB* 3: no 175.

é-ba-an, "pair", said of sandals and boots. A. Salonen, *Fussbekleidung*: p. 82-85, reads Ha$_x$-ba-an and thinks the term refers to the name of the city Ḫamban, see also his article in *BiOr*. 25 (1968): p. 101f. A. Goetze, *JCS* 9 (1955): p. 21, suggests the meaning "pair", however, cf. also W.W. Hallo, *BiOr*. 20 (1963): p. 138. This translation is strongly supported by a text discussed by P. Steinkeller, *OrAn*. 19 (1980): p. 87 n. 15, where 1/2 $^{kuš}$súḫub ... é-ba-an is listed, which must indicate half a pair of boots, rather than half a boot from Hamban. B. Landsberger, *JCS* 21 (1967): p. 169 n. 128, suggests that é-ba-an is a variant for é-pa-na = *tāpalum*, "pair" (*AHw*: p. 1320). In *BIN* 10: no 85 the term is used for a pair of chairs.

*BIN* 9: nos 39, 88, 231, 232, 233, 238, 323, 324, 325, 326, 327, 328, 369, 382, 383, 384, 395, 397, 415, 420, 421, 422, 423, 424, 425, 426, 428, 431, 432, 436, 440, 460, *BIN* 10: nos 85, 117, 128, 149, *TLB* 3: no 75.

é-du$_6$-la = *edullû, CAD* E: p. 38, *AHw*: p. 188, "storage house or workshop", W.W. Hallo, *BiOr*. 20 (1963): p. 137. For the term in the Ur III period, cf. Th. Jacobsen, *Toward the Image of Tammuz*, Cambridge, Massachusetts, 1970: p. 424 n. 18.

*BIN* 9: no 438, *BIN* 10: nos 9, 53, *JAOS* 98: p. 252 no 2.

é-uz-ga = *bīt marîm*(?), "house of fattening sheep", A. Falkenstein, *AnOr*. 30: p. 142f., Å. Sjöberg, *TCS* 3: p. 120f., "house of birds", T. Jones-J. Snyder: pp. 227-232, S.B. Nelson, *Nasha: a study of administrative texts of the Third Dynasty of Ur*, Univ. Microfilms, Ann Arbor, 1975: p. 6-9. It could also refer to a religious building or part of a temple, J. van Dijk, *Götterlieder* II: p. 25. See also M. Green, *JCS* 30 (1978): p. 149.

*BIN* 9: nos 234, 339, 361, 390, 395, 401, 428, 436, *BIN* 10: nos 147, 154, 155, *JAOS* 98: p. 255 no 9.

ébiḫ (ÉŠ.MAḪ) = *ebīḫu*, "heavy rope", *CAD* E: p. 14, *AHw*: p. 183.

*BIN* 9: nos 233, 453, 526, *BIN* 10: nos 76, 81, 84, 136, 161.

ésir = *ittû*, "bitumen", *CAD* I/J: p. 310-2, *iṭṭûm, AHw*: p. 408, cf. D. Snell, *YNER* 8: p. 48. See R.J. Forbes, *SAT* I: p. 1-123, for the uses of bitumen.

*BIN* 9: nos 36, 238, 249, 307, 332, 346, 347, 350, 355, 360, 364, 387, 393, 402, 426, 438, 441, 443, 447, 450, 480, 523, 525, 532, 534, *BIN* 10: nos 1, 62, 92, 93, 97, 98, 100, 103, 104, 105, 130, 156, 158, 173, 193, *TLB* 3: no 175, *JAOS* 98: p. 252 no 1, *ASJ* 5: p. 56 no 6.

ésir-é-a = *kuprum* (?), "bitumen", *CAD* K: p. 554, *AHw*: p. 509.

*BIN* 9: nos 27, 30, 134, 139, 178, 197, 204, 206, 208, 212, 234, 250, 251, 259, 262, 339, 343, 344, 345, 346, 347, 349, 350, 359, 361, 362, 365, 358, 376, 377, 381, 387, 390, 391, 394, 395, 396, 397, 399, 401, 412, 415, 417, 428, 429, 430, 433, 436, 439, 442, 443, 447, 448, 449, 451, 452, 463, 465, 477, 479, 485, 491, 493, 495, 511, 516, 534, *BIN* 10: nos 2, 6, 14-20, 27-31, 36, 37, 41, 52, 62, 92, 97, 106, 107, 109, 127-129, 133-135, 137, 138, 151, 153-156, 162, 169, 170, 181, *MCS* 5: p. 121 no 7, *JAOS* 98: p. 256 no 14, Lindblom High School 1.

ésir-é-a-ḫád = *kuprum*, "dry(?) bitumen", *CAD* K: p. 553, *AHw*: p. 509.

*BIN* 9: no 136.

éš = *eblum, ašlum*, "rope", *CAD* E: p. 15, *CAD* A/1: p. 447, *AHw*: p. 183 and 81.

*BIN* 9: nos 29, 39, 246, 255, 257, 265, 324, 327, 378, 391, 395, 415, 424, 425, 435, 450, 458, *BIN* 10: nos 75, 114.

éš-ur-gi$_7$-ra, "dog-leash". Translation suggested by M. Civil.

*BIN* 10: no 101.

éš-ur-maḫ, "leash for lions(?)".

*BIN* 10: no 84

gá-nun = *ganūnum*, "storage house", *CAD* G: p. 42, *AHw*: p. 280, cf. M. Lambert, *RlA* 3 (1957-71): p. 141-146.

*BIN* 9: nos 511, 530.

gaba-ri = *gabarû*, "copy", *CAD* G: p. 2, *AHw*: p. 271.

*passim.*

$^{kuš}$*gabābum*, "a shield", *CAD* K: p. 1, "a sling", *AHw*: p. 414 s.v. *k/gabābum*. The translation "shield" seems more appropriate than sling, since in *BIN* 9: no 329, out of eight oxhides thirty-two plus two small $^{kuš}$*gabābum* are made. One oxhide for four shields seems more likely than for four slings.

*BIN* 9: nos 14, 85, 106, 111, 119, 123, 329, 330, 331, 338, 433.

gašam = *apkallum*, "craftsman, etc.", *CAD* A/2: p. 171f., *AHw*: p. 58, J.P. Grégoire, *AAS*: p. 134f.

*BIN* 10: no 222

$^{giš}$ge-en = *binâtu*(?), cf. A. Falkenstein, *ZA* NF 21 (1963): p. 61 and l. 53. *binâtu* is part of a boat or structure, *CAD* B: p. 237.
*BIN* 9: no 502.

gi-ra, "type of processed reed", A.L. Oppenheim, *Eames Coll.*: p. 46 s.v. E7.
*BIN* 10: no 47.

$^{gi}$gíd = *malīlu*, "flute", *CAD* M/1: p. 164, *AHw*: p. 595, cf. E. Gordon, *Sumerian Proverbs*: p. 212 s.v. 2.54, 12.
*BIN* 9: nos 359, 365, 368, 394, 395, 396, 397, 399, 402, 532, *BIN* 10: nos 103, 133, 158.

giš-ḫum = *gišḫummu*, "bench", *CAD* G: p. 101, *AHw*: p. 292. Perhaps it is the same as $^{giš}$ḫu-um, a structure on a boat to provide shade, cf. M. Sigrist, *JCS* 33 (1981): p. 182 n. 159.
*BIN* 9: nos 198, 482, 512, *BIN* 10: no 25

giš-nú = *aršum*, "bed", *CAD* E: p. 315, *AHw*: p. 246, cf. P. Steinkeller, *OrAn*. 19 (1980): p. 79 n. 1.
*BIN* 9: nos 183, 254, 255, 303, 348, 435, 438, 473, 491, 499, *BIN* 10: nos 53, 74, 79, 90, 113, 150, 187.

giš-nú-aš-nú = *d/tinnû(tu)*, "couch", *CAD* D: p. 150, *AHw*: p. 171, cf. A. Salonen, Möbel: p. 116, 139f.
*ASJ* 5: p. 57 no 8.

gu-dim$_4$-ba-gada. Type of linen, not discussed in H. Waetzoldt, *Textilindustrie*. In *BIN* 9: no 455, copper is used for the production of it and for green leather (kuš-du$_8$-ši-a). When gu-dim$_4$-ba occurs in the Ur III period, it always is found together with green leather, e.g., H. Holma-A. Salonen, *StOr*. IX/1: no 32, 1-2:

14 $^{kuš}$súḫub gu-dim$_4$-ba kuš-a é-ba-an
1 $^{kuš}$súḫub du$_8$-ši-a é-ba-an

H. de Genouillac, *Trouvaille de Dréhem*: no 62, 1-3:

10 $^{kuš}$súḫub du$_8$-ši-a é-ba-an
1 $^{kuš}$súḫub gu-dim$_4$-ba x[* ] / du$_8$-ši-a $^{kuš}$KI.KAL é-ba-an
24 $^{kuš}$súḫub gu-dim$_4$-ba / kuš-a é-ba-an

(* the broken sign may be gada, but this is very uncertain)
The gu-dim$_4$-ba seems to be applied to boots, may be as lining. In *BIN* 9: no 460, green gu-dim$_4$-ba linen is used for royal sandals.
*BIN* 9: nos 129, 428, 455, 460, *BIN* 10: no 132.

giš gu-za = *kussûm*, "chair, throne", CAD K: p. 587, *AHw*: p. 515, cf. A. Salonen, *Möbel*: p. 34-75.
*BIN* 9: nos 28, 86, 110, 150, 151, 180, 182, 183, 185, 186, 187, 201, 202, 228, 246, 247, 248, 340, 341, 342, 354, 378, 434, 435, 436, 437, 438, 439, 440, 480, 491, 497, 499, *BIN* 10: nos 10, 83, 92, 113, 143, 150, 162, 187, *JAOS* 98: p. 252 no 2.

giš gu-za-má-la$ḫ_4$ = *kussûm ša malaḫḫim*, "boatsman's chair", Salonen, *Möbel*: p. 42.
*BIN* 9: no 341.

giš gu-za-sìr-da = *kussî serdîm*, "sedan chair", *CAD* K: p. 588, *AHw*: p. 515 and 1037, Salonen, *Möbel*: p. 79-81.
*BIN* 9: nos 27, 30, 184, 185, 374, 430, 432, 462, *BIN* 10: no 85, *SET*: no 291, *JAOS* 98: p. 254 no 7, p. 257 no 16, *The Ancient Orient Museum* 3: p. 41f.

$gu_4$-gaz, "oxslaughterer". gaz = *dâkum*, "to kill, slaughter", *CAD* D: p. 35f., *AHw*: p. 152.
*BIN* 10: nos 102, 121.

$gu_4$-si-AŠ = *āšibum*, "battering ram", *CAD* A/2: p. 428, *AHw*: p. 412, E. Salonen, *Waffen*: p. 29-31. AŠ is perhaps to be read dili.
*BIN* 9: nos 103, 125, 197, 371, 463.

$gur_7$ = *karûm*, "granary, silo", *CAD* K: p. 228, *AHw*: p. 452.
*BIN* 9: nos 447, 508, *BIN* 10: nos 167, 174, 195, 225, 265.

gi gurdub(GÁxGI), "reed-basket", A. Salonen, *Hausgeräte* I: p. 235 s.v. gi PISANxGI. For the reading gurdub, see M. Civil, *RA* 61 (1967): p. 65 n. 2.
*BIN* 10: nos 235, 242, 244, 251.

giš ḫa-lu-úb = *ḫaluppum*, "oak(?)", *CAD* H: p. 55f., *AHw*: p. 314.
*BIN* 9: nos 16, 374, 499.

ḪI-lá, "decoration(?)", cf. M. Sigrist, *JCS* 33 (1981): p. 184f. When colored oxhides are applied to doors, the term used is ḪI-lá.
*BIN* 9: nos 174, 477.

*ḫurdum*, "doormat", *CAD* H: p. 250, *AHw*: p. 358.
*BIN* 9: no 426.

ì = *šamnum*, "oil, fat", *AHw*: p. 1157, cf. D. Snell, *YNER* 8: p. 223f.
*BIN* 9: nos 182, 184, 185, 198, 200, 211, 371, 373, 375, 468, 489, 512, *BIN* 10: nos 32, 44, 130, 150, 160, *MCS* 5: p. 124 no 10.

ì ba-a-dé, "strained(?) oil", i.e. poured through a strainer. dé = *šapākum*, "to pour", *AHw*: p. 1168. This type of oil is unknown so far. It is used in leather manufacture. Some relation may exist with ninda ì-dé-a = *mirsum*, "a confection made of dates, oil, butter, etc.", *CAD* M/2: p. 108, *AHw*: p. 646.

*BIN* 9: nos 182, 489, *BIN* 10: nos 130, 150?.

ì-giš = *ellum*, "sesame oil", *CAD* E: p. 106, *AHw*: p. 205, cf. D. Snell, *YNER* 8: p. 224.

*BIN* 9: nos 37, 181, 343, 370, 437, 505, *BIN* 10: nos 38, 49, 50, 83, *MCS* 5: p. 115 no 1.

ì-rá-rá = *raqqûm*, "oilpresser", *AHw*: p. 958. Cf. M. Gallery, *AfO* 27 (1980): p. 9 and n. 43.

*BIN* 9: nos 235, 270, 282, 287, 289, 298, 301, 306, 366, 400, *BIN* 10: nos 157, 159, 239, 245, 250, 263, LB 1102.

ì-šur = *ṣāḫitum*, "preparer of sesame oil", *CAD* Ṣ: p. 62, *AHw*: p. 1074f.

*BIN* 9: no 351, *BIN* 10: no 163.

ì-udu = *lipûm*, "mutton fat, tallow of sheep", *CAD* L: p. 202, *AHw*: p. 555, cf. Snell, *YNER* 8: p. 225.

*BIN* 10: no 51.

gišig = *daltum*, "door", *CAD* D: p. 52f., *AHw*: p. 154, cf. A. Salonen, *Türen*.

*BIN* 9: nos 11, 15, 71, 74, 77, 87, 106, 137, 138, 140, 147, 148, 149, 153, 155, 156, 157, 158, 159, 160, 161, 162, 163, 164, 165, 166, 167, 168, 169, 170, 172, 173, 174, 175, 176, 294, 344, 345, 426, 477, 498, 505, 525, 534, *BIN* 10: nos 70, 76, 77, 81, 83, 89, 92, 94, 96, 97, 126, 148, 153, 155, 158, 159, 169, 175, 178-180, 186, 188, 192, 193, *MCS* 5: p. 121 no 7, p. 124 no 10, *JAOS* 98: p. 253 no 4, *ASJ* 4: p. 68 no 17.

gišig-gi, "reed door", cf. gišig-gi-kid, "door of reed mats", A. Salonen, *Türen*: p. 20.

*BIN* 9: nos 343, 376, 377, 382, 439, 532, 534, *BIN* 10: no 155.

gišig-mi-rí-za, "door made of small boards", A. Salonen, *Türen*: p. 24f., E. Prang, *ZA* 66 (1976): p. 24f.

*BIN* 9: nos 178, 179, 346, 347, 349, 350, 442, 443, 447, 464, *BIN* 10: nos 127, 172.

im-babbar = *gaṣṣum*, "gypsum", *CAD* G: p. 54, *AHw*: p. 282. L. Matouš, *BiOr*. 13 (1956): p. 137, suggests that it was a tanning agent, but in the Isin texts it was only used by the reedworkers. In the textile industry gypsum was used to clean garments, cf. H. Waetzoldt, *Textilindustrie*: p. 173f. The use in reedwork is unclear.

*BIN* 9: nos 35, 79, 80, 178, 201, 202, 249, 250, 251, 260, 346, 347, 349, 350, 364, 440, 443, 477, *BIN* 10: nos 13, 100, 127, *JAOS* 98: p. 256 no 14.

im-KÙ.GI = *šaršerru*, "red paste", *illur pānim*, "rouge for the face", *kalûm*, "a mineral of yellow color", *lēru*, "mineral color", *AHw*: p. 1191, *CAD* I/J: p. 88, K: p. 94f., L: p. 147. Lit. "gold-colored earth", cf. P. Steinkeller, *OrAn.* 19 (1980): p. 97 n. 39, D. Snell, *YNER* 8: p. 224. The material is used to produce black color.
*BIN* 9: nos 81, 182, 198, 489, *BIN* 10: nos 5, 51, 83, 130, 150.

KA.AḪ, "unknown type of wool", H. Waetzoldt, *Textilindustrie*: p. 55f.
*BIN* 10: 116.

ka-dù = *ermum*, "cover", *CAD* E: p. 302, *AHw*: p. 242, cf. A. Salonen, *Hausgeräte* I: p. 191f.
*BIN* 9: nos 234, 330, 334, 379, 382, 433, 434, 435, *BIN* 10: nos 83, 159.

KA-gìr = *padānum*, "road, path", *AHw*: p. 807f., W.W. Hallo-J. van Dijk, *YNER* 3: p. 80. *AHw*: p. 808 and J.P. Grégoire, *RA* 69 (1975): p. 191 read gù-gìr perhaps because of the variant kun-gìr in Ḫḫ II 275, but the variant ki-gìr in the *Exaltation of Inanna,* suggests the reading ka-. The term may be in the Isin texts a variant of KA-gir and KA-gir$_4$, which designates a type of reed mat or something from which reed mats are made, cf. *UET* 3: nos 701, 845, *TCL* 5: no 6036 (suggestion M. Civil).
*BIN* 10: no 107, Lindblom High School 1.

$^{giš}$ka-kara$_4$ = *kanna/iškarakkum*, "type of table", *CAD* K: p. 149, *AHw*: p. 437. A. Salonen, *Möbel*: p. 194f. translates "table with drawers".
*BIN* 9: no 29, *BIN* 10: no 150.

ka-tab. The term is a matter of dispute. A. Salonen, *Hausgeräte* I: p. 163 and 167-170, proposes the translation "with double mouth, with two openings". This translation is also proposed by M. Sigrist, *JCS* 33 (1981): p. 189f. He equates ka-tab with Akkadian *šakarum*, but I am unable to find this equation in the lexical material. F. Stephens, *JCS* 13 (1959): p. 12-14, comes to the conclusion that it means "lid", cf. also S. Cohen, *AOAT* 25 (1976): p. 106f.: ka-tab = *katammu* (*CAD* K: p. 297). D. Loding, *A Craft Archive from Ur*, Univ. Microfilms, Ann Arbor, 1974: p. 114, also argues in favor of the translation "lid or cover" based on *UET* 3: no 1498 rev col I 27: 1 $^{giš}$pisan ḫa-lu-úb ka-tab nu-tuk tur, "1 small wooden container of oak(?), not having a lid". In the Isin material the translation "lid or cover" seems most suitable. The amount of leather used for ka-tab is often very small, e.g., in *BIN* 9: no 276, where 10 shekels sheepleather are used for one. Moreover, it seems unlikely that the workshop issued numerous "double-mouth vessels" without producing any other type.

*BIN* 9: nos 34, 36, 190, 217, 219, 220, 221, 222, 223, 224, 225, 227, 229, 230, 235, 236, 237, 238, 239, 240, 241, 242, 243, 244, 245, 268, 270, 272, 273, 276, 279, 280, 281, 283, 285, 286, 287, 289, 291, 293, 295, 297, 298, 299, 301, 304, 306, 310, 312, 313, 314, 315, 316, 317, 320, 321, 322, 339, 344, 345, 361, 363, 365, 367, 368, 376, 377, 389, 391, 393, 394, 395, 396, 397, 398, 399, 400, 401, 402, 403, 404, 405, 407, 408, 409, 410, 411, 414, 419, 429, 435, 438, 441, 447, 452, *BIN* 10: nos 93, 110, 128, 133, 153, 157, 160, 195, *MCS* 5: p. 116 no 2, p. 120 no 6, p. 123 no 9, *JCS* 19: p. 42 Pf. 3, *Or* 36: p. 426f., *ASJ* 5: p. 56 no 6, p. 57 no 9.

$^{giš}$kak-sal$_4$ = *saparrum* "chariot or cart", *AHw*: p. 1026 (suggestion G. Ferwerda).

*BIN* 9: nos 249, 250, 251, *BIN* 10: no 131, LB 1113.

kešda = *rakāsum*, "to bind, to wrap", *AHw*: p. 945, E. Sollberger, *TCS* 1: p. 140.

*BIN* 9: nos 27, 29, 30, 89, 192, 261, 332, 378, 382, 386, 426, 435, 449, 458, 459, 461, 462, 463, 464, 466, 470, 477, *BIN* 10: nos 90, 114, 164, 195?.

ki-a-nag, "libation place, place where liquid offerings to the dead were libated", C. Wilcke, *CRRAI* 19: p. 192 n. 58, P. Michalowski, *Or.* NS 46 (1977): p. 221 and n. 4.

*BIN* 9: nos 259, 440, *BIN* 10: no 138.

KI.KAL = *sassum*, "bottom", *AHw*: p. 1032, cf. M. Civil, *JAOS* 88 (1968): p. 13. Said of boots it means "soles".

*BIN* 9: nos 383, 388, 428, 469.

ki-sá-a = *kisûm, CAD* K: p. 429, *AHw*: p. 487f. For this term see, S. Dunham, *A Study of Ancient Mesopotamian Foundations,* Univ. Microfilms, Ann Arbor, 1979: p. 405-421. She comes to the conclusion from the references in *BIN* 9 that the term refers to that part of the wall which had a supporting abutment. All texts referring to work on the ki-sá-a date from I/–/I.E. 16 - V/–/I.E. 17, which can be brought into connection to the year name of I.E. 17 "year that the wall 'Eštar-loves-Išbi'erra' was built", cf. D. Frayne, *The Historical Correlations of the Sumerian Royal Hymns,* Univ. Microfilms, Ann Arbor, 1981: p. 337.

The term ki-sá-a seems, however, to have another meaning in the Isin texts: *ASJ* 5: p. 57 no 8 records 1 giš-nú-aš-nú / še-gín-bi 5 gín / šà ki-sá-a-ta, "one couch, its glue being 15 shekels, from the ...", and *BIN* 9: no 7 also seems to record receipt of leather from an office called ki-sá-a. Further occurrences in *BIN* 9: no 177 [é?]-gal-gibil ki-sá-šè and *BIN* 9: no 439, ká-é-máš-da-ri-a šà ki-sá-a, can be interpreted as referring to both meanings. Also in Ur III and Sargonic texts an accouting office may have been called ki-sá-a, cf. Ur III (Drehem), *BIN* 3: no 45: 1 máš-ga-gi / šà ki-sá-a, and Sargonic (Me-ság archive), *BIN* 8: nos 185, 328 and 512: udu-á ki-sá-a (cf. B.R. Foster, *Mesopotamia* 9 [1982] p. 69).

*BIN* 9: nos 7, 153, 155, 156, 157, 159, 160, 161, 162, 163, 163, 164, 165, 166, 167, 168, 170, 171, 173, 175, 176, 177, 194, 439, *BIN* 10: nos 22, 81, 125, 192, 272, *JAOS* 98: p. 253 no 4, *ASJ* 4: p. 68 no 17, *ASJ* 5: p. 56 no 7, p. 57 no 8, LB 1020, 1105.

gikid = *kītum*, "reedmat", *CAD* K: p. 475f., *AHw*: p. 495, cf. A. Goetze, *JCS* 2 (1948): p. 176-182.

*BIN* 9: nos 199, 234, 259, 332, 354, 358, 362, 395, 434, 439, 451, 463, 480, 497, *BIN* 10: nos 158, 166, 185, 189, LB 1110.

kin = *šiprum*, "work, act", *AHw*: p. 1245f.

*BIN* 9: nos 177, 179, 182, 191, 192, 193, 199, 206, 309, 341, 349, 368, 372, 380, 489, *BIN* 10: nos 82, 130, 147, 150, 170, *JAOS* 98: p. 255 no 11, p. 256 no 12, *ASJ* 5: p. 56 no 6.

ku-ša-nu-um, "cushion", *BIN* 9: p. 4, A. Salonen, *Möbel*: p. 90. It cannot be equated with the Akkadian *gusānum* (a leather cover and bag), *CAD* G: p. 142f., *AHw*: p. 299, cf. M. Stol, *RlA* 6 (1980-83): p. 537f.

*BIN* 9: nos 248, 342, 434, 437, 438, 439, 440.

kù-dím = *kuttimmum*, "gold- or silversmith", *CAD* K: p. 608f., *AHw*: p. 518.

*BIN* 9: nos 28, 150, 206, 264, 378, 379, 380, 381, 418, 467, 470, seal impression H, *JAOS* 98: p. 256 no 12.

kun-zi-da = *miḫrum* "weir", *CAD* M/2: p. 54, cf. S.T. Kang, *SACT* II: p. 437f.

*BIN* 10: no 208, LB 1119.

kurum$_7$ = *piqittum*, "inspection", *AHw*: p. 865, J.P. Grégoire, *AAS*: 200.

*BIN* 10: no 222, Lindblom High School 2.

kuš-a-GAR, short for kuš-a-GAR-nag/kú-a, L. Matouš, *BiOr*. 13 (1956): p. 137.

*BIN* 9: nos 3, 77, 197, *The Ancient Orient Museum* 3: p. 41f.

kuš-a-GAR-nag-a, "dehaired skins". Note that only in the Isin texts the term a-GAR-nag-a occurs. In Ur III economic texts the term is always a-GAR-kú-a, cf. D. Loding, *A Craft Archive from Ur*, Univ. Microfilms, Ann Arbor, 1974: p. 179 (Ur), T. Fish, *MCS* 6 (1956): p. 24 (Umma), p. 58 (Lagash), and p. 87 (Drehem). The translation of the term is not entirely clear. A. Salonen, *Fussbekleidung*: p. 68-70, suggests that the term reflects a method of tanning leather by soaking it in water = "chamois" method. It seems, however, that the skins were called a-GAR-nag-a before the tanning took place. The term refers to the fact that the skins were treated with the a-GAR. This possibly could stand for a-gar-gar = *piqannu* "dung" and refer to the process of bating, but several Ur III texts suggest that flour was used in the a-GAR, see M. Stol, *RlA* 6 (1980-83): p. 531, where, e.g. še zì-a-GAR-kú-šè (*MVN* 3: no 259). The a-GAR was thus probably the ooze in which the hides were placed for drenching before tanning, cf. A.L. Oppenheim, *Eames Coll.*: p. 35, and *CT* 50: no 185 (Sargonic): kuš ... a-GAR-ka nu-ni-gar, "hides not placed in the a-GAR. In the Isin texts the kuš-a-GAR-nag-a are differentiated from hairy ones (kuš-síg-mú, e.g., *BIN* 9: nos 63 and 101), although it seems that the hides had gone through the entire pretannage stage, and were not just dehaired. The translation "dehaired" is thus not entirely accurate, but will be used here. Note that in *Iraq* 23 (1961): p. 162 l. 87 the skin of a fish is said to be GAR-kú-a which probably refers to the fact that the skin is does not have any hair, cf. M. Civil, *ibid.*: p. 172.

*BIN* 9: nos 6, 14, 55, 58, 63, 87, 90, 93, 98, 101, 112, 116, *BIN* 10: no 23, *JAOS* 98: p. 256 no 13.

kuš-du$_8$-ši-a "green leather", cf. M. Stol, *RlA* 6 (1980-83): p. 534. Perhaps du$_8$-ši-a = *dušûm*, "color of the *dušûm*-stone, either yellow or orange", *CAD* D: p. 200-202, cf. A. Salonen, *Fussbekleidung*: p. 71, but it is unclear how copper could produce this color. Note that *AHw*: p. 179, translates "untanned leather", which is impossible since in *BIN* 9: no 460 du$_8$-ši-a occurs as specification of both leather and linen.

*BIN* 9: nos 13, 87, 107, 187, 193, 198, 234, 354, 397, 426, 427, 428, 429, 434, 436, 439, 454, 455, 460, 470, *BIN* 10: nos 83, 117, 130.

kuš-e-rí-na, seems to be a variant of red leather (kuš-ú-ḫáb), since Ḫḫ III 495 equates giš-erina (MUŠxMUŠ) with *ḫūratu*, cf. M. Sigrist, *JCS* 33 (1981): p. 162f. The term seems to refer basically to the fact that the skins were treated with an extract of roots (cf. M. Stol, *RlA* [1980-83]: p. 535). V. Crawford, *Terminology*: p. 16-19, translated "water resistant leather" which seems very likely in the contexts provided by the Isin material. For further references, see M. Civil, *JCS* 15 (1961): p. 125 s.v., and D. Loding, *A Craft Archive from Ur*, Univ. Microfilms, Ann Arbor, 1974: p. 127f. Note that in *BIN* 10: no 273 leatherworkers are said to be e-rí-na-íl-me, which may refer to their treating skins with this root.

*BIN* 9: nos 37, 226, 234, 307, 339, 343, 364, 425, 438, 445, 446, *ASJ* 5: p. 57 no 8.

kuš-síg-mú, "hairy skin". V. Crawford, *BIN* 9: p. 41, "seems to mean 'fresh' and therefore 'hides or skins still having the hair'". A. Salonen, *Fussbekleidung*: p. 68, "in the Isin period the hair of such hides was sometimes combed, which is called *maški šapātim* in O. Ass. texts". Note that the text Salonen refers to, *BIN* 9: no 129, does not mention hides but felt (made) of combed wool, cf. P. Steinkeller, *OrAn.* 19 (1980): p. 88.

*BIN* 9: nos 3, 4, 6, 11, 14, 15, 19, 20, 21, 23, 24, 46, 55, 57, 58, 59, 61, 63, 90, 93, 96, 98, 101, 102, 207, 233, 249, 250, 251, 334, 349, 350, 434, 437, 442, 443, 477, 489, *BIN* 10: nos 23, 68, 127, 148, *MCS* 5: p. 115 no 1.

kuš-zag-bar, "leather scraps". For zag-bar as "clippings" in metallurgy, cf. H. Limet, *Métal*: p. 148. In the leather industry it seems to refer to small amounts of leather, therefore probably "scraps".

*BIN* 9: nos 88, 106, 248, 378, 403, 404, 438, 440, *BIN* 10: no 63.

$^{kuš}$lu-úb-BÚR, probably stands for $^{kuš}$lu-úb-sir = *nēpeštum* (M. Civil, *MSL* 12: p. 200), "bag to carry precious metals", *CAD* N/2: p. 168 s.v. 5.

*BIN* 9: nos 139, 141, 142, 143, 144, 204, 205, 207, 208, 209, 210, 465, 483, 488, *BIN* 10: no 71.

$^{gi}$ma-an-sim = *nappītum*, "sieve", *CAD* N/1: p. 312, *AHw*: p. 740, cf. A. Salonen, *Hausgeräte* I: p. 71f.

*BIN* 9: nos 355, 433, 439, 443, 450, *BIN* 10: nos 98, 154, 185, 211, *JAOS* 98: p. 252 no 1.

$^{giš}$ma-nu = *e'rum*, "fruit of(?) a native tree", *CAD* E: p. 318f., "Kornelkirschbaum(?)", *AHw*: p. 247. A.L. Oppenheim, *Eames Coll.*: p. 54 n. 71, translates "wooden sticks". P. Steinkeller, "Foresters of Umma" (forthcoming), proposes the translation "willow". D. Snell, *YNER* 8: p. 221 is uncertain whether a fruit or the wood is intended, but since the product is used in the Isin workshop, the second possibility is more likely.

*BIN* 9: no 531.

*malkum*, (a god or chthonic demon), *CAD* M/1: p. 168, cf. *AHw*: p. 596 s.v. 2.
*BIN* 9: no 440.

*mārītum*, "musical instrument", *CAD* M/1: p. 282, *AHw*: p. 646, *MAD* 3: p. 182, s.v. *mā/īrītum*.
*BIN* 9: nos 253, 496.

kuš*mašlium*, "leather bucket", *CAD* M/1: p. 380, *AHw*: p. 628, s.v. *mašlûm, MAD* 3: p. 270f.
*BIN* 9: no 327.

gišmes = *mēsum*, "a tree", *CAD* M/2: p. 33f., "Zürgelbaum(?)", *AHw*: p. 647, cf. A. Salonen, *Möbel*: p. 220f.
*JAOS* 98: p. 252 no 2.

naga = *uḫūlum*, "alkaline plant", *AHw*: p. 1404, cf. D. Snell, *YNER* 8: p. 228.
*BIN* 9: nos 37, 489.

naga-si-è, "sprouted alkaline plant", D. Snell, YNER 8: p. 229.
*BIN* 9: nos 81, 82.

nagar = *nagārum*, "carpenter", *CAD* N/1: p. 112, *AHw*: p. 710.
*BIN* 9: nos 191, 192, 193, 228, 341, 349, 368, 374, 380, 489, *BIN* 10: no 82, *JCS* 20: p. 40 no 5, *JAOS* 98: p. 254 no 6, p. 256 no 12, *passim* in the worker lists.

*naḫbātum*, "cover", *CAD* N/1: p. 135, *AHw*: p. 714. In Ḫḫ XI, 105 (*MSL* 7: p. 127) *naḫbātum* = *išpatum*, "quiver", *CAD* I/J: p. 257, *AHw*: p. 397, but in the Isin texts a broader sense of cover must be assumed for *naḫbātum* is often used for musical instruments (e.g., *BIN* 9: nos 38, 127), cf. L. Matouš, *BiOr*. 13 (1956): p. 138.
*BIN* 9: nos 38, 127, 225, 233, 333, 334, 335, 343, 355, 361, 395, 398, 408, 421, 425, 431, 437, 447, 490, 491, *BIN* 10: nos 8, 112, 116, 195, *MCS* 5: p. 115 no 1, *Or*. 36: p. 426f.

níg-dab$_5$, "offering", E. Sollberger, *TCS* 1: p. 156f.
*BIN* 9: nos 368, 396.

níg-šu-tag$_4$-a = *šūbultum* "official present", *AHw*: p. 1258. M. Powell, *ZA* 68 (1978): p. 181-191, in his lengthy discussion of the verb TAG$_4$, read taka, translates šu-taka as "to make an official present of something" (*ibid.*: p. 189 s.v. P). In the Isin texts the term always occurs when objects are issued to another town, country, or people, especially the Amorites. This group of signs is read in several ways in the previous literature. V. Crawford, *Terminology*: p. 121-127, reads níg-kad$_5$-a and connects this to kad$_5$ = *kaṣārum*, "to tie, bind" (*CAD* K: p. 257, *AHw*: p. 456), a reading also proposed by K. Oberhuber, *Or*. NS 36 (1967): p. 427 n. 8, who considers it a possible sumerogram for an unattested *makṣārum*, and R.D. Freedman, *JAOS* 98 (1978): p. 261, who translates "bundled goods". D.O. Edzard, *Zwischenzeit*: p. 62, reads níg-šu-peš and regards it as goods for a type of people whom he calls "Fänger".

*BIN* 9: nos 224, 225, 226, 227, 233, 242, 244, 269, 272, 280, 282, 283, 286, 289, 290, 293, 301, 310, 314, 316, 317, 324, 332, 369, 383, 384, 391, 395, 400, 403, 405, 408, 409, 410, 419, 433, 452, 491, *BIN* 10: no 165, *JAOS* 98: p. 253 no 3, p. 254 no 7, p. 257 no 16, *SET* no 291, *Or* 36: p. 426f., *MVN* 4: no 143, LB 1106, 1126.

níg-U.NU-a, "thread". The product is made of goat's hair and low quality wool, cf. H. Waetzoldt, *Textilindustrie*: p. 121. He equates U.NU with NU.NU = *ṭawûm* "to spin", (*AHw*: p. 1382), cf. W.W. Hallo, *Jones AV*: p. 9. NU.NU appears in literary texts (Dumuzi and Enkimdu and *SLTN* 35, cf. Hallo) and lexical texts after the combing of wool or weaving. Note, however, that the equation U.NU = NU.NU is uncertain, cf. G. Farber, *ZA* 68 (1978): p. 308f. n. 9. H. Waetzoldt, *Textilindustrie*: p. 121f. translates níg-U.NU-a as "auf U.NU-art gesponnenes Garn", i.e. warp-thread spun in U.NU manner. He thinks níg-U.NU-a and šà-U.NU-a refer to warp-thread (= ŠID, *ibid.*: p. 123-6) and woof-thread ( = šà, *ibid.*: p. 126-8). From the use of them outside the textile industry, is seems, however, that the term has to be taken broader as, simply, "thread". The variation níg-U.NU-a / šà-U.NU-a may refer to two ways of spinning, with šà-U.NU-a the less common, for it is only attested twice in the Isin archive. NU in its meaning *ṭawûm* "to spin" probably has to be read nu, cf. Th. Jacobsen, in *Studies in honour of I.M. Diakonoff*, 1982: p. 136 n. 6.

*BIN* 9: nos 30, 31, 37, 134, 136, 139, 141, 142, 194, 197, 205, 206, 210, 247, 249, 250, 254, 258, 264, 303, 332, 355, 366, 382, 388, 392, 421, 422, 423, 426, 430, 438, 443, 448, 451, 462, 463, 466, 482, 489, 518, *BIN* 10: nos 54, 71, 74, 104, 114, 130, 131, 136, 139, 140-142, 144, 145, 162, 163, *ASJ* 5: p. 57 no 8.

níg-U.NU-a *zibbatum*, "special type of thread", cf. *CAD* Q: p. 332, s.v. **quzippu*. H. Waetzoldt, *Textilindustrie*: p. 60 and 122, thinks the thread is made of a special type of wool from the tail of the sheep, síg-*zibbatum*, cf. also I.J. Gelb, *MAD* 3: p. 308.

*BIN* 9: nos 139, 142, 143, 144, 194, 197, 209, 463, 466, 482, 483.

giš nu-kúš = *nuku(š)šû*, "doorpivot", *CAD* N/2: p. 332f., *AHw*: p. 803, A. Salonen, *Türen*: p. 69f.

*BIN* 9: nos 350, 442, 534, *BIN* 10: nos 89, 155, 169, 193.

nu-úr-ma = *nurmû*, "pomegranate", *CAD* N/2: p. 345f., *AHw*: p. 804f. For its use as tanning material, cf. H. Hoffner, *Alimenta Hethaeorum*, New Haven, 1974: p. 119f.

*BIN* 9: nos 182, 489, *BIN* 10: no 130.

nu-úr-ma-duru$_5$, "moist pomegranate". duru$_5$ = *raṭbum*, "fresh, moist", *AHw*: p. 963. The product is measured as a liquid.

*BIN* 10: no 24.

*parūtum*, "sort of arrowholder", *AHw*: p. 837.

*BIN* 9: nos 14, 274.

peš-murgu, "date palm spine", B. Landsberger, *Date Palm*: p. 29.

*BIN* 9: no 490, *BIN* 10: no 78, *JAOS* 98: p. 255 no 9.

peš-giš nu-úr-ma, "pomegranate kernel/heart". peš = *libbum* "heart", *CAD* L: p. 165, *AHw*: p. 549, B. Landsberger, *Date Palm*: p. 5, b 158.

*BIN* 10: nos 24, 25. The PEŠ sign is written A.ḪA in both texts.

*puzirum*. Cf. *CAD* B: p. 322 s.v. *bunziru*, "a web". It may indicate a net-like cover (suggestion M. Civil). The term is possibly related to the root PZR "to protect".

*BIN* 9: no 334.

sa = *gīdum*, *CAD* G: p. 66, *AHw*: p. 287., Usually translated as "sinew" but since there is normally only one sa per hide (E. Sollberger, *TCS* 1: p. 163), it is probably catgut string, cf. K. Butz, *OLA* 5: p. 348 n. 238 and p. 350, F.R. Kraus, *Königliche Verfügungen in altbabylonischer Zeit*, Leiden, 1984: p. 365.

*BIN* 9: nos 37, 143, 326, 328, 382, 383, 388, 397, 398, 415, 421, 423, 424, 425, 426, 427, 428, 430, 431, 432, 489, *BIN* 10: nos 116, 117, 130, 149, *JAOS* 98: p. 257 no 16, *The Ancient Orient Museum* 3: p. 41f.

giš sag-gul = *sikkūrum*, "bolt, lock", *AHw*: p. 1042, cf. A. Salonen, *Türen*: p. 82-86.

*BIN* 9: nos 350, 382, 426, 442, *BIN* 10: nos 155, 169, 193.

SAGŠU = *kubšum*, "stopper, cork, cap", *CAD* K: p. 485, *AHw*: p. 497f., cf. A. Salonen, *Hausgeräte* I: p. 164 and 170 s.v. U.KA.

*BIN* 9: nos 197, 403, 404, 466.

*sekrum* (a class of women), *AHw*: p. 1036 s.v. *sekretum*.

*BIN* 9: nos 328, 341, 348, 350, 412, 444, 485, *JAOS* 98: p. 256 no 14.

síg = *šipātum*, "wool", *AHw*: p. 1244, cf. H. Waetzoldt, *Textilindustrie*: p. 36-60.

*BIN* 9: nos 181, 436, 534, *BIN* 10: no 79, 170.

síg-[giš]ga-ríg-ak = *pušikkum*, "combed wool", *AHw*: p. 883, cf. H. Waetzoldt, *Textilindustrie*: p. 115-7 s.v. [giš]GA.ZUM-ak. For the reading, cf. M. Civil, *JNES* 26 (1967): p. 210f., and *AOAT 25 (1976): p. 94.*

*BIN* 9: nos 32, 128, 129, 328, 341, 417, 429, 524, *BIN* 10: nos 10, 42, 43, 136, *ASJ* 5: p. 57 no 8.

síg-gi, "wool of the uligi-sheep", H. Waetzoldt, *Textilindustrie*: p. 73.

*BIN* 10: nos 73, 74.

síg-gin, "wool of ordinary quality", H. Waetzoldt, *Textilindustrie*: p. 47f.

*BIN* 9: nos 32, 128, 129, 328, 341, 429, 430, 438, 453, 518, 524, *BIN* 10: nos 9, 42, 43, 85, 86, 136, 140, 141, 142, 144, 145.

síg-$ud_5$ = *šārti enzi*, "goat's hair/wool", *CAD* E: p. 181, *AHw*: p. 1191. Cf. H. Waetzoldt, *Textilindustrie*: p. 75. For the reading $ud_5$ for ÙZ, cf. *MSL* 8/1: p. 28: 192a and note.

*BIN* 9: nos 29, 39, 81, 105, 112, 233, 246, 255, 257, 265, 324, 326, 327, 348, 351, 378, 391, 395, 415, 424, 425, 435, 450, 458, 500, 501, 517, 526, *BIN* 10: nos 3, 9, 10, 11, 21, 35, 54, 60, 61, 64-66, 69, 71, 72, 75, 76, 101, 104, 106, 114, 130, 131, 139, 140-142, 144, 161-163, *JAOS* 98: p. 154 no 6.

simug = *nappāḫum*, "smith", *CAD* N/1: p. 307-310, *AHw*: p. 739.

*BIN* 9: no 381, *BIN* 10: no 170.

su = *nabātum*, "to shine", *CAD* N/1: p. 22, *AHw*: p. 697.

*BIN* 9: nos 467, 469.

su-si-ig, "skinflayers, specialists in the skinning of animals and the preparation of the skins", J. Finkelstein, *RA* 63 (1969): p. 61-64, K. Butz, *OLA* 5: p. 350-353, F.R. Kraus, *OLA* 6: p. 430-432, *Königliche Verfügungen in altbabylonischer Zeit,* Leiden, 1984: p. 350-366.

*BIN* 9: nos 114, 151, 303, 376.

$sub_6$(TAG), "to coat", cf. J. Bauer, *W.O.* 9 (1977): p. 4. The reading is confirmed by the phonetic complement $sub_6$-ba in *BIN* 10: 170, and the variant su-ba in *BIN* 10: 92.

*BIN* 9: nos 326, 343, 362, 376, 377, 391, 451, *BIN* 10: nos 92, 170.

[kuš]súḫub = *suḫuppatum*, "boot", *AHw*: p. 1054, cf. A. Salonen, *Fussbekleidung*: p. 44-53.

*BIN* 9: nos 107, 128, 328, 385, 397, 426, 428, 431, 469, *BIN* 10: nos 10, 33, 117, 250.

šà-ra, "lining", perhaps to be read šag$_4$-ráḫ, cf. P. Steinkeller, *OrAn.* 19 (1980): p. 86 and n. 10, A. Salonen, *Möbel*: p. 89.
*BIN* 9: nos 395, 408, 436, 438, 440, 473.

[giš]ŠÀ.TAR, "a musical instrument(?)". Unknown but since it appears in a list of musical instruments in *BIN* 9: no 496 and *BIN* 10: no 82, it is probably also one.
*BIN 9: no 496*, *BIN* 10: nos 82, 104.

šà-tuku$_5$(TAG) = *šē/ī'tum*, "mattress", *AHw*: p. 1221, cf. P. Steinkeller, *OrAn.* 19 (1980): p. 80-83 for complete discussion.
*BIN* 9: nos 348, 351, 417, *BIN* 10: nos 66, 113, ASJ 5: p. 57 no 8.

šà-U.NU-a = šà-NU.U-a, "thread". H. Waetzoldt, *Textilindustrie*: p. 121f. translates as "auf U.NU-Art gesponnener Schussfaden" i.e. "woof-thread woven in the U.NU way", because šà = "woof-thread", cf. *ibid.*: p. 126-128. But the equivalent warp-thread = ŠID is not attested with U.NU-a (although Waetzoldt assumes it is níg-U.NU-a). Since both šà-U.NU-a and níg-U.NU-a (q.v.) are used outside the textile industry, Waetzoldt's translation of weft- and warp-thread seems too limited. The variation níg-U.NU-a / šà-U.NU-a may refer to two different ways of spinning since a distinction is made between géme-U.NU and géme-šà-U.NU-a (H. Waetzoldt, *Textilindustrie*: p. 122). šà-U.NU-a occurs only twice in the Isin archive, *ASJ* 5: p. 57 no 8 and *BIN* 9: no 481, where šà-NU.U-a *zibbatum*. It seems thus to refer to a less common type of spinning.
*BIN* 9: no 481, *ASJ* 5: p. 57 no 8.

[dug]šáman = *šappatu*, "bowl", *AHw*: p. 1175, cf. A. Salonen, *Hausgeräte* II: p. 124f., 132-136.
*BIN* 9: nos 215, 217, 219, 220, 223, 224, 225, 227, 243, 244, 269, 270, 276, 277, 279, 280, 281, 282, 283, 286, 287, 289, 291, 293, 299, 300, 301, 306, 310, 313, 314, 315, 316, 317, 318, 319, 320, 343, 360, 391, 400, 403, 404, 405, 407, 408, 409, 410, 411, 414, 416, 418, 435, 437, 438, 450, 452, 491, *BIN* 10: nos 128, 157, 160, 164, *MCS* 5: p. 120 no 6, *Or* 36: p. 426f.

še-gín = "glue". Usually equated with *šimtum, šindu*, "dye-paste", *AHw*: p. 1238, cf. A. Salonen, *Türen*: p. 115, and *Möbel*: p. 259, W.W. Hallo, *BiOr.* 26 (1969): p. 175. This equation does not make sense in many contexts where še-gín is used. Moreover, the coloring of leather is done with other products. A. Salonen, *Fussbekleidung*: p. 71, equated še-gín with *allaḫarum* based on the Practical Vocabulary of Elam (*RA* 18 [1921]: p. 65 VIII 4f.) where the sequence ŠE.GÍN(!), SA.DIB, *al-lu-ḫa-ru-um*, IM.UD.UD, which suggests rather a difference than an equivalence between the two products. še-gín is used in the Isin texts both with wood and leather. It is applied (gar) to furniture (e.g., *BIN* 9: nos 341, 374), doors (e.g., *BIN* 9: nos 346, 347), chariots (e.g., *BIN* 9: nos 372, 446) and leather products such as sandals (e.g., *BIN* 9: nos 415, 421), boots (e.g., *BIN* 9: no 428), and bags (e.g., *BIN* 9: no 309). A number of texts record leather which was weighed (ba-lá) before the application of še-gín (še-gín-šè, e.g., *BIN* 9: nos 106, 125). The translation "glue" seems to fit all this situations better than any other, cf. M. Sigrist, *JCS* 33 (1981): p. 157-9, and note M. Civil, *AS* 20: p. 132. From *BIN* 9: no 103 it is clear that glue could be applied to leather after it had been in use:

| | |
|---|---|
| 50 ma-na-kuš-gu$_4$ | 50 minas of oxhide |
| gu$_4$-si-AŠ-ta gur-ra | returned from a battering ram |
| še-gín-šè ba-lá | weighed for gluing |

It seems thus that some objects had to be reglued after they had been in use.

*BIN* 9: nos 12, 16, 27, 28, 29, 30, 31, 33, 35, 121, 122, 124, 130, 131, 132, 133, 134, 135, 140, 145, 146, 147, 153, 154, 155, 156, 157, 158, 159, 160, 161, 162, 163, 164, 165, 166, 167, 168, 169, 172, 177, 178, 179, 182, 187, 188, 189, 191, 192, 193, 194, 195, 199, 201, 202, 203, 212, 247, 252, 253, 258, 260, 262, 263, 266, 294, 309, 326, 328, 332, 333, 341, 346, 347, 349, 350, 352, 353, 354, 355, 360, 366, 369, 372, 374, 378, 379, 380, 382, 383, 388, 395, 397, 398, 415, 421, 423, 424, 425, 426, 427, 428, 429, 430, 432, 436, 438, 440, 441, 442, 444, 445, 446, 447, 449, 450, 454, 456, 457, 458, 459, 462, 466, 467, 469, 489, 491, *BIN* 10; nos 5, 51, 63, 70, 82, 90, 104, 114, 116, 117, 127, 128, 130, 149, 162, 176, 177, *MCS* 5: p. 121 no 7, p. 123 no 9, *ASJ* 4: p. 68 no 17, *ASJ* 5: p. 54 no 1, p. 57 no 8, *JAOS* 98: p. 255 no 10, p. 256 no 12, p. 257 no 16, *The Ancient Orient Museum* 3: p. 41f.

še-gín-bábbar, "white(?) glue". Maybe has to be read še-gín-ḫád, "dry glue". It is used in the manufacture of doors, and weighed.
*BIN* 9: no 157.

šitim = *itinnum*, "builder", *CAD* I/J: p. 296, *AHw*: p. 404.
*BIN* 10: nos 212, 215-217, 276, 277, 279, 280, 282-285, 287-290, 292, 305.

šu-e-sír, "shoe-mold(?)", cf. Crawford, *Terminology*: p. 131-133.
*BIN* 9: nos 88, 324, 325, 326, 327, 382, 395, 415, 422, *BIN* 10: no 149.

$^{giš}$ŠU$_4$.A is an earlier spelling of $^{giš}$ŠÚ.A = *littum*, "stool", *CAD* L: p. 219, *AHw*: p. 557. Cf. P. Steinkeller, *OrAn.* 19 (1980): p. 97f. n. 40
*BIN* 9: nos 334, 336, *BIN* 10: no 4, *SET* no 291.

$^{giš}$šudun = *nīrum*, "yoke", *CAD* N/2: p. 260f., *AHw*: p. 793f.
*BIN* 9: nos 256, 437.

$^{giš}$taškarin = *taskarinnum*, "boxwood", *AHw*: p. 1336f.
*BIN* 9: no 499, *BIN* 10: no 88.

tibira = *gurgurrum, qurqurrum*, "metalworker, coppersmith", *CAD* G: p. 137, *AHw*: p. 929.
*BIN* 9: nos 260, 366, 380, 381, *JAOS* 98: p. 256 no 12.

túg-du$_8$, "felter", P. Steinkeller, *OrAn.* 19 (1980): p. 85-94.
*BIN* 9: nos 246, 341, *BIN* 10: nos 60, 130, *passim* in the worker lists.

túg-du$_8$-a = prob. *kiššu*, "piece of felt", P. Steinkeller, *OrAn.* 19 (1980): p. 86-91.
*BIN* 9: nos 128, 129, 328, 341, 355, 361, 385, 397, 428, 430, 469, 473, *BIN* 10: no 33.

túg-du$_8$-a-babbar, "white felt", P. Steinkeller, *OrAn.* 19 (1980): p. 88.
*BIN* 9: nos 129, 395, *BIN* 10: no 116.

túg-du$_8$-a SU.A, "... felt", P. Steinkeller, *OrAn.* 19 (1980): p. 88.
*BIN* 9: no 129, *BIN* 10: no 85.

túg-guz-za, "*guzza*-cloth", H. Waetzoldt, *Textilindustrie*: p. 174 n. 129, H. Limet, *RA* 65 (1971): p. 15 n. 4.
*BIN* 9: no 467.

*tuksium* = *tukšum*, "shield", *AHw*: p. 1368.
*BIN* 9: no 312, *BIN* 10: no 97

tùn = *bisrum, tākaltum*, "bag", *AHw*: p. 130, 1304, *bisru, CAD* E: p. 268.
*BIN* 9: nos 37, 226.

ú-ḫáb = *ḫūratu*(?), A.L. Oppenheim, *JCS* 21 (1967): p. 242 n. 19, based on Ḫḫ III: (*MSL* 5: p. 137) where giš-ḪAB = *ḫūratu*. Although this equation is thus not totally assured, there is little doubt that the same product is intended, cf. B. Landsberger, *JCS* 21 (1967): p. 169f. This is also strongly suggested by a comparison of the early Isin texts with a late Old Babylonian tablet from Tell Rimah; in the Isin texts ú-ḫáb and *allaḫarum* are always found together, while in S. Dalley, *OBT Tell Rimah*: p. 102 no 128 l. 16-17 *ḫūratu* and *annuḫarum liqtum* (= *allaḫarum liqtum*) are requested together for the leatherworkers. The following succession of terms can thus be outlined:

| | |
|---|---|
| Isin | ú-ḫáb and *allaḫarum* |
| O.B. Rimah | *ḫūratu* and *allaḫarum* |
| 1st mill. | *ḫūratu* and *gabû* |

F. Thureau-Dangin, *RA* 17 (1920): p. 27-30, identified *ḫūratu* (read *pagratu*) as "gall-apple", a view adopted by V. Crawford, *Terminology*: p. 43-49, cf. W.W. Hallo, *HUCA* 29 (1958): p. 82. M. Stol showed, however, convincingly that *ḫūratu* is madder, Latin *Rubia tinctorum*, a product used to color textiles and leather red (*RlA* 6 [1980-83]: p. 534f.) and attested in Greek and Roman sources (R. Reed, *Ancient Skins*: p. 91). Although Stol insist upon distinguishing ú-ḫáb from giš-ḪAB (*RlA* 6 [1980-83]: p. 532), I believe the sequence of terms presented above suggests very strongly that ú-ḫáb and *ḫūratu* are the same. ú-ḫáb is measured by weight.

*BIN* 9: nos 80, 84, 105, 467, 470, 489, *BIN* 10: no 130, *MCS* 5: p. 110 no 4.

ú-ḫáb-duru$_5$, "fresh, moist madder", B. Landsberger, *JCS* 21 (1967): p. 169. duru$_5$ = *raṭbum, AHw*: p. 963. Measured by weight.

*BIN* 9: no 84.

ú-ḫáb-ḫád, "dried(?) madder". ḫád = *ablum CAD* A/1: p. 54, *AHw*: p. 6, E. Sollberger, *TCS* 1: p. 130. Measured by weight.

*BIN* 9: no 84.

$^{giš}$ù-suḫ$_5$ = *ašūḫum*, "fir tree", *CAD* A/2: p. 478, *AHw*: p. 85, cf. D. Snell, *YNER* 8: p. 222. W.W. Hallo - J. Curtis, *HUCA* 30 (1959): p. 137, translate "cedar". Both translations are impossible, however, since the tree was cultivated in S. Mesopotamia, M. Stol, *On trees, mountains and millstones in the Ancient Near East*, Leiden, 1979: p. 19 n. 68.

*BIN* 10: nos 53, 57, 88, 91, 95, 96, 175, 183, 186.

umbin. For furniture = *ṣuprum*, "legs", *AHw*: p. 1113, A. Salonen, *Möbel*: p. 153-6. *CAD* Ṣ: p. 250, translates "a claw-shaped ornament". For chariots: = *magarrum*, "wheel", *CAD* M/1: p. 32, *AHw*: p. 575.

*BIN* 9: nos 151, 191, 456, 459, 499, *BIN* 10: nos 77, 90, 150.

$^{kuš}$ummu(d)(A.EDIN.LAL) = *nādum*, "waterbag", *CAD* N/1: p. 100, *AHw*: p. 704. For reading, cf. M. Civil, *AOAT* 25 (1976): p. 91. See the detailed discussion by M. Stol, *RlA* 6 (1980-83): p. 536.

*BIN* 9: nos 34, 36, 39, 118, 127, 150, 199, 211, 228, 229, 230, 233, 325, 326, 327, 344, 345, 361, 363, 365, 368, 376, 377, 382, 388, 389, 390, 391, 392, 393, 394, 395, 396, 397, 398, 399, 401, 402, 415, 416, 421, 422, 423, 424, 425, 435, *BIN* 10: nos 110, 119, 128, 130, 133, 135, *ASJ* 5: p. 57 no 9.

$^{giš}$zà-mi = za-mí(?) = *sammûm*, "harp or lyre", *AHw*: p. 1018. Since the product is mentioned in *MCS* 5: p. 115 no 1 in a list of musical instruments, the equation zà-mi = za-mí seems certain, cf. L. Matouš, *BiOr.* 13 (1956): p. 138.

*BIN* 9: nos 150, 185, 257, 352, 353, 354, 444, 496, *BIN* 10: nos 82, 104, *MCS* 5: p. 115 no 1.

zé-na = *zinûm*, "midrib of the frond of the date palm", *CAD* Z: p. 123, *AHw*: p. 1529, B. Landsberger, Date Palm: p. 25-8.

*BIN* 9: nos 490, 519, *BIN* 10: no 78.

zì = *qēmum*, "flour", *AHw*: p. 913. The product is used as glue.

*BIN* 9: no 340.

zì-gu, "... flour", J.P. Grégoire, *AAS*: p. 149. Used as glue.

*BIN* 9: no 203, *BIN* 10: nos 98, 185.

zì-sig$_{15}$ = *ḫišiltum*, "coarse flour", *CAD* H: p. 205, *AHw*: p. 349, cf. A. Salonen, *Türen*: p. 117 for its use as glue.

*BIN* 9: no 169, *BIN* 10: no 70.

zì-še-gín, "mixture of flour and glue", cf. A. Salonen, *Türen*: p. 118-120 for its use as glue.

*BIN* 9: no 486.

*zaḫirum* is probably *šāḫirum*, "straps", known from the Old Assyrian texts, cf. *AHw*: p. 1132.

*BIN* 10: no 149, Ash 1932-280.

*zamirītum*, "household utensil or weapon", *CAD* Z: p. 39, *AHw*: p. 1508f., W.W. Hallo, *BiOr.* 20 (1963): p. 140. Note *MAD* 3: p. 182, s.v. *mirîtum*, and M. Sigrist, *Or.* 48 (1979): p. 73: a musical instrument.

*BIN* 9: nos 338, *BIN* 10: nos 67, 118, 124.

# INDICES

## A. Subject matters

ORIENTALISTE, P.B. 41, B-3000 Leuven